Cole City

Book 1
Ten Years and a Day

Garry Hundley

ISBN 978-1-0980-6363-4 (paperback)
ISBN 978-1-0980-6364-1 (digital)

Christian Faith Publishing, Inc.
832 Park Avenue
Meadville, PA 16335
www.christianfaithpublishing.com

Printed in the United States of America

Chapter 1
The Incident

In the late summer of 1890, they hanged Bernard Waller for his part in killing a man in a botched robbery in Murphy Hollow. My name is Tobias Oliver, and along with Waller, I was found guilty of the crime. But because I turned state's evidence, I received a more lenient sentence of ten years and a day of hard labor in the mines at Cole City. I would soon come to understand that Waller was the lucky one.

Daniel Hardy worked as a free laborer at the Cole City Prison Camp and lived in a boarding house there. Hardy had spent much of the evening in the saloons in Murphy Hollow, drinking, gambling, and looking longing at the working girls that he couldn't afford. Just after sundown on this particular evening, Hardy, who had had more than enough to drink, felt the call of nature and went into the bushes close by the last salon to relieve himself.

Murphy Hollow was just beyond the eastern limits of Cole City, where Hardy worked, south of the Tennessee State Line in Georgia. A rutted and always muddy dirt road connected the Cole City Prison Camp on top of Sand Mountain with the southern end of the Murphy Hollow. A road that was aptly named Hales Gap continued past the Murphy Hollow cut off and went on down the mountainside to intersect with the main road between Chattanooga and Birmingham in the valley below. This road was the only road in or out of Cole City. The road was used mostly by travelers on horseback or in a horse-drawn wagon. The preferred route for the free laborers working at the prison camp on top of the mountain was by a well-traveled footpath.

Since Cole City prohibited the sale or use of alcohol, nearby Murphy Hollow was the ideal location for a saloon—so much so that by 1890, there were more than a dozen of such establishments along the Murphy Hollow Road. The concentration of so many such businesses created a burgeoning entertainment district where the working-class men of Cole City could blow off a little steam.

A narrow-gauge rail spur connected Murphy Hollow to the main rail line running between Chattanooga and Nashville. The rail spur made Murphy Hollow easily accessible for folks from Chattanooga, less than an hour away by train. Passengers traveling by rail between Chattanooga and Nashville would often get off the train where the Murphy Hollow spur line connects to spend some time and money in the establishments of Murphy Hollow. The walking distance from Murphy Hollow to the Cole City Prison Camp was less than two miles along the footpath and only slightly farther along Hales Gap Road. Since Murphy Hollow was about halfway down the side of Sand Mountain, both the road and the footpath make for a steep climb on the way home. For those disinclined to climb the thousand feet up the mountain from Murphy Hollow, there was a sporadic rail service on the spur line from Murphy Hollow north to the town of Whiteside, Tennessee. It's a quick train ride westward on the main route to the next town of Shellmound, Tennessee. There was a spur line from Shellmound six miles up Nickajack gulch to a dead end at Lower Cole City. The Dade Coal Company operated a cable incline running from Lower Cole City up the thousand feet to the top of the mountain to the prison camp at Upper Cole City. The train ride from Murphy Hollow to Lower Cole City took longer than it did to walk up the footpath. So the train ride was usually preferred only when there were goods to be carried or the traveler was sick or drunk.

Along with the saloons came gambling and working girls. And with all this came a deserved reputation as a lawless and dangerous place. The county sheriff, based in Trenton about five miles down the valley toward Birmingham, turns a blind eye to all that transpires in Murphy Hollow except for the most egregious offenses. Even still, Murphy Hollow takes up more of the sheriff's time and energy than the entire rest of Dade County.

Having finished his business, Hardy began to make his way to the train platform. Being too drunk to walk home, he hoped to catch the next train. And if he'd missed the last train, then he might be lucky enough to find an empty railcar where he could sleep it off. As he made his way down the darkened dirt main street, Hardy was waylaid by the two of us. Both Waller and I lived in Upper Cole City, with Waller having come here from McMinnville, Tennessee, the year before, to work as a free laborer. I grew up in Trenton and, like Waller, worked as a free laborer at Cole City. Both Waller and I did various odd jobs for the Dade Coal Company at the prison mining camp known as Cole City. Mostly we took care of the mules that pulled the coal tubs and trams at the mines, making sure that they were fed and their stalls mucked out.

Like most free laborers, we never worked alongside the prisoners in the mines, at the ovens in Nickajack gulch below, or minding the related equipment. Such work was usually reserved for the prisoners serving time. I knew Waller from our work in Cole City and from the fact that we both had rooms at one of the boarding houses there. We had become friendly over time, and on this night, we traveled to Murphy Hollow with a plan to find a drunk to relieve of his money. It's not something that either of us had ever attempted before, but we proceeded with confidence in the outcome. I'm not sure of the exact amount, but I believed that we got less than $2 for our effort. Hardy resisted our demands for his money much more vigorously than either of us expected. In the melee, Waller stabbed Hardy in the chest with a hunting knife. Hardy fell to the ground in a heap and was still. A commotion arose as passersby found Hardy dead in the street and began to raise the alarm. Someone in the small crowd that was gathering saw me and Waller making our way down the main street and called out to us to stop. Fearing pursuit from the group, we of course did no such thing, and our climb up the mountain went without further incident. Early the next morning, the Dade County sheriff came to the boarding house and found both me and Waller asleep in our beds. We were arrested and tried at the recently completed new courthouse in Trenton. I turned state's evidence and told the sheriff where Waller had hidden the bloody murder weapon.

For this, I received a lighter sentence of only ten years and one day to be served in the prison mining camp at Cole City. By having "one day" added to my sentence, I would not be eligible for parole or early release and would have to serve my full sentence. Waller was ordered to be hung by his neck from a gallows erected for this purpose at Trenton's courthouse square.

Three days later, as I awaited transport to Cole City, I had a clear view of the hanging from the window of my second-floor cell across the street from the courthouse. The victim wasn't well known around town, so there was little civil outcry due to his killing. Of the few people who attended the hanging, most did so out of curiosity. Waller, by contrast, was well known as a hothead and a scoundrel. Many of the townspeople gathered to watch the hanging out of interest for his demise. A black hood was placed over Waller's head. And, without delay, the floor of the gallows, where Waller stood, gave way beneath his feet. Waller dropped like a stone. The preceding unnatural quiet gave way to what was a soft murmur, and as Waller swung from the noose, the murmur rose to a more boisterous cheer. I considered myself lucky not to be swinging from the gallows alongside Waller. I didn't know then that I would soon have reason to question this conclusion. I was only twenty-four years old, far too young to die in such a way in my estimation. If I would live long enough to serve my time at Cole City, I would still be young enough to have a life once I get out.

Early the next morning, I was taken from my jail cell, placed in handcuffs and leg irons, and locked inside a Black Maria to be carted to Cole City. The eight-mile trip on the often steep, always rutted, and muddy dirt road took a good part of the day. Looking back, this was unarguably the least difficult of my coming travails.

I have ten years and a day of hard labor yet to be served in this godforsaken place.

Chapter 2
Cole City

Cole City, located in the far northwestern corner of the state of Georgia, is near the Tennessee and Alabama state lines. Cole City proper is high atop Sand Mountain where the mining operations were. The area atop Sand Mountain, all of which is in Georgia, is referred to by everyone associated with Cole City as Upper Cole City. A thousand feet below in the Nickajack gulch are the ovens used to convert coal into coke. The area in Nickajack gulch is referred to by everyone associated with Cole City as Lower Cole City.

Before the Civil War, the Cherokee Indians in the region were marched off to be resettled out West, and the lands that had been theirs was parceled out to white settlers. The property in the vicinity of Cole City being rugged, remote, and mostly untenable went largely unsettled and remained in the ownership of the state of Georgia. Then about thirty years ago, coal was discovered under the northernmost portion of Sand Mountain in Georgia. Nothing happened with the coal for a long while because of the war, but then, in early 1873, the governor got the state to grant him the mineral rights for the Sand Mountain plateau. The governor formed the Dade Coal Company, and shortly after that, Cole City was incorporated. To work the mine, the governor took advantage of a convict lease system that the state of Georgia had put in place just after the war. Back then, and even now, there aren't many places to house prisoners. During the war, the Yankees burned most of the jails and prisons throughout the state and the entire South. Leasing prisoners to private business was a way to incarcerate prisoners without the need to invest in building new prisons. The state could wash its hands of the prisoners, and not coincidentally the governor could get the laborers that he needed to work the mines at Cole City. I understand that the governor's coal company paid the state just $10 a year for each prisoner. The remote location of Cole City meant that the prison had to be mostly self-sufficient. The lease agreement with the state required that the prisoners will be used for mining and related work only. The jobs needed to provide support for the operation went to free laborers like me. Free laborers raised hogs for meat and tended a forty-acre garden for vegetables to feed the prisoners. They also tended to the livestock, prepared meals, cleaned, and did laundry and many other tasks. More than a thousand nonprisoners were working and living in Cole City.

Of the five hundred prisoners at Cole City, four hundred were Negro, and most of the Negro prisoners were former slaves. All the prisoners were serving long sentences. One in every six prisoners was serving a life sentence. None of the prisoners were serving less than five-year sentences. Yet the offenses that brought many of the prisoners to Cole City were relatively minor. Some were guilty of nothing more than a failure to pay some undisclosed fee that they were unaware of before their arrest. These phantom fees were the construct of racial bias meant to subjugate the Negro population and supply a steady stream of workers for the mine.

Although the stated purpose for the prisoner's presence at Cole City was to pay their debt to society, the real reason was much less noble. Prisoners were there to mine coal in support of revenue production for the white owners.

*****

The mule team pulled the Black Marie up the mountain one slow step at a time. Each step drew me farther away from civilization. The remoteness of Cole City made it an excellent place to dispose of the unwanted refuse of society.

The governor of Georgia, who signed the predatory laws that sent so many innocent Negro men to Cole City, was also the principal owner of the mine there.

Having worked there, I was familiar with much of Cole City. But as we arrived, it was as if I was seeing it for the first time. Prisoners slept in ram-shackled barracks constructed of wooden planks, harvested from the forest, and sawed at the company's sawmill. In addition to the barracks, the town had several single-family homes, a blacksmith shop, a stable, a stockade, a barn, a large vegetable garden, a corral, a company store, a rough-hewn log commissary with a post office, a small school, two boarding houses, the mining office building, and a cemetery with row after row of graves with unmarked headstones. Beyond the confines of the town was the mine entrance, a rail yard, mine processing equipment that I could not yet name, and endless stretches of loose slate covering the hillsides. Smoke rising from what I knew were almost three hundred coke ovens, a thousand or so feet below in Nickajack gulch just beyond my line of sight, lent a thick haze to the scene before me. There was a set of wood rail cross ties, running alongside a small stream at a right angle to the road on which we approached the office building. These rails extended out of sight behind the office building heading in the direction of the smoke rising from Nickajack gulch below. The track goes over a slight rise where it disappears as if taking flight over the valley. Another set of rails approaches from the right and merges in with the other track. This second set of rails runs alongside a muddy road on which I observed a mule coming toward me, pulling a cart that was filled with coal. The cart rolled on metal wheels that turned on the rails. An older man was coaxing the mule with a piece of rope tethered to the animal's bridle. I assumed that their destination was the coke ovens in the valley below.

A thick blue haze blankets Cole City. The haze is most abundant over the valley, and I recognized the characteristic discharge coming from the coke ovens. Adding to the haze is the smoke from numerous smaller coal fires supplying heat for steam-operated equipment. Along with the visible haze that stings the eyes, there is an assault on the sense of smell. I could smell, along with the smoke, decaying garbage, fresh manure, human waste from numerous latrines, and, worst of all, the distinctly offensive smell of pig shit—but mostly pig shit. I found it odd that working here as a free laborer, I never noticed the smell of pig shit, and now I can smell little else.

The main mine at Cole City is known as the Slope Mine because of the descending slope of the entry of the tunnel. The mine entrance was visible as we approached the center of Upper Cole City. My impression of the mine entrance was one of foreboding. The mine opening looked to me like the open maw of some huge mythical beast, with nothing inside but darkness. Around the mine entrance were enormous piles of gray rock heaped higher than a man's head for as far as the eye could see. Here the forest had been denuded and replaced with desolation. Tendrils of smoke could be seen rising from the rock piles like the fires of hell itself. I would learn later that the gray rocks, referred to as slate, are the tailings from the mine and that the smoke rising from the slate comes from a smoldering fire deep in the slate pile. The slate itself is mildly combustible, and when exposed to a surface conflagration can burn indefinitely. I would also learn that it is from this same slate that, through processing, we get the coal oil used in the lanterns for the mining camp. Some areas of the slate pile have turned a deep shade of red from burning and then cooling. These red tailings are called red dog by the prisoners. The side of the mountain just above the coke ovens was covered from top to bottom in red dog from years of the dumped slate burning almost endlessly.

As we drew near the center of Upper Cole City, prisoners could be seen carrying out several tasks that I was yet to understand. Their distinctive dress was readily recognizable. Each prisoner was wearing the same stained and dirty prison garb with broad horizontal gray stripes on a once white background. They walked with an awkward gate, due to their leg irons. Their heads were bowed low as if concentrating on a potentially critical next step.

I wondered, *Is this what is to become of me?* I could not imagine a more depressing sight or a more anguished thought. As the Black Marie drew to a halt in front of the office, I whispered a prayer in the hope that a merciful God would save me from this hell. I imagined the hell that was yet to come, but the real meaning of this hell was beyond me.

Chapter 3
Orientation

We arrived in Cole City by midafternoon and, without ceremony, went directly to the Dade Coal Company Office, which served as the prison's main office. Once the deputy had secured the mule team to the hitching post, he went into the office building, where he found interest sufficient to keep him for fifteen to twenty minutes. When he finally returned, there was a well-dressed middle-aged man smoking a cigar standing at his elbow. As the deputy attended to unlocking the chains that bound me to the Black Marie, the cigar-smoking man introduced himself to me. His tone was friendly, no different than I'd expect from someone attending a church social. Such was my first impression of Col. Willard Towers, the superintendent and principal keeper of the prison. I soon learned that my first impression of Colonel Towers was off the mark. I was escorted across the plank sidewalk that separates the muddy street from the office and escorted into an antichamber. The room was void of furniture except for an old wooden desk in the center of the room and two straight-backed wooden chairs. I was summarily deposited in a straight-backed chair, while Colonel Towers made himself comfortable behind the desk. The deputy locked me to an iron ring on the wooden floor using a sturdy metal chain. The deputy then departed without further comment, leaving me alone with Colonel Towers.

Colonel Towers occupied himself with a stack of papers on the desk and seemed to be unaware of my presence for several minutes. During this time, I kept respectfully quiet and still. As I waited for Colonel Towers to address me, I looked around the small room to occupy my mind. There was a single small window, not big enough for a man to crawl through, to my right as I faced inward. The front door where I entered was of heavy wood construction that had heavy metal hinges on the inside and a double-throw metal lock. There was a narrow set of wooden stairs with no handrail to my left that disappeared into a second story and two doors on the opposite wall. One door was swung wide open, and I could see a long row of shot-guns leaning upright against a gun rack beyond. The other door had frosted glass in the top half with the words "Superintendent: Private" stenciled on it. There were no pictures on the walls and no curtains on the window, giving a drab unwelcoming impression.

Colonel Towers rose from his seat and went directly to the front door, which he locked before returning to his place. Colonel Towers turned to me and, in a voice gruffer than the one he used to introduce himself to me, said, "Is your name Tobias Oliver?" When I said yes, Colonel Towers lurched upward from his seat and, leaning across the desk, bellowed out, "That's your first mistake, laddie. I am Colonel Towers sir to you, and you best never forget it. Now let me ask you again, are you Tobias Oliver?"

I replied meekly, "Yes, Sir Colonel Towers."

The color returned to Colonel Towers' face, and he resat himself behind the desk. Having regained his composure, Colonel Towers went on to say, "We only have a few rules here, laddie, and if you learn them and live by them, then in ten years and one day, you'll again be a free man. Listen to me carefully because if you ever have to be reminded of any one of these rules, it'll be because you've already gotten yourself into more trouble than you want.

"Rule number one. If there is ever a need for you to come to this office, you will be escorted by a guard. You are never to come to this office otherwise. Understood? Any prisoner who shows up here without an escort will be shot on sight."

Without waiting for me to reply, Colonel Towers continued, "Rule number two. You may notice that we have no walls surround-ing this penitentiary. We don't need 'em. It's a thousand feet down to the valley floor, and the slope is more than sixty degrees. Then its six miles more to reach the Tennessee River where the main rail line runs. With leg irons on, there ain't much chance of you getting that far, especially with a team of bloodhounds on your tail. There have only been four attempts to escape this camp, and all the prisoners who tried died in the process. One was shot in the back with a load of double-ought buckshot from a Long Tom ten-gauge. It blew a hole in him big enough to throw a cat through. The other three attempts were all one-offs, and in each case, the dogs got to 'em. Gotta be a horrible way to go, don't you think?

"So the second rule is a simple one—you run, you die. Lastly, there's rule number three. You do what you're told. You do it the first time you're told. You do it without question or hesitation. You carry your weight all day every day. You may wonder what happens to you if you get lazy, or want to back talk a guard, or get into a fight with another inmate. There's no solitary confinement here. There are no inmate beatings. After all, we're paying the state for you to work, and we want to keep you fit. We've tried various ways to incentivize prisoners to do what they're told, and everything we've tried fell short of the desired result, that is, until about a year ago when a particularly stubborn convict had a finger cut off as punishment for his insolence. Pretty soon, the word spread among the prisoners that getting out of line meant losing a finger. Since then, we haven't had much trouble with prisoners getting out of line. But you need to know this—if you turn out to be a troublemaker, we won't just cut off a finger. We will strip you naked, hang you from our gallows till your dead, and feed your sorry ass to the hogs. The state will have a replacement for you here the next day."

I would learn later that Colonel Towers was not prone to exaggeration and that the taking of a prisoners finger for the more grievous acts of disobedience was no idle threat. It was not uncommon to see a prisoner with a finger missing.

"I want to impress upon you that this is a godless place. You can call upon the Lord to save you, but you can expect no answer here. There's a tent set up behind this building with split logs for pews. And every Sunday morning, a service will be held there for anyone who wishes to attend. What you hear there is a bunch of horseshit, and I only tell you about it because I want to impress upon you the need to be a good prisoner, and I know that the sermon you'll hear each week will encourage you accordingly."

I would learn when I attended my first worship service that the God-fearing congregants were Campbellites who were viewed by Baptist, of which I am one, and other mainstream protestant denominations pejoratively. I see no value in sharing my view of the Campbellites with the colonel.

While Colonel Towers was speaking, he got up from his desk, walked over, and unlocked the entrance door. A large man with shaggy red hair and a matching bushy mustache came in and stood at the door as Colonel Towers finished his speech.

Colonel Towers continued to say, "Now it's dinnertime for the prisoners, so I'm going to hand you over to the guard captain who'll walk you through all the particulars of your stay with us and help you to find your assigned bunk in the barracks."

"I hope you'll remember our little talk, laddie, and that when your ten years and a day are up, you'll be leaving with all ten fingers cause that'll mean you didn't give us any trouble. Captain, this here is Tobias Oliver. He's all yours."

The guard captain unlocked the chain binding me to the floor of the office; and with my leg irons securely in place, he put his hand under my arm, lifted me slightly, and angled me out the front door. This posture continued as the guard captain encouraged me forward along to a low-slung one-story plank building that served as a laundry, not far away. At an open window, I was given the prison garb that would be my clothing from now on. I signed a log showing the date and a number signifying that I received the clothing and heard the laundry worker say that I could get a clean set in a week provided I brought the dirty clothes back. The number on the back of the shirt just given me matched the number in the log I'd just signed.

The guard captain escorted me to an adjoining lean-to-type structure that turned out to be a bathhouse. He instructed me to take off all my clothes, including my boots. He pumped water into a bucket from a cast-iron pump on the floor by jacking the handle up and down. I was told to scrub myself clean using lye soap provided on a shelf there. I deposited my original clothes in a barrel situated just outside the bathhouse. I did as I was told without question or hesitation. As I did so, the soapy water cascaded off my body and flowed down into a small stream just outside the bathhouse. Once this task was completed, I put on the clean prison garb. The guard captain removed my leg irons just long enough for me to put on the trousers, and he locked my leg irons in place once again. I put my boots back on and waited for the guard captain to tell me what was next. The guard captain had engaged in conversation with a passerby who was wearing ordinary clothes. I assumed he was a free laborer. Their discussion was in hushed tones, and I could not make out what they were saying, but their faces bore an appearance of earnest that suggested this wasn't a pleasant howdy-do. Their conversation lasted several minutes and ended with the passerby continuing on his way and the guard captain returning his attention to me once again.

We walked on to a larger, low-slung shedlike building with open walls. There I saw several long tables set in rows and split log benches set on either side. Prisoners sat shoulder to shoulder at each of these tables, eating from metal plates and drinking from metal cups. It was dinnertime at Cole City, and this was the dining hall where all the prisoners convened for their meals. From the yet-to-be finished meals on the plates, I could tell that they were eating some sort of stew, and I could make out what looked like small chunks of some vegetable in a brown broth. Everyone was eating with spoons or with their hands. There were no knives or forks for apparent reasons. The guard captain brought me to a table near the center of the dining hall and stopped next to a man sitting at the head of the table wearing prison clothes but without leg irons. The guard captain introduced me by my last name only to the man that he referred to simply as Sarge.

Sarge was a trustee who served as a straw boss for several prisoners, all of whom sleep in the same barracks along with him. The guard captain explained to Sarge that I was new and had just finished new inmate intake and that he was now handing me over to Sarge as a replacement for one of Sarge's crew who was no longer there. I remember thinking it odd at the time that there was no mention of why the missing crew member wasn't there. Had he completed his sentence? Had he died or, worse, been killed? I wouldn't learn until much later that the missing crew member had been a longtimer who had grown to be too sick to work. He had developed a cough that had gotten worse and worse over the last several months and that he'd been put on sick list a week before my arrival, only never to return or be heard from again. The inmate who told me this said that I should never ask about it again for fear that Sarge would know we'd been gossiping and take retribution on us for this behavior.

Sarge only glanced at me briefly before turning to the guard captain to say that he had it from here. The exchange between the guard captain and Sarge seemed to conclude, and the guard captain took his leave without further comment. After what seemed like several minutes, Sarge pushed his now empty plate aside and turned his full attention to me. He spoke in a voice not much more than a whisper, explaining the difference between an ordinary convict and a trustee.

A trustee, he said, "is an inmate who has been given the responsibility to run a crew of prisoners in their daily activities." He said that I should think of him as a straw boss whose instructions and commands carried the weight of a guard and that to cross him in any way will bear the same consequences as crossing one of the guards. As I continued to stand, the prisoners at the table finished their meals and, one by one, pushed their empty plates aside. Sarge, with a slight grin, went on to tell me that I'd missed dinner and that I should follow the lead of the other prisoners at the table as they went about their usual routine. I followed the prisoners as they rose from the table and walked single file to the back of the dining hall where they deposited their dirty plates and cups into designated tubs. Those who had spoons tucked them away in their clothes or boot, signifying that the spoons were the property of the prisoners who possessed them. Having done so, they then walked single file in silence to a barracks building a few hundred yards away. It was dark now, and without light, I stumbled on the uneven surface. I noted that no one else stumbled, suggesting to me that they must have walked this path often.

The barracks buildings were much like the other buildings that I'd seen with wood plank walls. The buildings were low-slung and elevated on rock piers about three feet off the ground. I was escorted to one of ten similar buildings. These buildings were about sixteen feet wide and 140 feet long. Each building had forty bunks, enough for four crews of nine prisoners plus one trustee for each crew.

The plank floors and walls were roughly sawn hardwood measuring two inches thick and a foot wide. The floorboards were laid side by side and nailed to wooden floor joists. The floorboards were warped and uneven, leaving cracks between the boards of up to an inch in width. I envisioned this being much more of a concern when the cold winter wind starts to blow, but for now, it being summer, this wasn't yet a problem. There's a sizeable potbellied stove in the center of each building and plenty of coal to feed its fire. There were clay chamber pots for use by those who have an urgent need during the night. At night, the doors were locked, and no one was allowed to leave the building until the next morning. The lowest member of each crew had the job of emptying the chamber pot for their crew in the latrine each morning. Being the newest member of the crew, this became my responsibility right away. I never thought of prison as a pleasant place, but by the same token, I never imagined that I'd be emptying chamber pots every day. And making the thought even more depressing was the fact that I would continue to have this responsibility until the crew loses yet another member. There's no telling how long that might be.

The barracks had double-tier bunk beds along the walls, and Sarge directed me to one such bunk, a bottom one. The bunks were all constructed of hardwood frames with rope strung tightly in a cross-hatched pattern as support for the bedding. On top of the rope web was rolled-up ticking with what I'd soon discover was sawdust filling, which would serve as my mattress. The ticking was stained and soiled and had a strong odor of old sweat and urine. The crew member I was replacing had this bunk, which was the only reason that I was allowed to have a preferred lower bunk—no one else wanted it.

The day's events had been overwhelming, and I found myself in dire need of sleep. But sleep didn't come right away. I lay awake with runaway thoughts in my head that I couldn't seem to control. I thought about all the horror stories that I'd heard about this place. But mostly, I thought about my place in this godforsaken hellhole. I tried to concentrate on that which I could see and hear and feel as I lay awake. I could see nothing in the blackness of night. I could feel the unevenness of my mattress and the ropes that supported it and nothing more. There was much, however, that I could hear—snoring, farting, groans, the grinding of teeth, and the sounds of restless movement of other prisoners tossing about in their bunks. From the bunk beside me came the constant sound of hacking, wheezing, and coughing. The prisoner in the next bunk was experiencing what sounds like symptoms of some fatal malady. I would later learn that the man's name was James Sobel and that he had been at Cole City for almost thirteen years. And like the man whose bunk I inherited, he was afflicted with the black lung.

As I lay there listening to Sobel's death rattle, I remembered the story I'd heard about an insurrection that occurred here a few years ago. The insurrection had been put down in a brutal fashion. I also remembered the story about the young girl who had been raped and the lynching of her attacker. I also remembered the story about all the miners who drowned in Pump Hollow.

Then, mercifully, sleep overtook me only to yield to one nightmare after another.

Chapter 4
A Lynching

Lying in my bunk that first night, unable to sleep, I recalled a story that I'd heard of a lynching that occurred at Cole City a few years back.

Eight of the ten barracks at Cole City housed Negro prisoners, all of whom live segregated from the white prisoners. The Negroes ate separately and slept separately and used a separate bathhouse and latrine. They worked with their kind, and the straw bosses were all Negroes. The guards were all white men, though. The white prisoners didn't have much contact with the Negroes except on Sunday mornings when we all attended church services together. But even then, the Negroes sat together at the back of the tent. I heard that most of the Negro prisoners were former slaves. I guess that would be true considering that the slaves were freed about twenty-three years ago. Only a few of the Negro prisoners were of a young enough age that they never served as indentured slaves.

Miss Hargrave, who was thirteen years old, lived with her father and her older brother in an apartment in Lower Cole City. The apartment was one of many along the road that ran through Nickajack gulch.

Miss Hargrave had been visiting with a friend in Upper Cole City after church services one Sunday morning.

A Negro trustee, named Jed Johnson, was working with a crew maintaining track nearby. Johnson saw Miss Hargrave as she made her way down the footpath that meandered from Upper Cole City on top of the mountain down to Lower Cole City in the valley below.

Johnson was familiar with this path as it was the same one taken by prisoners traveling daily between Upper Cole City and the coke ovens below. Johnson made an excuse to the guard of needing to relieve himself and disappeared from the guard's view and made his way to the footpath just ahead of Miss Hargrave. As she approached, Johnson sprung from the bushes and wrestled Miss Hargrave to the ground, knocking the air out of her. As the young girl lay on the ground unable to scream, Johnson struck her on the head with a rock the size of a cantaloupe rendering her unconscious. Johnson dragged Miss Hargrave into the bushes and ripped away her clothing as she lay unconscious. Johnson raped her and left her for dead.

Later that day, a different Negro trustee, walking along the same footpath, heard a commotion in the bushes and went to investigate. He found Miss Hargrave still alive and semiconscious but severely injured. The trustee hurried up the mountain to raise an alarm that was responded to by the two white free laborers who worked at the stables nearby. They rushed together back down the mountain to where Miss Hargrave had been attacked and found her in tattered clothes and bloody and nearly naked. They retrieved her dress and petticoat and draped her in them for modesty's sake and then carried her to the infirmary. Doctor Street was summoned from his home and, arriving at the infirmary, took charge of Miss Hargrave's care. Miss Hargrave was grievously injured, and Dr. Street was unsure whether she would survive. Word went out to Miss Hargrave's father, who was called to the infirmary. Reverend Pickett, who was enjoying a meal of fried chicken with the superintendent, was summoned. The reverend and Miss Hargrave's father anchored, a bedside vigil.

The Negro trustee, who had discovered Miss Hargrave, was initially thought to be culpable. He was charged with the crime by the guard captain and was thrown in the stockade. The following day, the guard on duty nearest the crime scene the day before came forward to say that he believed Johnson to be the one they were after. He told the captain about Johnson taking leave of his work and having been gone for an inordinate length of time. He told the captain that Johnson had blood on his clothes when he returned and that he had no explanation for this.

Miss Hargrave slowly began to regain her senses and described her attacker as a tall Negro man. Because Johnson was much taller than the trustee who discovered Miss Hargrave, the evidence began to point away from this trustee and toward Johnson. Johnson was then brought before the guard captain and placed in the stockade. At first, Johnson denied any knowledge of the whole affair, but when confronted with the evidence against him, he admitted his wrongdoing. The guard captain decided that he would be held for the grand jury and tried for his crime. The Good Samaritan trustee was released.

The entirety of the population of Cole City was up in arms demanding swift justice. And by nightfall of the second day, the word had spread throughout Dade County and the neighboring area of Tennessee and Alabama. A crowd of people from the area gathered in the yard in front of the stockade. The sheriff, who had been on-site for some time now, was expecting trouble, and he had brought with him several recently sworn-in new deputies. The peace officers stood ready to defend Johnson against the gathered crowd, but the sheriff, seeing the futility of such a quest, instructed the guard captain to release Johnson to his custody. The guard captain flung open the front door to the stockade and tacitly invited the sheriff inside where Johnson was unchained and marched out across the yard to the gallows where a rope noose awaited him. The mob, which had until now been boisterous, fell eerily quiet. Johnson was stood up on the trap door and the noose secured around his neck without undue delay. But before the trap door was released, a man from the mob ran up the gallows steps and, with a slashing motion, eviscerated Johnson from his navel to his sternum. Johnson would have fallen to his knees had there been sufficient slack in the rope to do so. Instead, he hung there, gagging and choking from the noose around his neck. The mob suddenly regained their voice and shouted out, "Kill the Nigger." The man with the knife turned to face the crowd and shouted out, "Take him, boys." Then at his behest, a barrage of gunfire erupted from the mob aimed at Johnson's still-breathing body. Johnson, whose body was riddled by this gunfire, succumbed to his many injuries.

The mob was not, however, sated. En masse, the crowd turned away from the gallows and began to rush toward the nearest Negro barracks with shouts of "Kill the Niggers" or "Burn 'em out." As the mob approached the barracks with torches in hand, aiming to burn the building down, they were met in force by the sheriff, his deputies, and the prison guards. The peace officers didn't so much disagree with the mob as they were compelled to protect the assets of the coal company. The loss of any number of Negro prisoners at one time would strike a severe blow to the operations of Cole City, for some time to come. Discretion was said to be the better part of valor, and with this, in mind, the guard captain spoke to dissuade the mob from their intent. The mob disagreed with the guard captain, but the peacekeepers easily outgunned the mob, leaving little recourse but to comply.

Johnson's mutilated body hung from the gallows for two full days. During this time, Miss Hargrave was moved from the infirmary to her father's apartment in Lower Cole City, where she received ongoing care and many well-wishing visitors.

As the weeks passed, Miss Hargrave began to show, and since she professed to have never lain with anyone of her own accord, the bastard child was from Johnson's seed. Miss Hargrave was sent to live in exile with an aunt in Baltimore and never seen or heard from again. Miss Hargrave's father and brother soon quietly left Cole City as well, and their whereabouts remained unknown to all.

Chapter 5
My First Day in a Coal Mine

On the first full day at Cole City, I was wakened from my fitful sleep by the sound of what I might have mistaken for a church bell had it been a Sunday. The sun had yet to make an appearance over Upper Cole City but would come shortly. In the valley where the coke ovens lay dormant, the sun would not appear overhead for a few more hours due to the height and steepness of the surrounding mountains.

I awoke to what felt like a hundred mosquito bites. As I scratched the many bites, I shook out my clothes to dislodge any nighttime creatures that may have taken up residence. I shook out the bug-ridden mattress upon which I'd spent the night. Scorpions, although not big, were common, and although their sting was not lethal, I would prefer not to endure the pain they inflict. With one inch or bigger cracks between the floorboards, my other concern was for snakes. Rattlesnakes were common and plentiful in these mountains, and even worse, there were the more aggressive copperheads. Prisoners called a copperhead a two-step because once bitten, you only have two steps before you're dead.

I'm sure that this was a myth, but I have no interest in disproving it. When it came to snakes and my fear of them, I border on the fanatical. To my mind, the only good snake is a dead snake. Learning of my fear of snakes, the members of my crew began to make sport of me. They told me about a prisoner who was bitten by a rattlesnake while working in the camp and was dying. I was told another story about a rattlesnake coming up through the floorboards of the barracks and ending up being tripped over in the darkness of night. I heard that the snakes around here could grow to be more than six feet in length but that I should be most cautious around much smaller snakes. I understand that the larger snake has more control over the amount of venom injected during a bite and generally do not pump as much venom as they could. But the smaller snakes, being less mature, tend to pump their full load of poison when they strike.

The result being that contrary to what you might expect, the bite from a larger snake is less likely to kill me. I found this to be a less than comforting fact. I was also told of a prisoner who got into bed only to find a large rattlesnake to already be in occupancy. Then there was the story of a prisoner reaching for his boots in the morning and grabbed a rattlesnake by mistake. Rattlesnake Creek nearby was, I'm told, aptly named because of the number of snakes observed there. Whether the stories were true or not, it provided the other prisoners with a source of much amusement. And it had the effect of fanning my fears. I made a promise to myself that I would judiciously check around my bunk and in my shoes for the presence of a snake.

The bell tolled incessantly, urging the prisoners out of bed and to the latrines for their morning business. Being unsure of the protocol, I have held my water throughout the long night and now have an urgent need for relief. My rush to the latrines was delayed while I sorted through the pile of boots at the door looking for my own. I shuffled out the door of the barracks down the three steps that brought me to ground level and followed the procession of prisoners, all of whom must have felt a similar urgency. The latrine was nothing more than a six-hole privy constructed of wooden planks. The configuration of the latrine did not allow for individual privacy but was instead communal in design. The latrine is built over a large hole in the ground that was half full of human waste. The noxious smell that you'd expect was partially subdued by the use of crushed limestone and limestone dust that was ladled into the latrine daily by some unlucky prisoner. After having to wait my turn, I entered and found every shithole occupied. When, at last, there was room for me to join them, I hurriedly loosened my prison trousers and let go of a stream with the vigor of a youngster. Such a feeling of relief was found in only a few of life's endeavors, and I must confess that I enjoyed the release immensely. The urgency of my need to relieve myself had blocked out all other thoughts, and only now did my attention turned elsewhere.

As I left, the latrine Sarge took hold of my arm and encouraged me along the pathway back toward the barracks. Without a word, he pointed to one of the chamber pots on the floor. As the newest member of the crew, I understood that it was my job to empty the chamber pots from this section of the barracks. The chamber pots were made from clay and held as much as five gallons. The chamber pots had grip handles built into the walls to aid in lifting and carrying. The chore was not a strenuous one but was a most unpleasant one. By the time I got the first chamber pot to the latrine, there was, to my good fortune, no one left in line. I dumped the chamber pot into one of the holes and repeated the whole process over and over. Along the way, I noticed a hole dug in the ground a few yards away from the latrine. I later learned that this hole was where the latrine will be moved too once the hole in use was full. The new hole was being dug well uphill and away from the creek and was to be dug as deep as possible before hitting the bedrock, maybe eight to ten feet below the surface. When the hole beneath the latrine was full, the building would move over the new hole and the nearly solid sludge in the old hole covered over with dirt. Such was the process of waste disposal for all the barracks. Most prisoners sought to relieve themselves as much as was possible during their workday when they can go in the woods near their work site, avoiding the unpleasantness of having to use the latrine.

On a return trip to the barracks to retrieve another chamber pot, I noticed what looked like a distorted body lying in the bunk next to mine. The lump was Sobel, and I assumed that he was the source of all the noise through the night. Sobel was a painfully thin old man with ribs jutting out from his emaciated torso. His thin gray hair fell wistfully over his shoulders, and his scraggly gray beard reached midway down his sunken chest. His bloodshot eyes were deep-set in dark sockets, and from the sunken appearance of his cheeks, I assumed that he had few if any teeth left.

Looking at Sobel wrapped in his thin blanket, shivering on his bunk and continuously coughing, I could not imagine him rising and going about the work of the day. The trustee jostled Sobel and yelled at him to get out of bed, but Sobel did not respond. The trustee left only to be replaced moments later by one of the guards. Sobel was once again directed to get out of bed. The guard impatiently grabbed Sobel by the arm and wrenched him from his bunk, forcefully pushing him toward the door. Sobel bent down and picked up his boots just before being pushed out the door by the guard. Sobel stumbled on the steps outside and fell on the ground. The guard again grabbed Sobel's arm and hoisted him to his feet. The last I saw of Sobel, he was duckwalked past the fence surrounding the kitchen toward the superintendent's office. That was the last I saw of Sobel until I returned to the barracks that evening.

Meanwhile, I was beginning to feel the discomfort of the morning chill and the hunger pain in my empty stomach. The mornings on the mountaintop could be brisk, so I took comfort in the prison-issued coat and turned my focus toward finding something to eat.

As it turned out, I, along with the other prisoners, had almost an hour of free time before roll call. From experience, I knew where to find the mess hall and proceeded there without delay only to find a line of prisoners waiting outside. So much for the hour of free time.

The mess hall was a long, low-slung single-story building of the same wood construction as most other buildings in Upper Cole City. The main difference was that the outside walls only went up about five feet and were open above. This feature not only allowed for air to circulate in the mess hall but also granted access by flies, which were everywhere. I suppose that they found some way to close off these openings in winter or inclement weather, but I didn't see how this could be done.

To the mess hall was attached an enclosed building that I take to be the kitchen. Separating the kitchen from the mess hall was a counter behind which were workers serving food to prisoners as they walked single file down the serving line. Steam filled the kitchen and spilled out over the serving line. I suspected that one of the best things about the food here was that it was hot. Prisoners sat shoulder to shoulder at long wooden tables eating at a leisurely pace without seeming to hurry in the least. The steam wafting over them was insufficient to gain their interest. I got behind the last prisoner in line with the resignation that roll call might come before I get any food. But much to my surprise, the line moved quickly. Soon I found myself taking a tin plate and cup from a pile just inside the door and having some gruel ladled onto my plate. I didn't recognize the food and did not find its appearance appetizing. But I was hungry and, therefore, grateful to have anything to quiet my starving stomach. I noticed that the other prisoners either ate with their hands or had makeshift spoons. I saw that the spoons were crafted from wood and were kept with them at all times for fear of losing them or having them taken away. Once I found a seat and began to eat, I discovered that the food wasn't as unfamiliar as I'd first thought. It was mostly just grits smothered in a flour-based gravy made from grease drippings. And there was a small piece of salt pork called streak o' lean alongside the gruel on my plate courtesy of one of the servers. I was allowed to dip my cup in the water bucket at the end of the chow line to provide me with a means to wash down my meal. The meal was salty and not the most nourishing, but it was filling and left me with a feeling of comfort that up until now I had not felt.

There was a bit of time before roll call commenced, leaving an opportunity for anyone so inclined to do a little horse-trading. Negotiations typically involved an exchange of cash for contraband, including tobacco and whiskey. One of the other prisoners in the barracks received a package from home the day before, and he was letting everyone know that he had tobacco to sell or trade. I had never developed a taste for tobacco and had no interest. Several others were, however, alert to the prospect, and I expected that whatever store of tobacco the prisoner had would run out by tomorrow. Rather than police such activity, the guards most often turn a blind eye to the goings-on. Sometimes, however, the guards involved themselves in the traffic and trade of contraband.

Prisoners often receive small amounts of money hidden away in packages sent to them from their families. Or they earn token amounts of money for performing extracurricular chores or favors for other prisoners or the guards. These favors may include protecting another prisoner from someone who means them harm or taking on some unpleasant task such as emptying chamber pots or sexual favors. Homosexual activities were frowned upon by the superintendent on religious grounds, but such behavior nevertheless occurred frequently. Certain prisoners referred to as cows make a habit of performing oral sex or allowing others to engage in anal sex with them. Some come to this behavior naturally and others, seeking to make their stay here less onerous, adopted such behavior. And, occasionally, especially with weaker new young prisoners, sex was not consensual.

Each crew of prisoners had a prisoner in charge. This prisoner had no formal authority or responsibility but was the one person everyone in a crew looked to for leadership. The prisoner at the top of the pecking order sometimes provided a measure of protection for the other prisoners in their crew. The top of the pecking order for the crew that I now belonged too was a man named George Prosser. Prosser was doing a long stretch for manslaughter. He was a tall man standing perhaps six feet three inches and big-boned. Prosser was muscular, which came, I suspect, from years of swinging a pick or handling a shovel for long hours of work every day in the mines. He was a quiet man with little to say to anyone. The prisoners in my crew knew not to try to engage Prosser in idle conversation. But the thing more than any that let them know that Prosser was at the top of the pecking order was the little differential gestures made toward him by the other prisoners. Prosser was always at the front of the chow line, his blanket was less worn, and his boots were newer and sturdier. More subtly was Prosser's detached dismissive nature, when dealing with Sarge or another trustee or a guard. Everyone gave Prosser a full birth. I've made a mental note to keep my head down in the hope that Prosser will take no notice of me.

Protection included shielding the weaker prisoners from unwanted sexual attention. In our crew, this responsibility also fell, by default, to Prosser. But the dirty work that would usually be expected to fall to Prosser, such as enforcement matters and oversight of the sex trade, was in the purview of another prisoner whose name was Henri Moran. Moran was Prosser's second in charge.

Like Prosser, Moran was physically imposing. He had the attributes needed to be an effective enforcer in this place. A Frenchman from parts unknown, he was serving a life sentence for stabbing a man to death during a card game in Savannah a couple of years previous. Unlike Prosser, however, Moran was always talking and was quite the loudmouth. Moran relished his role as a bully over this small crew. He was, however, less demonstrative when it came to dealing with his rivals elsewhere in the barracks or the prison proper. Underneath all his blustering, Moran was, I believe, a coward. But it must be remembered that being killed by a coward does not leave you any less dead. Moran, like Prosser, was someone to avoid as much as possible.

Many times, the packages sent to prisoners were inspected thoroughly by the guard captain, who kept whatever money he finds. But there were some prisoners in particular whose packages did not receive such a vigorous inspection. In such cases, the captain was rewarded for his willingness to turn a blind eye. More often, contraband, including tobacco and whiskey, were brought in by the free laborers or the guards who were known as bootleggers.

From my observation, it was clear that there was a simple measure of fitness to be the prisoner at the top of the pecking order. The longer a prisoner has been here was a factor, but only to a point. A ten-year veteran would most often be higher in the pecking order than any prisoner with a fewer number of years served, but not always. The stronger prisoners would always have dominion over the weaker prisoners regardless of the number of years served.

Prisoners like Sobel, who have been weakened by illness, were easy prey for ruffians. If not protected by Prosser and Moran, they would fall victim to thugs and goons from other crews and unscrupulous guards. It was unlikely that Sobel would be able to hold on to his prized possession, his spoon, for much longer. And without his spoon, he'll be reduced to the indignity of eating with his hands.

Then it was time for roll call.

Prisoners from each barracks would line up in front of their barracks. Guards would pass by each group one at a time and ask the trustee if all prisoners were present. If not, then the guard would put the missing prisoner on report, and a determination would be made then and there whether the prisoner had an excused absence or was absent without authorization. When the guard queried Sarge, he advised the guard that Sobel was missing and that he had been taken away before breakfast by a guard named Murdock. Sarge said that he did not know where Murdock had taken Sobel. This guard called out across the open area to Murdock, who was taking roll at the nearby barracks. Murdock turned when he heard his name and shouted, "Sobel is on special assignment." He went on to say, "You'd know this if you'd been where you were supposed to be this. I'm getting tired of covering for your lazy ass. If you want Sobel, he's swabbing out the office." The guard making the inquiry about Sobel made a mark on the piece of paper he was holding, issued an incoherent guttural grunt, and then turned his attention back to his roll call duties.

Every prisoner was frisked for contraband, concealed weapons, or food hidden away in their clothing. The guard didn't find anything except wooden spoons that the guard ignored. The guard proclaimed in a loud voice that the crew was all clear. He then turned to the crew to tell us that we'll be working in the main west tunnel of the Slope Mine today. I didn't know it at the time, but the main west tunnel of the Slope Mine was where I'll work almost every day. The crew trudged off together in the direction of the Slope Mine entrance stopping as we passed the toolshed to have a pick or a shovel handed to us through a window. Each prisoner also received a lantern filled with coal oil. As we entered the mine, the trustee would strike a match and light the lamps for each prisoner. If during the day the lantern went out, Sarge will have to be summoned to relight it as the prisoners were not allowed to have matches. I thought this ironic because every prisoner who smoked had matches. None of the prisoners let on to this fact. And I kept my thoughts to myself.

Sobel was sitting on his bunk when we returned from the mine. He still looked like death, with eyes sunk in their sockets, his cheeks were drawn, and he had a sickly yellow pallor. He explained to no

one in particular that the guard had taken him to the superintendent's office. He said that he'd expected the worst, but to his surprise,
he'd been directed to spend the day not in the mines, as usual, but
cleaning the floor in the antichamber.

Recognizing that the guard had let him off the hook for the
day, Sobel worked at a casual but steady pace. The job of scouring
the office floor is a job that usually falls to the trustee assigned to the
superintendent. But the trustee appointed this task is a lazy slug who
discovered that he can "borrow" a prisoner from the sick list to do
his job for him. Whether the prisoner's illness is genuine or feigned,
it made no difference to this trustee. Sobel was relieved to have light-
duty work and did his best to endear himself in so doing so that he
may be afforded the same consideration in the future.

I can already tell that life as a prisoner here is like a dance, and
I am just now beginning to learn the steps.

Chapter 6
More Ways to Die

Prison life at the mining camp at Cole City and coke oven operations was brutal and dangerous. Malnutrition, unsanitary conditions, and the absence of even essential medical treatment doomed the weak and the infirm. Tuberculosis, typhoid fever, pneumonia, and syphilis took many lives. But worst of all was the always constant dampness and cold from which there was no escape. After a while, death became preferred over the daily monotony and discomfort. Many prisoners chose suicide over the continuation of their misery. Suicide was easily accomplished by simply making a break for freedom. The guards, with their ten-gauge shotguns, were happy to oblige. Murders and deadly accidents were commonplace. Prisoners were made to mine the coal regardless of their health. Those who were unable to continue were allowed to die if it didn't take too long. Otherwise, their demise was hurried along.

Countless lives had been taken, and I believe that the souls of the unfortunate haunt these mines.

On the second night of my sentence, I was brought face-to-face with the cruel nature of Cole City. In the middle of the night, I was awakened by a rustling near my bunk. My head was turned in that direction so I could open one eye just slightly to see what the commotion was all about. In the darkness, I saw Moran bent over Sobel's bunk with something in his hand. Whatever he was holding, he was using it to cover Sobel's head and press him into the bunk. Sobel, weakened by his illness, lacked the strength to resist Moran, and within a short time, his protestation subsided. Moran stood statue-still for a long moment more and then turned his head toward me. My heart raced, and I nearly jumped up from my bunk to fight off Moran's murderous intent. But I fought the urge and lay perfectly still. Moran must have concluded that I had not awakened, and he, as quietly as possible, went back to his bunk. The next morning, Sarge found Sobel dead in his bunk. Sobel's body was quietly removed, and the rest of us went about our business as usual.

Sobel's murder may have been an act of mercy considering his condition and the absence of any prospect for his improvement. But I doubt that there was any charity in the act. Sobel could no longer aid in the mining process or provide other value in his condition. One of the unspoken rules of Cole City was if you can't work, you die. Sobel's death was an everyday kind of occurrence. I didn't know what happened with Sobel's body, but I heard rumors that range from his burial in an unmarked grave to being fed to the hogs.

So many men were subject to appalling conditions with an absence of charity, making this existence loathsome and hopeless. The exact number of prisoners who died in Cole City may never be known for sure, but without doubt, the number is in the hundreds.

The heart of Cole City and the extent of my world is the three-square-mile area around the entrance to the Slope Mine. Upper Cole City, at the very center of the town, is the nucleus of the prison camp activities and is the locus of all that is genuinely evil about this place. If there are such things as ghosts, then Upper Cole City, where so many died violently, must be a place that they haunt. Lying awake in my bunk at night, I could hear the voices of those lost souls in the whispering of the wind. I listened to them call out for me to join them, and from what I have learned about life here in these first few hours, I believe it likely that I would do so before my sentence is up.

The entrance to the Slope Mine in Upper Cole City is on a thirty-degree slope, which makes for treacherous footing for the first three hundred feet. Beyond that, the floor slopes less and less until once well inside the mine, the walking surface is more level. Mules are remarkably sure-footed animals and can negotiate the sloped floor easily. Inside the mine, mules are used to pull carts called tubs along rails to bring coal to the surface. Sometimes the distance can be miles along these rails. At the mine entrance, where the floor slope is steepest, a cable system hoists the tubs. Tubs ride on a single set of tracks with a cable attached to a large drum above the mine entrance. The drum operates on a cog gear powered by the piston of a steam engine fired by the same coal that we mine.

Once the coal tub reached the outside, the coal was dumped onto a steam-powered conveyor for "breaking," a manual process by which prisoners separate the impurities from the coal. The conveyor was the superintendent's most prized piece of equipment. It seemed that some fellow working for the Thomas Edison mining company up north had come up with an idea for moving material from one place to another by mechanical means. The colonel, learning of this revolutionary idea, had to have it. The contraption used a belt made out of something called vulcanized rubber. The coal, along with the tailings, was moved along the conveyor on this belt. The conveyor, like many new inventions, didn't always work well. In the winter, the cold weather would cause the belt to become brittle and prone to breaking. In the heat of a summer day, the belt would become slick and slip on its rollers. I've never seen the like, and I must admit to being fascinated by all the moving parts. When it worked, it was a marvel to behold. When it didn't work, the prisoners had to revert to moving materials by hand.

The coal was the obvious prize, but coal shale also had value, although much less so, for making coal oil used in the lanterns. The tubs carried coal, coal shale, and tailings to the surface where the three materials were separated in a process known as breaking. Breaking is a manual process in which the prisoners use their bare hands to separate the materials on the conveyor belt. The uneconomic fraction called tailings were discarded, the coal shale saved for future processing, and the coal sent on to the coke ovens in the valley. It was a job that was tough on the hands and the cause of many minor nuisance-type injuries. Because the coal was slick with moisture, the prisoners couldn't get a grip wearing gloves, so the hardship was something that was endured. More severe injuries occurred occasionally. These were mostly due to clothing getting caught in pinch points where the belt passes over the drive pulley or idler drum or where the belt passes over intermediate rollers.

The drive pulley was powered by a steam engine that also had several exposed pinch points where a prisoner could get caught in the mechanism. The result was crushed fingers and hands, broken wrists and arms, and shoulder separations. Unfortunately, there was no quick way to stop the machine in an emergency. There was at least one past incident in which a prisoner's sleeve was caught, pulling his upper torso into the works crushing him to death. Early on in my sentence, being the lowest seniority member of the crew, I'd have to substitute for a breaker in their absence. And the unpleasant nature of the work gave reassurance that those given this duty on an ongoing basis would find ways to get on the sick list as often as possible. One trick was to pack tobacco in the rectum, which resulted in an elevated fever and nausea, just enough to get a trip to the infirmary and a day off.

Once the coal was separated, it was dumped from the conveyor into tram cars below the tipple. The tram cars carried the coal over the edge of the precipice high above the coke ovens in Lower Cole City. The tram was attached to a cable allowing the tram full of coal to be lowered on a steep incline railway to the valley floor. This railway had a forty-five-degree slope and from all appearances was the most hazardous proposition. The incline railway had a dual track such that as a full car was lowered, an empty car was being raised, allowing for continuous operation. A third rail accommodated a small cab designed for up to four passengers to be carried up and down the mountain. I remembered hearing about an incident involving the passenger car that occurred shortly before my incarceration. A Georgia senator, accompanied by his wife, visited Lower Coal City to see the coke ovens. While there, he accepted an invitation from Colonel Towers to travel up the mountain to see the miraculous new coal conveyor. The party went up in the cab of the passenger car and after a tour returned to the valley floor in the same manner. As the car was repeating its climb up the mountain, it had nearly reached the top when the cable broke, allowing the car to plunge headlong into the valley below.

Fortunately, the cab had been empty at the time. One observer was said to remark that there wasn't enough left of the cab to make a decent toothpick. As fortune would have it, the senator, his wife, and Colonel Towers were uninjured. Colonel Towers launched an investigation that revealed that this was no accident. The cable had been sabotaged. This incident was a case of attempted murder. But unless the culprit was apprehended and talked, it might never be known who the attempt was on. A trustee was eventually charged with the crime, but no evidence of his guilt was ever found. The lack of evidence did not, however, prevent him from being sent to the gallows. The free laborers working in the vicinity were all fired, and the prisoners working under the guilty trustee were reassigned to duties as a breakers at the Slope Mine where they remain to this day.

*****

My crew entered the Slope Mine around daybreak and worked with only one midday ten-minute break and the occasional water break until the evening. Such a timetable left us without knowledge of what it was like to feel sunlight on our faces. I welcomed the rare chance to work as a substitute breaker. The work was horrendous, but at least I get to be outside for a little while. I enjoyed the short-lived change from endlessly toiling in the darkness of the mine.

The seam of coal that we worked inside the mine was, at this point, only about three feet in depth. The prisoners, therefore, had to lie on their sides to pick the coal. A great deal of shale and slate had to be removed above and below the coal seam to allow the seam to be fully exposed. Once broken free, the coal and tailings were shoveled into the tubs that were pulled to the mine entrance. The face of the seam where we worked now was perhaps two miles from the mine entrance. So deep were we under the earth that vertical air shafts had to be dug, allowing air from the surface to get into the tunnel where we worked. These air shafts were just holes in the ground that were surrounded by high rock walls to prevent anyone from accidentally falling in. The holes themselves might be as much as several hundred feet deep, and a fall from that height would most certainly be fatal.

The face of the coal seam was full enough for three workers using picks to work at the same time. Three other prisoners shoveled the coal and tailings into the tubs, and two prisoners had the job of leading the mules pulling tubs back and forth to the entrance. The job of handling the mules was less work than the other jobs, so you might think this job would go to the weakest crew members, but the pecking order didn't work that way.

The pecking order within the crew was mule handler first, followed by the prisoners shoveling, and finally the pickers. The order for who does what was predetermined by each prisoner's relative station within the crew. The job of mule handler went to whoever was at the top of the pecking order, which in this case were Prosser and Moran. I was new to the crew and no one to contend with either Prosser of Moran, so I was relegated to the job of picker. I, therefore, spent my first full day on my side, swinging a wood-handled pick into the coal seam ahead of me.

The mines were always cold, and a coat was necessary even on the hottest summer day, that is, until the strenuousness of the work was enough to raise a sweat. The mine was as black as coal itself, and all of the work had to proceed using lanterns. The coal tubs had lanterns affixed to the carriage so that it could be determined when the tub was fully loaded, and so the mule pulling the cart back toward the entrance could be coaxed along in an otherwise blinding darkness.

Besides the cold and the darkness, there's the dust that was thick and constant, making it hard to breathe, especially during a period of exertion. Prisoners would scrounge rags to carry with them into the mines so that they could wrap them around their nose and mouth as protection against inhaling the coal dust. On my first day in the mine, I had no such protection. And throughout the day, I steadily breathed in the thick dust with every breath.

I quickly learned that to last the entire shift in the mine, I had to pace myself to dig no faster than necessary but fast enough to not invoke the ire of Sarge or worse yet the guard. Fortunately, the guards didn't often come into the mines, preferring to stay on the outside except when the weather was terrible. The guards kept close track of how many tubs were brought out by each crew as their way of assuring that no one was lax. Sarge's presence was a constant as he stood just behind the pickers holding a lantern aloft in one hand and a handkerchief over his nose and mouth with the other and shouting out encouragement whenever he thinks someone is slacking off. Sarge had been a farmer before coming here, and his demeanor was much like you'd expect of a farmer. Unlike Moran, Sarge was less prone to hyperbole or demonstrative behavior and never raised his voice to anyone, whether his equal or occupying a station either above or below him on the pecking order. But underneath that calm exterior was a man with whom few were foolish enough to challenge.

Sarge was, I'm told, at Cole City for beating a neighbor man to death over a land dispute. The neighbor in his zeal to drive home his argument had made the mistake of thinking Sarge's soft-spoken nature was a sign of weakness and had crossed some imaginary line between civility and impropriety. The neighbor's broken body was a testament to the wisdom of never pushing Sarge too far. But you didn't have to know Sarge's history, because one look at his barrel chest and bulging biceps would tell you that he would not be someone that you'd want to piss off. Neither Prosser nor Moran would challenge Sarge's authority directly or talk back to him when he addresses them. He was diligent in performing his duties as a trustee and steadfast in his belief that the only road to salvation for prisoners here was through hard work.

By the midday break, my arms ached from the exertion, and the muscles in my shoulders felt as if I wouldn't be able to go on. My plan to pace myself to make it through the day needed reassessment. During the midday break, Sarge, who was typically urging workers on, told me that I needed to slow down a bit. Otherwise, I wouldn't make it to the end of the day and that that would lead to a whole litany of other issues. He also handed me a piece of rag with which to cover my nose and mouth. Looking back on Sarge's behavior, I have come to understand that it was a case of enlightened best interest. Sarge was not my friend. I retrieved a dipper full of water from the water bucket and went back to work.

The rest of the day passed slowly and monotonously without incident. Slowing my pace of work, I was able to make it to the end of the shift, but just barely.

38

Trudging back to the barracks, the crew passed by the hog pen with its collection of porcine prisoners, all of which serving a death sentence themselves, to the wash shed for just long enough to wash the coal dust from their face and hands with the lye soap provided for this purpose. The dirty water ran steadily from the shed down into a small creek just below the shed and on, eventually, to Cole City Creek. The water ran black.

There was about ten minutes of free time before the call to the mess hall. This short reprieve found most prisoners catching a quick twenty winks out of desperation. Then one at a time, each crew and each barracks were summoned to the mess hall for the evening meal. I retrieved a tin plate and a cup and took my place in line. During the day, I had kept an eye out for any piece of slate that I might be able to use as a makeshift spoon and was optimistic that the piece of shale I concealed in my boot would suffice. It was as simple as it was effective. The "spoon" was a piece of slate about a quarter of an inch thick by six inches long by an inch wide. The size and shape would serve the purpose, but it remained to be seen whether the piece of slate was sufficiently strong as not to break during repeated use. Only time would tell.

The food being served up was referred to by the prisoners as gruel, and I could think of no more fitting term for the appearance of the food. It had the consistency of a stew, which had the occasional chunk of something more substantial. I would learn that these more massive components of the gruel were chunks of squash. The squash came from the enormous vegetable garden on the edge of the camp. Since it was the middle of summer, squash was one of the more bountiful vegetables and an obvious choice for inclusion in the gruel. Other vegetables grown in the garden could be found in the gruel when they ripen. Summer meals may include tomatoes, green beans, okra, and corn. Winter meals may include cabbage, onions, and potatoes, which were harvested and stored for use through the winter. If you were fortunate, you might find a small bit of pork in the gruel. This welcome morsel could be a shred of shoulder meat, a knuckle, or even an eyeball. Nothing went to waste, and nothing went uneaten.

Chapter 7
Insurrection

It had been six months since I arrived at Cole City, and much to my surprise, I'm still alive. These first few months had been challenging but were lacking in any high drama, that is, until now.

It is winter now, and Ernest Shackleford genuinely believed that he would not survive another harsh winter at Cole City.

Shackleford, who was serving time for murder with no chance of ever getting out, was a malcontent and a troublemaker. Shackleford had managed to foment unrest among the prisoners over the fact that most did not have blankets and the ones who did took little comfort from their threadbare condition. The prisoners were cold and miserable. During the evening meal, Shackleford, who had spent considerable time inciting the prisoners, successfully instigated an uprising. There wasn't much to the incident at first. But the guards overreacted, and a couple of them fired shots into the mob that had formed, wounding two prisoners. Mostly, the prisoners just wanted blankets to stave off the cold of January. But the shots fired gave the mob a renewed purpose. It was now a life-and-death situation; and in response to the guards' ill-advised actions, the prisoners overpowered them, took their guns, and began to beat them. The ruckus spilled out of the mess hall and onto the prison yard, and an alarm went up. Prisoners in one barracks after another joined the fracas until almost the entire prisoner population was involved. The guards in the mess hall didn't stand a chance against the mob. With the prisoners running amok, the guards' lifeless bodies were torn shred from shred, leaving little to be recognized. Not yet fully sated, the prisoners began to strike out against each other, using the occasion as an opportunity to settle old scores with those for whom they held a grudge. The chaotic free-for-all spilled over into other areas until most of Cole City's center was engulfed.

The guards understanding the futility of trying to quell the uprising at its most volatile point withdrew some distance and observed. One barracks was set afire and was left to burn. Livestock was set loose. Pent-up anger overtook the prisoners as if it had a mind of its own, and the end to the hostilities was long in coming. As the night approached daybreak, the mob lost its momentum, much like the way an afternoon thunderstorm yields its fury to a calming rain. The inevitable surrender to the guards came without fanfare, and the guards began to corral the wrongdoers by the dozens. But the leaders of the revolt were nowhere to be found.

During all the confusion, a small group of prisoners, who were the ones to ignite the riot, broke away and found their way to the blacksmith shop. They quickly found the tools needed to remove their leg irons. They stormed the prison office, and finding the gun room unguarded, they helped themselves to the Long Tom shotguns racked there. The group, which numbered six in total, set out on foot to leave Cole City by the road leading to Hales Gap. They had gotten no more than a half mile when they heard the dogs on their trail. The guards were satisfied to let the riot run its course, but they weren't about to let this group escape. Hiding behind Cooper's barn alongside the road, the prisoners took up positions in anticipation of a gunfight with the guards closing in on them.

Among the guards were two brothers named Sam and Daniel Jackson who handled the dogs, which were six in number and of the bloodhound breed. The brothers, pulled by the dogs, were well out in front of the armed guards who pursued the escapees. The two brothers were dragged by the dogs on their leashes round the bend in the road just before Cooper's barn. Shackleford stepped out from the shadows and let go a blast from the mighty shotgun from less than ten yards away. The blast struck Daniel Jackson squarely in the chest, and he fell to the ground releasing his hold on the dogs. The other Jackson brother dropped the leashes holding his dogs as well.

All six dogs charged into the pack of escapees growling, snarling, and viciously biting them. All the escapees, except for Shackleford and one other, dropped their weapons and fell to the ground. They tried to cover their faces with their arms in a vain attempt to stave off the attack of the bloodhounds. Shackleford reloaded quickly and struck one of the dogs with the gun barrel. He then leveled the gun and pulled the trigger, killing the dog instantly. By now, the guards were within range, and they let go with a barrage of shots that ripped Shackleford's body to shreds. The other escapee who had remained standing was also killed by gunfire. The dogs were retrieved, and the four remaining escapees, mangled and mauled by the dogs, were rounded up in short order.

Meanwhile, the riot was wearing itself out as the inmates' enthusiasm for the conflict waned. Under threat of being shot by the armed guards, prisoners began to return to their barracks, that is, all except for the forty whose barracks burned to the ground. The guards quickly designated a refuge point, and these forty prisoners were assembled there soon enough. The mess hall would serve double duty as both a mess hall and a makeshift barracks until the barracks were rebuilt. The prisoners would have to sleep on the wood plank floor without the benefit of blankets. The mess hall's potbellied stoves would be kept burning all through the night, but they would provide little comfort against the January wind.

The four escapees were marched back to the center of Upper Cole City, where they were once again placed in leg irons. Instead of being returned to their barracks, however, the escapees were chained to a large oak tree, one of the few such trees to be found in Cole City, where they spent the cold night without the blankets that they had sought in the first place. Huddled and shivering, the escapees spent the night wondering what would become of them. They didn't have to wait long for an answer. With the sun rising in the east, the escapees were unchained from the tree and marched two hundred yards to where the gallows stood. The gallows were a permanent fixture of Cole City, but only a few have ever seen it put to use. Under armed guard, the other prisoners were ordered outside their dormitories and marched to the site of the gallows.

With everyone watching, Colonel Towers addressed the gathered crowd, saying, "In a failed attempt to escape Cole City Prison, these prisoners have taken the lives of three guards and one of our prized bloodhounds. Two of the guards had families that will forever bear the burden of having lost their father and husband and breadwinner. For their role in this shameful episode, they are to be hung by the neck until dead." With their hands tied behind them, rope nooses were placed around their necks, and a large trap door beneath their feet was released. The site was one that no one who witnessed it will ever forget. Eyes bulging and tongues lolling out of their mouths, the prisoners who weren't killed immediately by the snapping of their necks choked to death. The hanged escapees let go first their bladder and then their bowels, shitting their pants, and it was over. The prisoners did not get the addition blankets they'd sought.

Later that same day, another six prisoners were hanged. It can't be proven that these six prisoners struck the death blows against the deceased guards, but someone had to pay, and it might as well be them.

Later that day, Colonel Towers sent an urgent telegram to the state attorney general. The colonel downplayed the details of the insurrection, but nevertheless asked for an additional twelve prisoners. Operations at Cole City must not, after all, be interrupted.

Chapter 8
My Second Day in a Coal Mine

Other than Sobel's death, my second day at Cole City went much the same as the first. I found Sobel's spoon lying under his bunk and quickly stuffed it in my boot. I hadn't gotten to know Sobel and felt no remorse for his absence. I couldn't believe my luck to happen upon such a badly needed utensil at just the right time.

Although my body ached from head to toe from the previous day's exertion, I went about the morning routine like everyone else. I caught a glimpse of Moran staring at me and suspected that he was trying to decide whether or not I saw him murder Sobel the night before. I did my very best to not behave in any way different to feed his suspicions. I was unsure of Moran's motive for his actions and wondered if perhaps it had to do with an old score to be settled. But more likely, I think Moran was just doing what he'd been told to do. By taking care of this chore, he had solved a problem for the mining company having a prisoner too sick to work. Moran's action enabled them to replace Sobel with a healthy, hopefully, more productive, prisoner. Doing so would, no doubt, provide Moran the opportunity to garner some favor with the guards or even the superintendent himself. Or Moran may have seen a chance to take a life without worrying for the consequences. To think that there was one among our small group who would kill a man just for the sport of it was too worrisome to contemplate.

On my first day in the mine, I learned about pacing myself. Today I could complete my shift with more ease and with less discomfort. I returned to the barracks at the end of the day exhausted but feeling optimistic that perhaps I could survive the whole ordeal after all.

I was amazed at how quickly I had fallen into the daily rhythm of Cole City. Upon return to the barracks, I fell upon my bunk to take full advantage of the short break before the evening meal. I had been using the thin blanket that I'd gotten as a pillow. I found the blanket, instead, spread across the sawdust-filled mattress, and as I lay on top of it, I felt something beneath me. As I rose up, I pulled the blanket back, and there in the middle of my bed was a snake fully four feet in length. Being deathly afraid of snakes, I couldn't help but let out a scream that could have easily be mistaken as having come from a little girl. I jumped back, lost my footing, and fell on the floor all the while scrambling to gain purchase to allow me to escape. The other crew members, and indeed the entire barracks, including Sarge, were hysterical with laughter at my expense. As I scrambled up off the floor and made for the door, I turned to see Moran holding the snake up as he laughed. It turned out to be nothing more than a king snake and a dead one at that. While I suspect Moran to be behind this joke, I'll never know for sure who played this cruel trick on me, so revenge was beyond consideration. I vowed that from that day forward, I'd never lay upon my bunk without first checking for unwanted visitors.

Chapter 9
Pump Hollow

Death came to many of the prisoners working at Cole City. Of the many that entered there, few walked out alive. Most deaths were a result of the common causes such as illness from exposure to the elements such as the constant presence of coal dusts, the cold and damp work environment, and industrial accidents and, of course, acts of violence. Less often but still significant were deaths from falls from heights, snake bites, and even drowning. Cole City Creek ran fast and was in places quite deep. A prisoner falling into the swift water wearing leg irons had little chance for survival. But such occurrences were infrequent and were the cause of few deaths. Therefore, death by drowning at this mountaintop location was unusual, that is, except for the incident at Pump Hollow.

The main seam of coal that I worked was the Dade Seam, which was accessed by the Slope Mine that is entered from the opening near the center of Upper Cole City. A second seam, found deeper under the mountain, was accessed by a separate mine entrance on the opposite side of the mountain. This mine, known as the Rattlesnake, was worked daily by the prisoners from Cole City.

The Rattlesnake Mine entrance was along Rattlesnake Creek, which was little more than a trickle at this point except when it storms. There was a large spring located in Rattlesnake Gulf just below the mine tipple, where the creek would grow to a significant size. I'm not sure whether the mine entrance got its names from the stream or vice versa. Either way, Rattlesnake Mine was aptly named due to the number of such snakes found there. Daily about twenty to thirty prisoners could be found working the mine. I was never called upon to work this mine, and what little I knew about it came secondhand. The Rattlesnake Mine had a lateral entry instead of the slopped entrance of the Slope Mine. Like the Slope Mine, the coal was brought out in tubs pulled by mules along a narrow-gauge rail line that ran the full length of the excavation. Once outside, the coal tub would be pushed onto a tipple where the coal was dumped into tram cars below. There's a double-track incline rail system with a hoist at the top of the mountain that was used to lift the coal out of the Rattlesnake Gulf. The tram carried a mixture of coal and tailings to be dumped onto the breaker conveyor once the tram reached Cole City. Here the coal from the Rattlesnake Mine was sorted along with the coal from the Slope Mine. Except for the trustees and a handful of prisoners that were charged with conveying the coal out to the tipple, everyone associated with the operations at Rattlesnake Mine worked at coal extraction deep inside the mountain.

The Rattlesnake Mine was a wet mine, meaning that there's always some seepage of water into the mine. Other than causing wet feet, this characteristic of the mine was little more than an inconvenience.

On occasion, in the past, the prisoners working the seam would have a breakthrough to a small underground stream or reservoir. The prisoners would get wet, but their work would go on mostly uninterrupted.

I was told of an incident that occurred two years previously. During a period of much mining activity deep within a side tunnel, the wall sprung a leak. The straw boss instructed the miners to keep digging, expecting that as in the past the amount of water coming from the wall wouldn't be a problem. But on this day, the leak didn't diminish but got stronger and stronger. Now the miners were up to their knees in water with it ever rising.

Then suddenly, the wall disappeared under a torrent of water that rapidly flooded the tunnel. The prisoner's leg irons were like anchors pinning them to the floor of the tunnel. The miners had no chance to get out before the water filled the tunnel. Twenty-six prisoners inside of the mine drowned.

The only two prisoners to survive were outside the mine entrance at the time. They heard the screams deep inside the mine and started to rush in only to be met by a wall of water coming out. They were washed down the mountainside into Rattlesnake Creek below, which had grown to be most forceful as the water sought its level.

It was concluded that the miners had inadvertently broken into an underground stream that fed the downstream spring. In so doing, the miners had redirected the full flow of the stream into the mine tunnel. Within a few minutes, the flow began to ebb somewhat but it remained steady, and the damage was done.

The Rattlesnake Mine remained closed for some time after the disaster. Eventually, steam-powered pumps were brought in to keep the water level in the mine at a manageable level, allowing the removal of the corpses and a return to mining operations.

From that day on, the Rattlesnake Gulf up the stream from the mine entrance was known as Pump Hollow.

Chapter 10
A New Addition

Without Sobel, the work in the mine was more taxing than it would be if there was a strong back to replace him. It's now been ten days since Sobel died without any word about a replacement. As we sat at the table finishing our evening meal, I saw out of the corner of my eye a guard approaching with a prisoner in tow. The new prisoner was the replacement for Sobel, so we were quite naturally pleased to have him join us. More than anyone else, I was glad to see the new prisoner arrive because I get to move up one rung in the pecking order. That means that I would no longer have latrine duty. My euphoria would, however, be short-lived.

The new prisoner came from the prison at Marietta, where he had been confined to his cell for twenty-three hours a day ever since his incarceration more than six months ago. He was a big man, even bigger than Prosser, but he was quite young, perhaps no more than eighteen years old with a youthful round face that was both beardless and handsome. His head was sheared, leaving only short stubble, but from this, you can tell that he has blonde hair. Razors aren't allowed in Cole City, so all the prisoners sport full unmanaged beards. In this, the new prisoner was different because his beard was sparse and scraggly, most likely due to his tender age. From the very first impression, it was natural to take a liking to this young man.

Sarge introduced the young man James Wildeman, another farm boy, from Alabama. He was serving twenty years for crushing, with his bare hands, the skull of a rival for the affections of a young lady. The victim had survived, but his injuries had resulted in permanent brain damage; he would always be an idiot for the experience. Because the idiot had survived, Wildeman had gotten twenty years instead of being hanged. This knowledge should have put the rest of us on notice to be cautious around Wildeman, but things being what they were, caution was flung to the wind. Sarge went through the same routine with Wildeman that he had with me on my arrival, including giving him to know that latrine duty was to be his for the foreseeable future. Wildeman remained impassive while listening to Sarge. The young man remained very quiet the rest of the evening, laying on his bunk and turning his face to the wall. When the morning tolled, we got out of bed as usual. I was quite pleased not to have to carry the chamber pots to the latrine. Wildeman did not, however, make a move to undertake this chore. When Sarge once again told him that this duty befell the last man to join the crew, he continued to look impassive and still made no move to undertake the task. Finally, in a small voice that belied his size, Wildeman told Sarge that someone else could empty the chamber pots. He went on to say that he'd be happy to persuade anyone who disagrees. Since no one else but me had a dog in this fight, no one stepped up to challenge Wildeman. It was a short trip to the conclusion either that I had to continue to empty the chamber pots or that I'd have to convince Wildeman to do so. Since Wildeman outweighed me by probably a hundred pounds and had the physique of a farm boy, I didn't like my chances of convincing Wildeman of anything. So, one by one, I once again emptied all the chamber pots. I went to Sarge and pleaded my case asking for his intervention. Sarge did not hesitate to tell me that this was my problem and that I'd have to find a solution on my own.

Later that day, deep in the mines, Wildeman once again attempted to exert dominance over me and showed his disregard for my place in the established pecking order. The most senior prisoner on pick duty always worked the middle of the seam with those lower in the pecking order on either side where there were more tailings to be removed. The lowest prisoner in the pecking order was always left of center because working backhanded was more tiring for anyone who is right-handed, as most prisoners were. I had just been promoted because of Sobel's death to work on the right side of the center with the lower pecking order position to the left of the center going to Wildeman. After only a very few minutes, Wildeman proclaimed that he would have the right-hand place and that I had to move back to the left-hand position. Wildeman ordered me to "move shit heel, or I'll move you" and proceeded to shove me aside. I looked at Sarge, whose shrug told me all I needed to know about his lack of willingness to intervene. I now knew why Wildeman had been locked in his cell at Marietta for twenty-three hours a day. I also knew that I had to take matters into my own hands now before things got any worse.

I stepped back from the face of the seam to where the tunnel ceiling was high enough for me to stand upright and swung my pick broadside at Wildeman's left knee. Wildeman went down to one knee with a scream of pain and anger. As he bent over from the waist, I kicked Wildeman in the face as hard as I dared with my boot-covered right foot. Wildeman went over backward as blood gushed from his nose and mouth. Wildeman rolled over onto his right side with his face pointing away from me. I planted the toe of my boot into the small of his back, where I thought one of his kidneys would be. Again and again, I kicked Wildeman until he stopped moving. Only then did I comprehend the laughter and cheers coming from my crew. Even Prosser, who'd just arrived with a mule-towed tub, had a chuckle. The pecking order was preserved, and Wildeman reluctantly assumed his proper role. Lucky for me, the guard was back at the mine entrance out of earshot and was unaware of the fracas. I had taken an awful risk by my actions. Had the guard been aware of my actions, I would surely be disciplined, perhaps losing a finger for my effort. Wildeman carried his bruises well and made no complaint to the guard. The other crew members afforded me an increased measure of respect commensurate with someone not to be trifled with, and Wildeman didn't try to bully me again. The next morning, he could be seen emptying the chamber pots at the latrine.

In the coming weeks, I would learn, little by little, how to get along and what was expected of me in this place. The lessons were sometimes brutal and always had the effect of impressing upon me the experience to be learned. But my education would not be extended beyond that which was necessary. My crew was assigned to work the Dade seam of coal in the Slope Mine. Nothing more, nothing less.

The mines themselves had numerous other openings cut into the mountainside. But my crew never got to these more remote locations. Every day we would enter the Slope Mine and make our way to where we left off the day before. There were miles of underground passageways, honeycombing the entire area, interconnecting the various entrances. If not for the rails that led unerringly to the outside, many a prisoner would likely end up wandering aimlessly in the tunnels for days with little hope of finding their way out.

Chapter 11
The Coke Ovens

The area around Cole City was free of all vegetation and quite desolate. The steady plume of dense smoke from the ovens left a constant cloud lying across the valley floor that was deadly to the plant life. Rising from the valley below the smoke ascends the steep mountain to infringe upon the highest peaks rendering the mountainside landscape void of life. The entirety of Cole City was shrouded in a dull cloud that imparted a bleak and dreary feeling of dread and foreboding to the place. At night, the fires from the ovens lend a tinge of red to the smoke, reminiscent of the biblical description of hell's inferno.

The long row of dome-shaped ovens was arranged side by side, hugging the base of the mountain along Cole City Creek. Extending for more than a half mile toward the terminus of the small-gauge railroad coming up from Tennessee, the ovens dominated the landscape. The brick-lined ovens were as high as a man was tall. In the ceiling of the dome, just beyond a man's reach, was a hole in the top. Coal was charged through this hole in the roof. The hole, equipped with a damper, was also used to regulate airflow in the oven. The oven had a diameter of more than twelve feet and had a brick floor. At the base of the oven was a larger opening big enough for a man with a wheelbarrow to enter. The coal was ignited using tinder and the ensuing fire allowed to engulf the face of the coal pile. Then, when the fire was burning well, the damper was closed to restrict the flow of air into the oven. The discharge door was bricked up and sealed with mud. The coal would cook very slowly over the next two to three days, becoming almost pure carbon. Once the coal was sufficiently carbonized, water would be dumped through the roof hole to stop the process and cool the coke.

Once the coke cooled, the discharge door was broken open to allow a man to get inside to shovel the coke into a wheelbarrow to be rolled out and dumped onto a railcar. Impurities in the coke coagulated as slag during the process and were removed and discarded as unwanted waste. Accumulations of slag were visible in all directions for as far as the eye could see.

The ovens operated twenty-four hours a day, year-round, rain or shine. The work was hot and strenuous, especially in the summer months. Since the work was done mostly by free laborers, the method of payment was based merely upon their production. This arrangement allowed for the concentration of effort to be at night and in the early morning hours of the summer months. A worker could charge two ovens a night on average and was paid $1 per oven. Such work for such little pay meant that the least employable among the free labors were drawn to the job. Still, about 175 people, free laborers, and prisoners altogether worked at the ovens. The free laborers were mostly immigrants from Italy, many of whom speak little or no English, and Ireland, who's English was often undecipherable.

As occupants of the lowest social station, these free laborers were sometimes prone to drinking too much and getting into fights. On occasion, these tendencies interfered with their availability to work the next day, and since the ovens never stopped, someone had to fill in for these absentee workers. On such occasions, prisoners served as substitutes to do manual labor. In such cases, a prisoner would be assigned to a free laborer, and the two work together. Working as a team, the two could handle three ovens allowing the free laborer to earn a dollar extra. The prisoner, of course, was not paid for his effort. The prisoners chosen as free labor substitutes at the ovens were those who ordinarily had other duties around the ovens such as shoveling coal and slag. Prisoners would be reassigned from mining duties to help out at the ovens when needed. On summer nights, especially Sundays, after having finished a full day in the mine, I was sometimes called upon to spend the night tending the ovens for some hungover free laborer. I came to know about the operations of the coke ovens in this way. And such was how I came to loathe the free laborers who worked there. Given the opportunity to succeed undetected, most prisoners would be pleased to slit the throat of the bastards.

The 150 or so free laborers who tended the ovens lived in shanties or derelict apartment buildings built alongside Cole City Creek in Lower Cole City. The apartments were small, dingy places stacked one on top of the other, three and four high, that afforded neither luxury nor privacy. On Sundays, a few of the free laborers, mostly wives and children, attended church service in Upper Cole City. Most of the men spent the day recovering from a Saturday night spent drinking. It was in one of these apartments that the Hargrave girl lived on the day that she was raped. Her family, along with six others, occupied the same building in what was a typical scenario for the families of the coke oven free laborers.

Working at the ovens was somewhat less treacherous than working in the mines with fewer opportunities to suffer severe injury or death.

Most but not all the ovens have well-established earthen coverings. I noticed, however, that the earthen cover of several of the ovens appeared to be relatively new. One day, I asked the free laborer that I was working with about this, and I learned of a great tragedy that had befallen those working at the ovens. As I've said before, the ovens lie alongside Cole City Creek as it rushed headlong off the mountainside toward the Tennessee River. Under normal conditions, the creek was most formidable with the rushing water creating rapids that forbid traversing under the threat of death by drowning. There was one bridge over the creek in Lower Cole City and just one place upstream where the creek could be forded with any degree of safety. Prisoners risked their lives to construct a rock dam and spillway to divert some of the water from the creek to meet the needs of the ovens and to help control the raging flow. The dam had been washed out by heavy rains in the spring, and what little control there had been of the creek had been lost altogether. Company management eschewed the rebuilding of the dam in favor of keeping the workers and prisoners' efforts concentrated on mining and making coke. They reason that the probability of a second rain event of the size needed to threaten the operation of the ovens is unlikely to occur anytime soon.

Before the dog days of summer could come calling with their prolonged period of dry weather, a second summer storm of unimaginable fury occurred. The rainfall upstream at Upper Cole City was torrential, turning small branches into raging washouts. Prisoners in the mines had no idea what was happening until water began to wash into the slopped entrances and accumulate in the tunnels. Most of the rainwater deluge sought its level by cascading down the sides of the mountain. Workers in the mines were safe enough, but workers at the ovens saw the waters rising in Cole City Creek and began to seek higher ground. Some began to climb up the mountainside while other, less fortunate souls, believed that they'd be safe enough by climbing atop the ovens. The base of the ovens was, after all, a good twenty-five feet above the creek, and the ovens added height of another ten feet.

The raging creek rose rapidly and within minutes turned the event into what would be described by survivors as a flash flood. The rising creek breached the berm upon which the ovens lay and quenched the fires embedded in the ovens there. The ovens, not being designed with the intent to withstand the power of the rushing water, began to crumble and wash away, taking workers and prisoners with it. The storm didn't last long, and within an hour, the creek began to subside. Within two hours, the creek had returned to its usual course, but not before having washed away all or a big part of dozens of ovens, undercut a long section of the spur rail line, and upset the entirety of coke oven operations. Six free laborers drowned that day. But countless others saved themselves by either climbing the mountainside to safety or had swum well enough to find safe purchase downstream. The prisoners, all of whom wore leg irons, weren't so fortunate. The leg irons prevented them from climbing fast enough to avoid the surge of the flood. Once in the water, the prisoners' leg irons prevented them from saving themselves. Nine prisoners drowned that day. The bodies of the deceased free laborers and prisoners were recovered, loaded onto a train car, and moved to the cemetery at Whiteside Baptist Church where they were interned.

Colonel Towers spoke, quite eloquently, I'm told, at the memorial service where he praised the heroism of the fallen and pledged to rebuild what was lost. No prisoners were in attendance.

As soon as the prisoners lost could be replaced, work began once again on the upstream dam. The damage to the ovens was repaired without delay, the earthen covers restored, and production reintroduced.

Chapter 12
Pretty Boy Dupree

The coke ovens were located in Lower Cole City near the head of Nickajack gulch at the terminus of a six-mile-long rail spur off the main rail line at Shellmound. The ovens were in a valley two thousand feet below the center of the mining camp in Upper Cole City. The only access to Lower Cole City was via the spur line or by way of the two thousand feet descent from the mountaintop. Coal and the occasional passenger made the descent via an incline railway or a meandering footpath. The circumstance of the location made the prospects for prisoners to escape dim, but there would always be those who would try no matter the odds. Pretty Boy Dupree was one such prisoner.

Dupree had been sentenced to fifteen years hard labor for robbing a bank in Rome, Georgia, and was in his second year of confinement. A young and handsome man of about thirty, he was deceptively mean and adept at managing any situation. Dupree could talk his way out of almost any predicament, and when his words weren't sufficient, he could be a vicious and brutal adversary. One prisoner found this out the hard way when he pushed Dupree too far and lost an eye for his trouble.

To get special consideration, Dupree cozied up to the trustee for his crew with incentives such as tobacco and whiskey. Dupree was quick to volunteer whenever the guard came to the trustee in need of someone to work a double shift at the ovens. Dupree, being both intelligent and observant, thereby became very familiar with the operation of the ovens. For months, Dupree noted the repetitive

58

tasks associated with oven operations, when the ovens were charged with coal, when the coke was discharged, and how often the train operated. He also made a note of the guard's schedule and movement. With this information, Dupree could devise a detailed plan of escape, and on a night with no moon, he made his move. Just after the guard completed his rounds in the area where Dupree was working, he bashed in the head of the free laborer that he had been assigned to work with and made a break for the last railcar.

Knowing that the train was scheduled to depart on its usual run down to the mainline six miles away within moments, Dupree hurriedly stretched his leg iron across one of the rails just ahead of a train car wheel. The leg iron had just enough slack to allow Dupree to keep his leg and foot free of the path of the wheels. As the train began to roll, the wheel came into contact with the leg iron chain and began to push the chain along the rail. Dupree's heart pounded as he wondered if he'd made a miscalculation. Dupree was now being dragged along the ground by the chain as it slid on the rail. Then, at a junction where two sections of rail met, there was a slight gap, and the leg iron chain snagged in the gap. The weight of the train car rolling over the leg iron chain severed the chain in two places. Dupree scrambled to his feet and began to run alongside the moving train car. He only had seconds to spare before the car passed a guard station, so he had to be quick. Dupree placed his foot on the car's foothold and propelled himself up and onto the car. He quickly raked loose coke around himself as a means of camouflage and lay motionless as the car passed the guard station. Dupree was free. Later it was speculated that he had someone on the outside waiting somewhere near the junction of the spur line and the mainline who assisted him with the removal of the shackles, a change of clothes, and transportation. Such accouterments were indeed not beyond the means of locals whose allegiance to profit far outweighed any civic obligation. Dupree would be one of the very few ever to escape Cole City.

Few were aware of Dupree's success, but one who knew exactly how he'd accomplished it was the trustee that Dupree had been in cahoots with all along. Some months after Dupree's escape, the trustee whose name was Cuzzort managed to get himself assigned to a work detail at the oven one night and tried to duplicate Dupree's daring escape. Cuzzort, like Dupree before him, bashed in the head of the free laborer that he was assigned to work with and made his way to the train where he successfully severed his leg iron and mounted the train car. What Cuzzort did not know was that the guard at the only guard station to be passed had been instructed, under penalty of death, to carefully check every car as it left the yard for any hitch-hikers. Cuzzort managed to conceal himself well on the last car, and as it passed the guard station, he very nearly got away with his plan. Unfortunately, as the car pulled away, the guard, holding a lantern high aloft, caught a glimpse of a remnant of Cuzzort's prison garb protruding from the pile of coke and raised the alarm. But the train was on its way, and the engineer was unaware of any problem. It became a race to see if the guard could be roused in time to prevent Cuzzort from jumping off the car and getting away. The spur line being six miles in length gave the guards a measure of response time, and knowing that Cuzzort would have to wait until the train slowed near the junction with the mainline to safely jump overboard meant that the guards would be waiting for Cuzzort.

As the train began to slow, Cuzzort could see the light from several lanterns up ahead. He knew that it was now or never, so he leaped from the moving train. The berm where Cuzzort jumped was made of rock, and the fall was painful but not harmful to Cuzzort. He clambered to his feet and began to run through the brambles that tore at his clothes and skin. He could hear the sound of the blood-hounds coming for him and the shouts of the guards as they pursued him. Cuzzort could see just up ahead the opening of Nickajack cave and dashed toward the entrance. With the guards and dogs in hot pursuit, Cuzzort plunged headlong into the cave with no light to guide his way. The floor of the cave went from dry to ankle-deep water and then to chest-deep water as the bottom fell beneath his feet. Then just before the water would become too deep, the floor of the cave leveled off. Had the water gotten any deeper, Cuzzort would be in trouble as the remnants of his leg irons would prevent him from swimming, and he would surely drown. Cuzzort's only option was to continue in a direction away from the lights and the sounds of the dogs and guards. The dogs could not follow Cuzzort's scent in the water, and the guards were satisfied to sit and wait Cuzzort out—the thought being that sooner or later, he'd get cold and hungry and would surrender to them.

I've heard that Nickajack cave had been explored for as much as nine miles under the mountain. Someone said that the Confederate army stored munitions in the cave some fifteen miles from the entrance during the War Between the States. The vastness of the cavern had never been fully explored. Maybe Cuzzort found another exit from the cave and got away. Perhaps Cuzzort wandered in the dark until he met his demise, dropped to his death, found a poisonous gas pocket, or fell victim to a cave-in. It is more likely that Cuzzort got in over his head and drowned. The prisoners he left behind were eternally hopeful that Cuzzort had not merely gotten lost and died of exposure and starvation. A twenty-four-hour guard remained posted at the cave entrance for two weeks before being recalled to routine duties. Cuzzort was never seen or heard from again. Unlike the story of Dupree's escape that was hushed up, the story of Cuzzort's folly was widely disseminated among both prisoners and nonprisoners in the area. The superintendent wanted it known that Cuzzort's misadventure had resulted in his demise.

Chapter 13
Coal Creek War

The prison camp was entirely isolated, and little news of the outside world made its way to the prisoners here. What little "gossip" obtained was provided by the guards and from limited interaction with the free laborers working here. Occasionally we'd hear whispers about unrest among the free labor miners at coal mines in the region. Such rumors, having little to do with us, got little consideration, but their persistence over several months was met with growing curiosity among the prisoners at Cole City. The underlying issue related to the practice, employed by several mine owners, of replacing free labor miners with prisoners leased from the state. The revolt, centered in East Tennessee, pitted the free laborers against the mine owners over their use of cheaper convict labor. While the free laborers at Cole City were heard to grumble about the same situation at Cole City, it had not grown to open protest, much less revolt.

Then in 1891, word came that the situation had turned violent for mines at the northern end of Walton Ridge, about a hundred miles away. The conflict had given rise to a bloody labor confrontation between the free labor miners and the mining companies, supported by the state militia at the Coal Creek mine near Briceville, northwest of Knoxville. During the conflict, free labor miners attacked and burned down stockades and other mining company buildings at several mine locations in the vicinity, setting prisoners free in the process.

The conflict spread southward to Marion County along the Georgia border near Cole City and northward to Campbell County along the Kentucky State Line.

Cole City, being located in such a remote area of Georgia, was ignored. Then in the summer of 1892, free labor miners attacked the mine at Inman in Marion County, Tennessee, about twenty miles from Cole City. The stockade and prisoner barracks there were burned to the ground, and the prisoners were set free. Prisoners at Cole City overheard the guards' whisper with apprehension about the conflict. The number of guards doubled. What was heard from the guards soon spread by word of mouth throughout the barracks, putting both guards and prisoners on edge. The following day, a group of a hundred to 150 free labor miners from the region, including some from as far away as Kentucky, seized the train on the spur line at Shellmound and rode it to its terminus at Lower Cole City. Finding mostly free laborers with only a handful of prisoners there, the mob turned its attention to Upper Cole City and following the well-worn footpath climbed the mountain. A mass of armed guards met the mob at the top of Nickajack gulch. But the guards quickly realized that they were insufficient in number to dissuade the mob from its purpose, and fearing for their lives, the guards quickly lay down their guns. After setting the stockade, a Negro barracks, a barn, and the main office building ablaze, the mob set all the prisoners free. The white prisoners had their leg irons removed and were provided with food, water, and civilian clothes. Most of the black prisoners didn't have their leg irons removed and were not given any of the same consideration as the white prisoners. The escaping white prisoners, of which I was one, wasted no time in departing the mountaintop. Some of the recently released Negro prisoners, however, lingered, seeking some degree of immediate retribution against the guards and trustees. But the mob wouldn't hear of it, telling the prisoners that they must leave of their own accord and not engage in any further violence.

The white prison escapees split into two groups, one of which took off on foot in the direction of Hales Gap and the footpath to Murphy Hollow. The other group took off down the footpath toward Lower Cole City. The mob, having accomplished what it came to do, retreated down the footpath to Lower Cole City as well. Upon arriving at Lower Cole City, the escaped prisoners along with the mob boarded the train and headed off down the tracks toward Shellmound.

In response to this latest free laborer uprisings, Tennessee governor Buchanan dispatched six hundred militiamen to the area. Having learned of the mob's plan to attack Cole City, the militia was dispatched by train from Chattanooga to Shellmound. The mob and escaped prisoners were met at Shellmound by a contingency of as many as two hundred militiamen. The militiamen were well armed and well organized. The mob and escaped Negro prisoners hesitated only slightly before giving up without a single shot fired.

The white prisoners, unencumbered by leg irons, sought to make a break for open spaces at Shellmound. The militia, some mounted on horseback, made quick work of rounding up the remaining escapees. The white escapees who chose the route that led to Murphy Hollow were more successful, with about a dozen getting away completely. The successful escapees left behind a handful of prisoners who were too ill or infirm to go on. Another handful of escapees chose to stay in Murphy Hollow, enforcing their will on the saloon patrons and imbibing in alcoholic drink until they were recaptured by the guards.

The following morning, the militia swept the region, arresting dozens of escaped prisoners and free labor miners thought to have aided and promoted the insurrection. The arrested free laborers were held for trial in Tennessee and Georgia. No one from Dade County was found to have had a hand in the matter, and no arrests were made in Georgia. Over the following years, the number of free laborers convicted in the Coal Creek War overwhelmed the Tennessee prison system. With the collapse of the convict leasing system in that state, it was necessary to construct new maximum-security prisons.

The Coal Creek War was eventually quelled, but the damage had been done for the mines in East Tennessee, and most would never recover. The conflict had also struck Cole City. No one was killed in the incident at Cole City, but the impact on the operations as a result of the escaped prisoners would be felt for months while the last of the escaped prisoners were hunted down. Georgia continued the prisoner lease system for many years and slowly but surely rebuilt the slave workforce by transferring prisoners from other prisons in the state.

As a footnote to this story, Tennessee governor Buchanan failed to get reelected in 1892. The incoming governor, Peter Turney, seeing the convict leasing system as unprofitable to the state and increasingly unpopular among the voters, allowed the convict leases to the mining companies lapse, effectively ending the conflict.

Chapter 14
Internal Conflict

After the Coal Creek War incident, routine life at Upper Cole City resumed, and the little nuisances of daily life once again replaced the thoughts of more considerable concern in the minds of the prisoners. Prosser continued to enjoy his status as the top dog of the crew, and Moran continued to play the role of faithful sidekick.

Our crew was typical of the other crews composed of white prisoners in that we had some regular contact with the other white prisoners in our barracks but almost no interaction with the Negro prisoners in the other barracks.

Imprisoned men occasionally had conflict, and it was only natural. But such instances were of little consequence, that is, until Moran singled out a member of the crew adjacent to ours in the barracks over some minor grievance. No one remembered the details of the altercation, either real or concocted, and no one cared. But Moran, not being someone to let anything go and possibly seeking to enhance his reputation as an enforcer, pushed the issue beyond reason. Angry words were exchanged, and much blustering ensued. The other man was small of stature and slight of build but nevertheless unwilling to consent to Moran's demand for subservience. As the other man was outmatched by Moran physically, the prisoner at the top of that crew's pecking order took it upon himself to intervene on his young man's behalf. So Moran found himself face-to-face with a large Irishman named Fanning, who was looking to put Moran in his place. Now it was Moran who is overmatched, so he called upon Prosser for support.

Here's where things could quickly have gone off the tracks with an entire crew pitted against another crew for bragging rights. But Prosser, in his usual unruffled style, nodded to Moran and grinned, signifying to Moran, in no uncertain terms, that he had gotten himself into trouble and it was his responsibility to get himself out of trouble. Prosser went about whatever it was that he was doing and ignored Moran. Moran wasn't the type to back down even when it meant taking a beating, and that's exactly how this affair went. Fanning easily mauled Moran, pummeling him with one severe blow after another until Moran lay unconscious on the barracks floor. Sarge, like Prosser, choose to ignore all the excitement, but the commotion got the attention of a guard. Upon entering the barracks, the guard was met with the scene of Moran sprawled on the floor bleeding and Fanning standing over him with fists clenched.

These sorts of things happen occasionally. More often than not, there was little made of such things. But in this case, the guard had a genuine dislike for Moran and seized this opportunity to cause him some well-deserved pain. Moran was dragged out and to the infirmary where he soon regained consciousness. After being observed to be fit, Moran was moved to the stockade where he'll spend the night.

The guard filed his report with the superintendent, who read it with great interest. He too saw Moran as a troublemaker and decided that it was time to take action. Instructions were given to the guard, and preparations were made for a public display of disciplinary action. They planned to make an example of Moran.

At roll call the following morning, Moran was marched out in front of the gathered prisoners and placed in stocks that bound his head and hands. The captain of the guard approached and turned to the assembled crowd to say that Moran had run afoul of the accepted norm for prisoner behavior and that he was being punished accordingly. Another guard approached and handed the captain a large pair of long-handled pruning shears. The captain retrieving a mickey of whiskey from his jacket commenced to pour whiskey over the pinch point of the shears and put the bottle away. The crowd stood in complete silence as the captain extended the shears and quickly removed the little finger of Moran's left hand at the first knuckle. Moran howled in pain as blood gushed from the severed digit. The captain reached down and picked up the severed finger and held it aloft so everyone could see. He said that this is what happens when you break the rules and that this severed finger would be fed to the hogs. He added that a second offense would mean feeding the rest to the hogs.

Moran was led away and back to the infirmary where his wound was attended to and bandaged. Moran was sent out with the rest of his crew to spend the day in the mines. Bandaged and in pain, Moran went about his duties as if nothing had happened.

The object lesson here was that bad behavior led to swift punishment, but the lesson was lost on Moran. Instead of a commitment to change his ways, he committed to getting even with those who had wronged him. First on his list was Prosser for not standing for him and then Fanning for the beat down he'd received.

Revenge was something that required great patience here at Cole City, but Moran was not by nature a patient man. He'd have his revenge sooner rather than later.

Chapter 15
Prosser Is Murdered

Over the coming weeks, the tension between Prosser and Moran mounted. It was like listening to an old and mismatched married couple who couldn't agree on anything. Everyone knew that it was just a matter of time until things came to a head, and Prosser put Moran in his place. But surprisingly, things had been allowed to go on now for quite some time. Among the prisoners in the barracks, the odds on favorite to come out of the conflict ahead was Prosser. The other sure bet was that we wouldn't have to wait much longer for the issue to get resolved. And we were right.

During our daily routine, Prosser and Moran didn't often come into close contact. Prosser and Moran shared the task of leading the mules pulling the coal tubs from the excavation to the mouth of the mine. It seemed that one was always coming as the other was going, and the only time they saw each other was when they passed going in opposite directions, that is, except during the ten-minute midday break.

Moran's patience had run out, and his anger overpowered his reason. During a midday break, both Prosser and Moran happened to be at the excavation taking advantage of the brief respite. Prosser made the mistake of turning his back to Moran, and Moran saw the opportunity for which he had been waiting. Moran retrieved an idle pick and, before Prosser knew what was happening, buried the pick into Prosser's skull. Prosser was dead before his big body hit the floor. The other crew members wrestled Moran quickly to the ground, but there was no resistance from Moran. It was as if his blow to Prosser had taken all the wind out of him and he had no will to resist. Wildeman picked up Prosser's limp body and deposited it into the coal tub. I led the mule pulling the tub down the tunnel as Sarge and Wildeman escorted Moran a few steps behind. When we got to the mouth of the mine, Sarge told the guard what had happened and turned Moran over to him.

The guard, a young man who hadn't been on the job very long, seemed bewildered and confused about what to do next, so Sarge accompanied him as he took Moran to the stockade. The rest of us stood around talking and wondering out loud what would happen to Moran until Sarge returned. Then it was back to work as usual.

Later at our evening meal and until lights out, the absence of Prosser and Moran was noticed and seemed unnatural. We kept looking for them to be there, but they weren't. Wildeman was particularly mournful as he had grown quite fond of Prosser as had we all to a greater or lesser degree.

There was no concern among the crew as to who would assume the role of new top dog for our little crew, but circumstance demanded that someone step up to take the job. We, as a group, had to show strength and resolve, or we'd fall under the control of one of the other crews. Wildeman was the logical choice because of his size and strength. The problem with choosing Wildeman was that he suffered a defeat at my hands and was therefore not seen as being strong enough. By default, it fell upon me to take my place at the top of the pecking order for our crew. The straw boss would now look to me to manage the small daily nuisance issues that inevitably arose and to mediate conflict between crew members. Nothing in my life, up to this point, had prepared me for this role. I felt quite sure that, before long, my ineptitude will result in a pick in my skull like Prosser.

But as luck would have it, Wildeman, who at first had been an adversary, would turn out to be my staunchest supporter. I was fortunate to have Wildeman, who was quite willing to serve as my second and be the muscle that will surely be needed. Wildeman and I assumed our place at the top of the crew's pecking order and took over the day-to-day jobs as mule leaders the next day.

We never knew what happened to Prosser's body and were probably better off for it. By contrast, we knew well what happened to Moran. At roll call the following morning, Moran was lead from the stockade to the gallows with his hands tied behind his back. He was marched unceremoniously up the steps to the raised platform of the gallows, and a noose was placed around his neck. The superintendent climbed the steps and took a position facing the assembled prisoners.

"Gentlemen," he said, "it gives me no pleasure to be here today, yet here I am. Even after being warned in a most demonstrative way, Henri Moran has chosen to break our most grievous rules. By taking the life of another, Henri Moran forfeited his right to live among us. It is, therefore, my duty to see that the sentence of death by hanging is carried out."

The superintendent then asked Moran if he had any last words. Moran replied by hurling a great gob of spit in the direction of the superintendent. He missed. The captain of the guard placed a black bag over Moran's head and stepped away. Without delay, the trap door opened, and Moran fell to his death as the crowd looked on in silence.

The superintendent faced the assembled prisoners again and said, "Let Moran's fate be a lesson to anyone who doubts our resolve to enforce our rules. Moran will not have the benefit of a proper burial but will have his worthless carcass feed to the hogs. Now get to work!"

We may never know whether the superintendent had Moran's body fed to the hogs, but I, for one, did not doubt that he did just that.

Chapter 16
Epidemic

Among the longtimers here at Cole City, there was a tremendous amount of hacking and wheezing and coughing up black mucus. From their haggard appearance, it was apparent that they were weary to the bone. But after a while, the hacking became just background noise, and no one paid much attention to it.

This was my first winter here and I had not yet become desensitized to the evidence of illness and despair. But it wasn't until someone remarked at the abnormal amount of misery that I began to notice that there was more sickness than there was just a few weeks ago. My first reaction to this realization was that it's only a product of the cold weather. But as more and more prisoners fell ill, I began to wonder if there's not more to it than that. It's not just the coughing but prisoners with diarrhea, vomiting, and a high fever. Some were unable to get out of bed due to weakness and delirium.

My crew was down to just three able-bodied prisoners. And even the straw boss was unable to go. There were more sick prisoners than the infirmary could deal with, and sick prisoners were told to stay in their barracks.

I was one of the fortunate ones who hasn't yet fallen ill, so I did what I could to bring comfort to the prisoners in my crew. I covered those that were having chills with blankets and tried to get them to take water. I kept the fire going in the potbellied stove, and I brought back sustenance from the mess hall for those who wanted it and could keep it down.

I went to the infirmary to find Doc Steele and was told by the orderly, who himself was a prisoner, that even the good doctor has fallen ill. The orderly told me that it's the flu and that there's no medicine left. He told me that everyone will get better and that we just have to keep giving them water and wait it out. Then prisoners began to die. One after another, the death toll mounted. The few healthy prisoners left standing dragged bodies out of the barracks and stacked them like cordwood in the prison yard to be dealt with later, if there's anyone left alive.

At the height of the epidemic, there weren't enough healthy workers to man the kitchen. Healthy prisoners were left to their own devices to scrounge whatever food they could. Many of the sick went without nourishment for several days, not that many of them complained, as they were too sick to eat anyway.

In the third week of the epidemic, the militia arrived bringing food and medicine, and within a day or two, things began to improve slowly. The kitchen reopened, and meals began to get prepared once again.

Remarkably none of the militia came down with the flu for reasons that I never knew. If it hadn't been for that fact, I suspect that most of the prison population would have perished. As it was, more than a hundred prisoners succumbed to the flu. I understood that the free laborers and their families who lived in or around Cole City experienced a similar fate with at least another hundred to two hundred of them dying.

Doc Steele, having gotten over the illness, returned to camp to oversee the recovery and, although still weak, spent many a long hour attending to the sick. One of the orderlies, who had been the doctor's favorite, would not survive, leaving that much more to be done by the few left to attend to the sick.

By the time the next thaw came, there were enough able-bodied prisoners to dig mass graves on the hill overlooking the Slope Mine entrance. The dead bodies were piled in the graves and covered over with six feet or more of dirt. When spring finally came, the epidemic was well behind us, and the superintendent, who had only barely survived the epidemic himself, said a few words over the grave. Otherwise, life went on.

The Black Marie was seen to arrive at the office regularly, bringing prisoners from Marietta and elsewhere to replace those who had perished. The two members of my crew who had died in the epidemic were replaced within another week or so.

I would learn later, from talking with one of the guards who had survived the epidemic, that Cole City had survived the flu epidemic better than some. The flu, it seems, had run rampant throughout the country, and many thousands of people had died as a result. Somehow that failed to give me solace.

Chapter 17
Camp Sumter

The newest addition to our crew was a quiet, unremarkable man of average height and a lean 165 pounds. In his midforties, he had the look of someone who has had a soft life. His hands were not callused and his shoulders were not stooped. He didn't walk with the bent posture of a man whose back was used to hard labor. And the shoes he wore when he arrived at Upper Cole City were expensive in comparison to the brogans worn by others. When asked the usual question as to what brought him here, he smiled and said, "A lack of good fortune," that is, until after being among us for a good long while, he at last shared his story. When he did so, the story he told us was a remarkable one.

Robert Wilcox, originally from Huntington, West Virginia, traveled to Charleston, West Virginia, to join the Cavalry Corps of the Union Army in 1864, as soon as he turned eighteen years old. Not long after enlisting, he served under Union Major General David Hunter at the Battle of Lynchburg in June of 1864. The Union forces were routed there and forced to retreat. A handful of Union soldiers were left behind during the retreat, and Wilcox was one of them. Along with two other soldiers, Wilcox hid out in the woods for several days but was eventually rooted out of hiding by a Confederate patrol party. The other two soldiers fought bravely but were shot and killed. Wilcox seeing the futility in continuing the fight against the rebels laid down his rifle and was captured. It was a time when most captured soldiers either Union or rebel would be shot on the spot rather than taken into custody. Wilcox benefited from an unexpected reprieve. He didn't know why he wasn't shot with his body dumped in a ditch, and he didn't ask. Perhaps his tender age and almost child-like appearance made his execution more than the rebel captain leading the patrol party wished to bear.

Wilcox was moved behind rebel lines, placed in restraints, and herded onto a train with dozens of other captured Union soldiers, many of whom were wounded and unattended too. Along with other Union prisoners of war, Wilcox was sent to Camp Sumter near the town of Andersonville in Southwest Georgia. There Wilcox found himself among thousands of other Union soldiers interned. Long after the war was over, he'd learned that at the time he was at Camp Sumter, there were more than 45,000 prisoners of war confined in an area of only sixteen acres.

Calling Fort Sumter a fort was a misnomer. It was essentially a prison compound consisting of a twenty-foot-high stockade fence with several guard towers surrounding a low-lying area. Situated twenty feet inside the stockade fence was a four-foot-high split rail fence. The space between the enclosure and the split rail fence was a no man's land. Any prisoner found in no man's land was shot. There were no buildings to speak of and few trees to provide shade against the hot South Georgia sun. The only source of water was a small stream that ran through the camp, which the prisoners used for both drinking water and for human waste. Prisoners slept on the ground out in the open, rain or shine. Lucky for Wilcox, it was August when he arrived at Fort Sumter, and August was the driest time of year in the South. Other than the occasional afternoon shower, Wilcox could stay dry. But that wouldn't last. As the summer days stretched into fall, the rains were more frequent, and before long, the ground of the entire camp had the consistency of a hog wallow. There was no escape from the constant dampness, and as the nights grew colder, the misery deepened. As November edged relentlessly toward December, the first frost would appear. While the days remained warm enough, the nights brought a chill to the bones. Prisoners would huddle together, trying with little success to ward off the chill. There was little else to be done but to shiver and shake until the morning sun returned to provide some relief.

Wilcox went on to say, "The camp is on half rations, and you'd be lucky to get even that. Fights broke out between prisoners over the smallest scrap of food. Hunger became a constant companion. There is talk of acts of cannibalism, and while I did not witness such, I am prone to believing that it may have been right."

"Escape is not an option as the prisoners were too weak to muster the energy needed for such an effort. And all the while, rebel guards with rifles kept a close eye on the camp. Anyone who approached the fence would be shot dead without as much as a warning.

"Every night, prisoners would be lined up along the fence, and guards would walk along the outside of the fence surveying the sea of humanity before them. Without exception, one prisoner would be selected each night and taken away never to return. I could still hear the screams and pleas for mercy of the unfortunate ones echoing through the night. The same young Rebel lieutenant selected an unlucky Yankee prisoner each night to get taken away. I will always remember his face as he came down the line to where I stood, shoulder to shoulder, with the other prisoners. When he got to where I stood, he paused for a long moment. Then raising his hand slowly, he pointed to the prisoner next to me. The prisoner, who I had come to know as a friend, was taken away. I have nightmares even still about this moment in time, and I can still hear the screams of my friend as he was dragged off into the night. We were left to wonder about his fate and the fate of all of those that got taken away. When left with only our imagination, the mind conjured up an endless array of cruelties and ways to die."

Wilcox was at Camp Sumter for ten months before the camp was liberated, and he was set free. Upon his arrival at Camp Sumter, Wilcox had been a youthful and scrawny 155 pounds. When he finally was released, his weight had dropped to just 92 pounds. Still, he was one of the most fortunate. Over 13,000 prisoners of war died while being held at Camp Sumter. Some were shot. Others were murdered by a fellow prisoner. Many succumbed to starvation and the unsanitary conditions that gave cause to any number of deadly illnesses. The dead bodies were so numerous that giving them a proper burial wasn't possible. Many of the unnamed dead were dumped into mass graves and covered over with dirt never to get identified.

After the camp was liberated, Wilcox was put on a train to Savannah and then a ship bound for a hospital in Baltimore. The worst was over, but it would take many months for Wilcox to recover from his ordeal fully. His body mended, but Wilcox would carry memories of his time at Camp Sumter for the rest of his life.

It was at this point in the story being told by Wilcox that he paused for what must have been a minute or more. In the silence, that minute seemed to go on forever. Then he spoke again, saying, "Cole City is as close to hell as any of you will ever get. But I have been to hell, and I'm here to tell the tale. You have a warm place to sleep and a bunk where you can lay your head. You get to eat two meals a day. You work set hours, and you have Sundays off to thank your maker. There's a camp doc to tend to injuries and illnesses, and you have latrines. These are things that the prisoners at Camp Sumter would have killed to have. So give that some thought the next time you feel like bellyaching about being here."

Wilcox had talked himself entirely out of breath and fell silent.

Later on, Wilcox told us that he had returned to Charleston after his discharge from the army and had taken a wife. He moved to the Nebraska Territory to try his hand at homestead farming. But he discovered that farming wasn't in his blood. He and his wife resettled in Omaha, and Wilcox found work as a clerk in a mercantile store. He and his wife tried mightily but were never able to have any children. Wilcox became a deacon in the church he attended, and the two of them settled into what became their life for more than twenty years. But it wasn't destined to be a happily ever after kind of life. Four years ago, Wilcox's wife contracted consumption and fell gravely ill. She would linger for two years, suffering from her illness all the while, before finally succumbing to the inevitability of death. During this time, Wilcox, believing that God had forsaken him, turned away from the church and took up the bottle.

Wilcox drank more and more heavily and would eventually lose his job because of it. After that, Wilcox roamed the country, finding work where he could and spending his earnings on whiskey. Most recently, he had been just down the road in Murphy Hollow, where he'd found a job as a bartender in one of the saloons there. The owner of the saloon accused Wilcox of skimming profits off liquor sales for himself. Wilcox was drunk when he was arrested for this crime. He had but $2 in his pocket, so it remained uncertain as to whether he was guilty or not. Nevertheless Wilcox was tried and convicted of embezzlement and sentenced to five years imprisonment. Like this, Wilcox came to Cole City.

All the prisoners at Cole City had to attend the Campbellite Church service on Sundays, and Wilcox was no exception. While sitting with Wilcox on one such Sunday, I observed Colonel Towers enter and take up residence in the very front row, as was his habit. At the same time, I noticed Wilcox become very restless, wringing his hands and fidgeting with his cap. Once the service came to an end, he couldn't get away fast enough. When I tracked him down in the camp yard, Wilcox was beside himself, rambling on about some non-sense that I couldn't quite make out. Only after a long while did he seem to settle down a bit and begin to speak coherently. He asked me who the well-dressed man that had come to the service late and sat in the front could be. I was surprised to know that Wilcox did not know who the colonel was and said so. Wilcox then told me that he had met the colonel before but not here, not at Cole City. When Wilcox had arrived here, he had been greeted by the guard captain and had not met the colonel at that time. Wilcox seemed quite alarmed at the fact that the colonel was the camp superintendent and wondered aloud how such a man could ever hold such a position.

When finally I got Wilcox to tell me what he was talking about, I learned that Wilcox thought that he knew the colonel from his days at Camp Sumter. Although it had been almost twenty-five years and the colonel quite naturally looked somewhat different now, Wilcox did not doubt that it was the same man.

The colonel was proud of his service in the Confederate States of America (CSA) and spoke of it often when addressing the prisoners. All we knew about the colonel was what he told us and now what we heard from Wilcox. The colonel had said to us that he was originally from Anderson, South Carolina, and that he'd enlisted in the CSA as a captain of Company E of the Georgia 8th Infantry in 1861. He told us that he'd been promoted twice and ended his service after Appomattox.

But no one knew for sure anything more about the superintendent's rebel army days, except for Wilcox. Wilcox told us that when he was at Camp Sumter, Colonel Towers had been a lieutenant and one of the officers overseeing the guards. Of all the Union officers that served at Camp Sumter, Lieutenant Towers was memorable because of his treatment of the prisoners in his charge. Towers was well known for having singled out individual prisoners of his choosing to have brought to him at his guard post. It was rumored that Towers would perform the most sadistic imaginable torture to see how long the prisoner could endure before they died. The rumors were widely believed because night after night, the prisoners could hear the screams and the begging for mercy coming from the prisoner in Towers' grasp. And not once was a prisoner that had been chosen by Towers returned alive. Some died quickly, but most took a long, long time with their pleas heard well into the night. Night after night, the prisoners listened helplessly to the sounds of one of their own dying a slow and horrible death.

Wilcox had this irrational fear that the colonel would recognize him from their days at Camp Sumter and that his fate would forever be sealed with a single knowing look. I argued with Wilcox that it was unreasonable to think that the colonel could pick out one in fifty thousand prisoners, especially after all these years. But Wilcox could never be convinced. Whenever Wilcox was in the vicinity of the superintendent, he would go to great lengths to make himself as inconspicuous as possible.

Seeing Wilcox this way, an entirely reasonable man in all other respects, gave credence to the belief that he must have truly endured hell on earth while at Camp Sumter. And after his first encounter with the colonel, Wilcox never spoke to me about his time at Camp Sumter again.

It's possible that Wilcox had it all wrong and that the lieutenant he knew at Camp Sumter was not the colonel who is superintendent of Cole City. Or it could be that the colonel was hiding the truth about his evil past. Perhaps we will never know one way or the other.

Chapter 18
A Passel of Hogs

Another winter was descending on Cole City, bringing with it an increased measure of misery. Winter here was a series of wet days with mild temperatures intermixed with bitterly cold days with snow and ice. It's as if Mother Nature can't decide which causes more misery, so she delivers a healthy dose of each, one after the other. On most winter days, the mines, with their constant mild temperature, were a welcome alternative to being out in the weather.

Ever since the flu epidemic of last year, there had been a shortage of prisoners. And it had been challenging to get free laborers to come to this remote place when they could find more available work for more money elsewhere. As a result, the superintendent had turned to the use of prisoners for jobs that would ordinarily be handled by either trustees or free laborers. Prisoners that had the least history of causing trouble were handpicked to take these other jobs. Notwithstanding the incident involving Wildeman soon after his arrival at Cole City, my record was clean, so I was selected for chores associated with the hog farm. As luck would have it, I got around the harsh work in the mines for now in favor of work out in the elements. With the warmth of the late autumn sun, I welcomed the chance to be outside. But as I said, winter was coming and I expected to miss the relative warmth of the mine soon enough.

The hog farm consisted of a fenced area of about forty acres adjacent to a similar-sized plot of land dedicated to growing vegetables in the summer. There were no trees for shade from the sun in the open pen, so a brush arbor had been constructed to give the hogs relief from the summer sun. No such favor was afforded the prisoner whose job it was to tend to the hogs. With winter coming, the lack of shade wasn't a concern at the moment, but come July and August, the coolness of the mines was a pleasant reprieve. Either way, it's not for me to choose the work, and I will do whatever was required of me regardless of the weather.

For the hogs' comfort in the summer, one corner of the pen had been dug out and was full of water to create a hog wallow. Even now, as the weather turned relentlessly toward the frigid days of winter, the hogs seemed to enjoy the wallow immensely. I could only imagine how unpleasant the hog wallow was come the harsh winds of January.

Last February, several brood sows gave birth to litters of piglets. Around 250 healthy piglets were kept, and after six to eight weeks, the overage was sold off to help pay for feed. Now the remaining piglets have grown to become mature barrows or gilts weighing over two hundred pounds. Starting in the fall, the responsibility for the care and feeding of which fell to me, at least until it came time to butcher the whole passel of them.

Twice a day, I collected scraps from the mess hall and mixed them with water and ground corn from the barn to make the mash to feed the hogs. I slopped the mash into troughs made from one-by-twelve boards nailed together to form a V so that every hog has a chance to get a share of the bounty. Altogether, I figured to deliver more than a ton of mash every day, so this task took up much of my day. The rest of the day was spent repairing the fence surrounding the hog lot. Rooting was in a hog's nature, and they would seem to have a fondness for rooting underneath the fence, causing me to have the endless burden of repairing the fence before any of the hogs managed to get out of the pen.

Since Thanksgiving, which was just another day on the calendar, the temperature had been mostly below freezing. As the days marched endlessly forward, the daily temperature had steadily fallen. That means that although it a bit earlier than usual, it's time to butcher the hogs that will provide Cole City with meat for the coming year. But the choice of day in which to slaughter the hogs depended on more than consistently cold temperatures. The wisdom of our elders told us that to prevent the meat from being tainted, the hogs must be butchered during a full moon. So the calendar was watched closely to be sure that this requirement was met.

As preparations were made for the coming full moon, I assumed that I would be returned to my regular mining duties, but I was told to return the next morning to assist in the butchering of the hogs.

I was roused quite early the following morning and was allowed the briefest of moments to quickly gulp down a bowl of gruel before being directed to the hog pen. As daylight broke upon the yard, two guards with Long Tom ten-gauge shotguns kept a watchful eye on all that was going on. There, set up close to the pen, were several large vats full of water. I was instructed to retrieve kindling and coal and build a fire under each, which I commenced doing without delay. Long wooden tables had been set up alongside the vats, which I assumed would be used for butchering the meat. Several free laborers and other prisoners were milling about with a handful working feverishly to kindle the fires under the vats. It wasn't until the vats of water were near boiling that activity increased. Then with a flourish, everyone was suddenly busy. I noticed that a gate was erected in the fence and that the opening beyond led a short distance to a dead end. The purpose of this structure was to allow one hog at a time to get separated from the passel. Once a hog was in position, one of the free laborers aimed a .22-caliber rifle at the hog's head and pulled the trigger. When struck by the bullet, the hog, which wasn't killed but only stunned, dropped to its knees or fell on its side. A second free laborer approached the stunned hog and, using a butcher knife with a thin blade of twelve to fourteen inches in length, made an incision in the hog's throat and then thrust the knife up to its hilt into the hog's chest. The objective was to puncture the hog's heart with the blade so that the animal would bleed out. The fallen hog was loaded into a wheelbarrow and rolled alongside one of the vats of steaming water where the hog was hung upside down with its front feet off the ground and allowed to bleed out. Two free laborers worked quickly to cut off the hog's head and set it aside on a table nearby to be used later to make head cheese. Using a gallon-sized wooden bucket, the men dipped hot water from the vat and doused the hog's carcass to scald it. Then using a special tool called a bell hog scraper, the workers removed the hair from the carcass.

Meanwhile, the prisoners were tending to the fires and replenishing the water in the vats to keep the vats full of boiling water at all times. One of the workers eviscerated the carcass allowing the intestines and internal organs to fall out and into a waiting wheelbarrow. The heart and kidneys were separated and placed on the table. The stomach and intestines were removed to a designated area where they would be hand slung to remove any undigested food and feces. The stomach and intestines were kept entirely separate from all other meat and thoroughly washed in lye to prevent contamination. The intestines were later made into chitlins. Unusable parts such as the lungs were deposited into barrels and saved for later use as hog feed. The carcass was then moved away and rehung nearby to allow the meat to cool naturally until the following day.

The process of singling out one hog at a time and preparing it to get butchered was repeated again and again until all 250 hog carcasses were hung up awaiting butchering the next day.

Only the brood sows and a single boar remain at the end of the day. The number of hogs was greatly diminished, meaning less work for me. But the need for attending to those who remain continued unabated. So I had to make sure the remaining hogs were fed and that the fence around their pen was maintained. Tending to the remaining hogs was in addition to minding the fires under the vats.

Early the following day, the butchering process began. Again my job was to keep the fires burning under the vats. In addition to heating water, some of the heated vats were used to render fat to make lard. The fat would melt under the heat of the fire and turn to liquid that would get poured into five-gallon tins. As the fatty liquid cooled, it would solidify and take on a pure white color and semisolid consistency of lard. In addition to sectioning the fat for rendering, the hogs were cut into shoulders, hams, ribs, bacon, and fatback and laid out on the tables.

The meat was thoroughly rubbed with a mixture of sugar, salt, and black pepper. The ribs, bacon, and fatback were then laid out on shelves in the smokehouses with plenty of the curing mixture and covered with cotton sheets. The hams and shoulders were put into empty feed sacks with the shank end pointing downward into a closed corner. Hams and shoulders, which number a thousand, were hung from the rafters of the smokehouses with the shank end pointing down to allow proper drainage. The meat would be left this way without being disturbed for six weeks. During this time, my duties at the hog farm were minimal, just feeding the brood sows and the boar and tending to the fence. Since the vegetable-growing season was over, the brood sows and boar were relocated to the forty-acre plot adjacent to their pen, used as a garden. The hogs were allowed to root for any leftover root vegetables such as turnips or potatoes. The purpose in this was to use this year's hog pen as next spring's garden plot. The hogs would have most effectively tilled the soil, and the hog shit, although foul-smelling, would serve as an excellent fertilizer. The whole process was repeated every winter, and every spring, a new brush arbor and wallowing pit were constructed. The fence around the garden plot was put there to keep out the deer, and I must improve it to hold swine. Once the fence was improved and the remaining hogs moved to their new pen, I had some time to attend to other less urgent matters. I was, for example, allowed to venture into the forest in search of chestnuts, which I gathered by the bushel to bring back for the hogs.

When it's time, the smokehouses, which were closed tightly to keep out vermin, were now even more tightly sealed for the meat-smoking process. Hickory wood would be gathered, split, and cured ahead of time as fuel for smoking. It only takes a small fire, but smoke must be continuously generated. Care must be taken to assure that the fire doesn't blaze up. Each smokehouse must be watched closely for the two weeks needed to smoke the meat. Once again, I had another new task added to my daily routine. It seemed that the reward for doing good work was getting more work.

Once the meat was cured, it was left in the smokehouses as long as the weather remains cool. Before the warm days of spring, the meat was moved to storage in the "cooler." The name cooler was a term used to describe an otherwise inactive area of the mine that was suitable for keeping meat and vegetables. Suitability means that the location was close to camp and far enough underground to benefit from the constant coolness there. The cooler has a vertical air shaft to promote air circulation and lower humid. Even though the cooler had much less dampness than elsewhere in the mine, mold growth on the meat was common. Mold growth was trimmed away when the meat was moved to the kitchen. Vegetables, including cabbage, turnips, and potatoes, and fruits, including apples and pears, were dry stored here to preserve them. Come spring, close to twenty tons of cured pork will also be dry stored here. It was from this store that the cooks would retrieve the ingredients they need for the daily meals for the prisoners throughout the year.

The last prisoner to have the task of tending the garden and the hog farm eventually made a trustee with the rank and privileges that accompany the position. He was one of the few prisoners to live long enough to complete his sentence successfully. I have hope that I may yet be able to survive this ordeal. Such thoughts flood my mind and lift my spirits.

Chapter 19
Fire

The flu epidemic depleted the ranks of prisoners and free laborers alike, and adjustments had to be made to deal with the manpower shortage. With fewer prisoners working in the mines, coal production was lagging. Most of the ovens that ordinarily operate continuously were cold. Crews were consolidated so that a smaller number of straw bosses could supervise them. Barracks were closed. But one strict unwritten and unspoken rule was observed without exception. The Negro prisoners were housed separately from white prisoners. Nor did they work alongside white prisoners in the mine. They did, however, work alongside free laborers, tending the few ovens operating just as they had done before the flu epidemic.

Food was plentiful, but there remained an insufficient number of kitchen workers to feed the prisoners adequately. And the quality of the food, already just barely edible, suffered greatly.

The prisoners double up on job duties working longer hours and get pushed to work harder. Without sufficient sleep, accidents became more commonplace.

There was much unrest in the camp as a result of the harsh conditions, and tempers were short. More than a few dustups occurred between prisoners, especially between whites and Negroes, who believed that they were being treated more harshly than the white prisoners. This grievance had been long-standing at the camp. And there was a great deal of truth to the notion. The Negro prisoners were seen as beasts on burden whose well-being was on little concern. Negro prisoners who were old enough to remember what it was like to be a slave working in the cotton fields long for the days of dragging an eleven-pound cotton sack in the hot sun.

This simmered for day after day until the situation finally boiled over during an evening meal when one particularly boisterous Negro prisoner loudly pointed out that his food ration was only half what the white prisoners got. The loathing felt by Negroes for whites and vice versa fueled what happened next. Within seconds, the latent hostility between whites and Negroes rose to a fever pitch. The Negroes shouted, threw plates and cups, and turned over several tables in the mess hall. White prisoners, although much fewer in number, made a motion to respond to the challenge, but before it could come to blows, the guards stepped between the two groups. One guard fired his Long Tom ten-gauge shotgun blowing a hole in the roof such that the stars above could be visible. Two other guards also stepped between the two groups standing with their guns at the ready as well.

The guards' intervention was just enough to quell the conflict for the moment. And the Negro straw bosses herded the Negro prisoners back to their barracks, to the jeers and cheers of the white prisoners, who eventually went back to their meals.

As the evening wore on the prisoners, both Negro and white settled in for the night. The potbellied stoves were stoked to fend against the night's chill. Boots were piled at the barracks door, and the prisoner shuffled across the bare floor in their leg irons and climbed into their bunks. Even after lights went out in the barracks, disgruntled whispers continued to be heard among the white prisoners. Many in my barracks thought that the Negroes were "uppity" and that they need to be taught a lesson. There were several comments about wanting to "put them in their place." Gradually the comments became less and less raucous, and eventually, silence befell the place.

Sometime in the middle of the night, I was roused from my sleep by a great commotion. Outside the barracks could be heard the sounds of men shouting. But there being no windows, we couldn't know the source of all the activity.

Suddenly the door to the barracks burst open, and a breathless guard yelled to those of us inside to get our boots on and follow him. As we poured out of our barracks, the night sky beyond our barracks was aglow. Following the guard around the corner of the building, the source of the commotion and the glow in the night sky was immediately evident. The roof of the Negro barracks that was the farthest from the center of the camp was ablaze.

Flames rose above the roof a full twenty feet into the air, creating a billowing column of thick black smoke. The single door to the barracks stood wide open with flames visible inside. Smoke seeped through the cracks in the walls, giving an otherworldly appearance to the scene.

A bucket brigade was formed, and Negroes and whites alike fought feverishly to contain the blaze. Bucket after bucket of water was poured on the fire with what appeared to be little or no effect. So those fighting the fire were told to "just let it burn itself out" and to begin throwing water on the next barracks to keep it from catching fire from the heat. For the next hour or so, we continued to douse water on the roof of the unignited barracks and nearest wall as the nearby fire raged. Eventually, the fire began to run out of fuel and lose its ferocity.

With the fire smoldering, roll call was announced, and all the prisoners assembled in the still dark camp yard. A head count revealed that all were present and accounted for. It had been something of a miracle that one of the guards had spotted the fire early enough to unbolt the door and get all the prisoners sleeping inside out to safety. But medals weren't handed out for saving prisoners' lives at Cole City, especially Negro lives. The only thanks he got was from the Negro straw bosses whose lives he'd saved, an all but imperceptible nod in deference.

With the number of prisoners diminished from the flu epidemic, there was no great challenge in finding bunks for the displaced Negro prisoners. The now homeless prisoners were settled in new quarters quickly, and the camp soon returned to its quiet nocturnal norm.

The next morning, as we assembled for roll call, the ashes of the burned-out barracks were still smoldering. Among the assembled prisoners, there was much chatter with accusations and innuendo flowing freely. Many of the white prisoners were gloating, saying that the Negroes had gotten what they deserved. Many of the Negro prisoners wondered aloud whether their misfortune was at the hands of some white prisoner or guard out to do them harm.

Cooler heads surmised that a white prisoner could not have set the fire as they were all locked down for the night. This conclusion seemed to provide a measure of satisfaction to many, but not all of the Negro prisoners. Then, the idea surfaced that perhaps the guard who had first spotted the fire had set the barracks ablaze himself. Some of the Negro prisoners noted that he had been the guard who had intervened between the white and Negro prisoners in the mess hall. All eyes of the Negro prisoners then turned as one to look at the guard in question. The guard, seeing that he was being accused, calmly pointed out that the fire started in the roof where the stove pipe exits the building and that it was probably overstoking the potbellied stove that caused the fire. He added that everyone should remember that he was the one who got them out of the burning building and that if he intended them harm, he wouldn't have been so quick to help them to safety. All his posturing served only to appease those so inclined to believe him from the outset. Those who were predisposed to blame the guard for the fire remained mostly unpersuaded.

Whether coincidence or not, the Negroes barely avoided their demise and, as a group, were, from that moment on, less boisterous with their grievances.

I saw no difference in the white prisoners' attitude toward the Negroes before or after the fire. The white prisoners had come from a society where Negroes were thought to be inferior in every way, and there was nothing that could be said or done to convince them otherwise. Yesterday's dustup in the mess hall wasn't the first of its kind, and I doubt that it would be the last.

Chapter 20
Tending the Garden

After the fire, things began to get back to normal, or at least the Cole City version of what's normal. The winter was starting to relent, and the promise of spring was buoying spirits. I have been busy tending to the brood sows and the boar at the hog farm, which included moving the pen to last year's garden plot. These duties took up a considerable amount of my time, but not all of it. I was lucky not to be sent back to the mines to help out with production and thankful to have any other task instead.

As luck would have it, I was assigned to work the garden, and with winter giving way to spring, there was much to be done in this regard. It seemed that my predecessor at the hog farm had also had garden responsibility, and this combination of duties had worked out well for him.

The garden plot for this coming year was last year's hog pen. As soon as I could get the brood sows and boar relocated to their new enclosure, I'll turn my attention to getting the new garden plot ready for planting.

The new garden plot was a full forty acres in size, and preparing a plot of that size for planting was a daunting task. Fortunately, the hogs had done a lot of the work for me by tilling the soil and contributing their waste to serve as a natural fertilizer.

As soon as the ground thawed sufficiently to be tilled, I would spend each day behind John or Jake, the two mules that were dedicated to farmwork at the camp. I'd never handled a plow or worked with a mule, and at first, it was quite strenuous work. But little by little, I learned to work with the mule instead of against him, and things went much better.

I learned much about gardening from the straw boss, whose name was Ahrens. Ahrens taught me that if you're not losing some plants to frost in the spring, then you're not planting early enough. He also taught me about planting by the signs. Once I came to understand and apply this knowledge, the rest, though complicated, began to make sense. It's March, and now would be the best time to plant cabbage, collard greens, and onions, among other things.

Planting root vegetables such as beets and carrots would be done in the summer months, and everything else would be planted in between those two seasons. Knowing when to harvest was much simpler. I simply waited until the crop was ripe. Harvesting started as early as May and continued until frost, usually sometime in early November, just in time to shift focus to slaughtering hogs.

One of the unusual aspects of my predecessor's gardens was his herb garden, where he grew the spices that made the gruel served up by the kitchen edible. Ahrens grew traditional herbs such as garlic, oregano, and sage. Medicinal herbs were also cultivated, such as chamomile flowers used for wound healing and to reduce inflammation or swelling; echinacea root used to treat colds, flu, and infections; goldenseal root used as an antiseptic; ginger used to relieve nausea and diarrhea; and castor beans used to relieve constipation. Ahrens consulted with Doc Steele about which herbs to plant, and Doc Steele made ample use of the product of Ahrens' effort.

Between my work in the garden and my work at the hog farm, I found myself on my own much of the time. And I didn't have much to do with most of the other prisoners. I still had to be at the top of the pecking order for my crew. But this duty was something that occupied little of my thoughts or time. More and more Wildeman had taken over the more cerebral aspects of this role to go along with the physical aspects that he has always had. I still answered to Sarge, who was still my straw boss. I also answered to those who had responsibility for the garden and the hog farm, including Ahrens. I always took meals with my crew, and I still bed down with my crew every night. But little by little, I was becoming more estranged from them. The newer crew members didn't know much about me, nor did I know much about them. In most ways, all these changes seemed to work in my favor. Of course, anything was better than working in the mines.

Chapter 21
Two Norwegian Brothers

Two Norwegian were the next to be introduced to the crew. From the similarity of their physical appearance and facial features, it was clear that they were brothers. Although not twins, they shared the same blond hair, dimples, and blue eyes. They were the same height, about six feet, and weight, approximately 160 pounds. They had the same mannerisms and the same heavily accented way of speaking softly. One was just a bit older than the other, but a casual observer would be unlikely to say which is which. There was no question that the two of them were quite young, but it was hard to get a fix on their age. They stuck together like, well, brothers. They ate together, slept in bunks that were near each other, and often seen sharing the same hand-rolled cigarette in the camp yard. They kept to themselves, only speaking to others when spoken to and then by saying as little as possible. They came to Cole City together in the Black Marie just a few days ago and had been acclimating to their new surroundings very slowly. They took turns emptying the chamber pots for the crew in the mornings, as was the custom for the latest member of the crew. They spent their days lying side by side, picking coal from the seam in the Slope Mine. During water breaks, they drank from the same dipper full of water. They spoke with an unfamiliar accent that at first was hard to decipher, but as time went on, we all got somewhat used to this.

Crew members come and go with murder and sickness being the usual cause for departure and, to a lesser degree, executions, drownings, cave-ins, falls, and such. Wildeman could be the source of any other crew member's demise, and with his quick temper, such an event wasn't out of the question.

Wildeman, now being the top dog for the crew, took it upon himself to try and get to know the new prisoners and attempted on several occasions to engage them in conversation. But between their heavy accents and Wildeman's poor language skills, these attempts were less than successful. It didn't take long for Wildeman to lose interest and, for the most part, leave the new prisoners alone. With their limited interaction with the other members of their crew, it was almost like the two brothers were an entirely separate crew unto themselves.

Sarge, who was still the straw boss for the crew, was his usual stoic self and involved as little as possible with anything related to, well, anything. He'd give direction to the two brothers as needed but offered no further conversation.

What the brothers failed to realize was that in a place such as Cole City, the straw boss was everything. A good rapport with the straw boss could make all the difference in the world, literally. And the failure to develop such a rapport could mean the death of you.

One day, after the brothers had been working in the mine for several hours, they, along with other members of the crew, became dizzy and disoriented. Within a few minutes, the crew members were overcome and fell to the floor of the mine unconscious. There's no telling exactly how long the crew lay motionless when Wildeman came along, leading a mule-drawn empty coal tub and discovered them this way. Wildeman, remembering a lesson driven home to him again and again during his introduction to working in the mine, knew to make a hasty retreat in search of better air. Wildeman found Sarge at the mine entrance chatting with the crew's other mule handler. Raising the alarm, Wildeman urged Sarge to do something. Sarge and Wildeman raced back down the mine tunnel but stopped short of the excavation where the other crew members lay motionless on the mine floor. Sarge threw a lantern ahead to where the bodies lay and was relieved when, as it crashed against a side wall, there was no explosion, which means that the crew had not been overcome with explosive gas. Digging into a pocket of methane was an unusual but not unheard of occurrence and could be a fatal hazard from both asphyxiation and explosion. With methane gas ruled out as the culprit, the logical options were either bad air or insufficient air. Sarge knew that to rush in would risk being overcome in the same way as the crew. Sarge immediately took off his jacket and began to fan the air ahead of him vigorously. Wildeman seeing this did the same. The mines had vertical air shafts to provide a steady flow of fresh air into the mines below, but the airflow could, on occasion, be insufficient, leading to the kind of problem before the Sarge at the moment. By agitating the air in the tunnel, Sarge hoped to cause enough circulation to prevent them from being overcome and maybe even save some or all the stricken crew members.

Sarge and Wildeman went in a single file about ten feet apart, taking one slow step at a time. Sarge first reached a fallen shoveler and dragged him by his jacket collar away from the excavation. The Sarge handed this prisoner off to Wildeman, who hoisted him up and into the coal tub. The two men repeated this process again and again for the other two fallen shovelers and then again for the nearest picker. But when Sarge reached for the second picker, one of the brothers, he became dizzy and fell to his knees. Wildeman seeing this sprang forward and caught Sarge before he fell over and dragged him away from the excavation. Sarge was hoisted into the coal tub, and Wildeman led the mule pulling the tub with Sarge and four others inside back to the mine entrance. By the time they reached the mine entrance, Sarge had fully regained consciousness, and the others in the tub were beginning to stir. The injured prisoners were unloaded from the coal tub, and Wildeman started back into the mine tunnel. Sarge stopped Wildeman saying it's too dangerous to go back in just yet. Sarge ordered Wildeman to stay where he was.

It's easier to choose not to risk life and limb if the people who were the subject of the rescue effort were strangers, and such was the case with the brothers from Norway. Had the brothers made an effort to develop a rapport with Sarge, then perhaps he would have been more inclined to risk his life in trying to rescue them from the mine.

It wasn't until much later that a rescue attempt was mounted. With prisoners leading the way back into the mine using the same single-file technique that Sarge employed, the two Norwegian brothers were reached. By now, the rescuers were able to breathe the air in the mine. The rescuers found the brothers lying next to each other on the floor of the mine near the excavation. Unfortunately, however, neither brother survived the ordeal.

Chapter 22
The King Is Dead

The colonel relied heavily upon the day-to-day assistance of the camp clerk. The clerk position was one of great responsibilities and importance held by a prison trustee. The camp clerk enjoyed the colonel's trust and confidence. Only the most capable and honest prisoner could hold this essential position. The trustee currently in this position had earned the colonel's respect by fulfilling his duties with effectiveness and efficiency and without significant oversight. The trustee, whose name was Weissman, had become a vital component of the camp's administration and was something of a fixture whose presence was presumed. Weissman handled all the paperwork associated with prisoner transfers and disciplinary actions. He completed the monthly production reports required by the mine owner. Supply and material requisitions were all managed by Weissman. It was said that no one took a shit without Weissman signing off on the associated paperwork. This observation was an obvious exaggeration of Weissman's powers, but the point was, nonetheless, well taken.

Weissman was not a young man, and he had many years of experience in administrative matters both inside and outside of Cole City. His eyesight began to fail some time ago, and he complained that it was getting harder and harder for him to see the work before him. He was never seen without the spectacles that had become an essential extension of him. The failing eyesight was but the first evidence of Weissman's advancing years. As time went by, he became frail and sickly. Eventually, the superintendent had no choice but to begin to groom a replacement for Weissman.

Word went out to the guards to identify any potential candidates for the assistant clerk job. Unfortunately, the lack of necessary business acumen and clerical experience of the typical prisoner made for a very short list of candidates. It turned out that there was only one prisoner thought to be a match for the job. That prisoner was none other than Wilcox, the one prisoner who most hated and feared the colonel.

Wilcox had no choice but to subvert his feelings about the colonel and embrace his new responsibility. The fact that this new responsibility led directly to the possibility of being promoted to trustee and after that avoiding the rigors of work in the mines seemed lost on Wilcox. He viewed the change in his work status as nothing less than disastrous. He was convinced that the colonel was the man he knew from his time at Camp Sumter and that he would recognize him and have him killed to preserve the secret of his past.

Wilcox was a capable administrator and quickly learned that which was needed to serve in the role of camp clerk. Wilcox was a quick study, which was a fortunate happenstance as Weissman's health deteriorated rapidly. More and more, Wilcox was relied upon to take over for Weissman. The rapidly changing landscape of Wilcox's world brought him inevitably to the colonel's attention, where Wilcox least wanted to be. But the colonel expressed no recognition of Wilcox, and as time went by, Wilcox began to wonder whether he might avoid identification—that is, until one day, in a particularly chatty mood, the colonel inquired about Wilcox's past. Wilcox's heart stopped, and he was frozen in his tracks. Had the colonel recognized him? Wilcox, being the intelligent man that he was, quickly recovered and began telling his life story to the colonel. But Wilcox was careful to leave out the part about his time at Camp Sumter in the hope that this wouldn't come up in their conversation. And much to Wilcox's relief, it did not. From all appearances, the colonel did not recognize Wilcox. But Wilcox wouldn't allow himself to believe that the colonel might not be who Wilcox thought him to be.

After the one chatty episode, the colonel reverted to his usual curmudgeonly self and showed no further interest in Wilcox.

A few months later, Weissman died, leaving Wilcox in sole charge of the camp clerk duties and into more direct contact with the colonel on an ongoing basis. Wilcox became increasingly convinced that his first recognition of the colonel as the lieutenant he knew at Camp Sumter was justified and that eventually, the colonel would recognize him. Wilcox greeted each encounter with the colonel as potentially pivotal and found himself growing increasingly anxious.

Wilcox became increasingly convinced that he had to do something before it was too late. It was with this feeling of desperation that Wilcox began to hatch a diabolical plan.

The colonel often demanded that Wilcox go to the camp kitchen and have the head cook prepare a meal that Wilcox would bring back to the colonel. The colonel didn't like the usual camp food, nor did he relish going to the mess hall, so this errand became a routine part of Wilcox's day. It would be easy, Wilcox thought, to take advantage of this situation and poison the colonel, if only he could put his hands on a lethal substance. Wilcox contemplated this dilemma for quite some time and, through casual conversation with me, learned about the plants growing in the herb garden. Wilcox knew that some of the herbs were used for medicinal purposes. Wilcox was determined to identify something in the herb garden that would serve his purpose. But he made his inquiries in such a way as to obscure this purpose. I proudly shared with him what I'd learned from Ahrens about the various herbs, their uses, and their risks. Wilcox was especially interested in what I had to tell him about the castor beans. The castor bean, as I explained to Wilcox, could be used to treat constipation; but because the beans were toxic, mishandling could lead the patient to have diarrhea, nausea, and in some cases even death. The proper method of handling was to separate the oil from the pulp. The oil was the main ingredient in castor oil, and the pulp, which contained the toxins, must be carefully discarded. The poison in just one or two beans could cause the exposed individual to become very ill, and only a bit more could cause death.

Wilcox waited patiently as the castor plants in the herb garden grew to maturity, then picked, and secreted several beans for future use. To assure that the colonel's death wouldn't get linked to castor beans, he decided to wait until well past the end of the growing season to execute his plan. Then when he thought the time was right, he crushed and ground eight castor beans into a pulp and slipped the pulp into a stew that the kitchen had prepared for the colonel. Wilcox worried that the stew would have an unpleasant taste and the colonel would refuse to eat. But Wilcox's fear was not realized as the colonel consumed the entire bowl of stew without complaint. Within a few hours, the colonel began to show symptoms of the poisoning, including nausea, diarrhea, dizziness, and weakness. Wilcox was called into the colonel's office and instructed to retrieve the doctor at once. Instead of heeding the colonel's demand, he provided the colonel with a wet cloth for his head and a glass of water. But the colonel wouldn't be distracted for long and insisted that Wilcox retrieve the doctor. Wilcox pretended to follow the colonel's order and left the office building but made no effort to summon the doctor. Wilcox, after a while, returned to the colonel's bedside and explained that the doctor wasn't in the camp and that a guard was dispatched to locate him and bring him as soon as possible. In the meantime, the colonel grew weaker by the moment and soon lapsed into unconsciousness. Wilcox continued to sit with the colonel and monitor his steady demise. Within six hours of having served him the poisoned stew, the colonel was dead. Wilcox removed all evidence of his deed by dropping the tainted stew and all evidence of having processed the castor beans into the latrine and washing the bowl and spoon. Then Wilcox pretended to discover the colonel and raised the alarm.

It didn't take much imagination for me to figure out what Wilcox did, but it was none of my business, so his secret was safe with me. No one else ever suspected.

There was a lavish funeral for the colonel in Marietta, where he was laid to rest in the city cemetery.

Wilcox capably carried on with the administration of the camp as if the colonel were still there and soon was elevated to the status of trustee. The guard captain quite capably managed the operations of the mines and ovens. And the task of replacing the superintendent began without delay.

Chapter 23
The Bourbon Triumvirate

Occasionally we would catch a glimpse of some well-dressed and upright dignitary about the camp. We assumed these dignitaries to be among the class of individuals who had control over our meager existence. None of the prisoners ever met these dignitaries, and what little we knew of them came secondhand from the guards. While we never met these men, it was with great certainty that we understood that it was their attitudes toward Cole City that dictated our purpose and the degree of our misery.

With the unexpected death of Colonel Towers, there was a need to find a new superintendent of Cole City operations. The responsibility for doing so fell squarely on the governor of Georgia, John Brown Gordon. This responsibility stemmed not only from the governor's position as the titular head of government for the state but also because the governor was so prominently involved with the ownership and history of Cole City.

Before the War Between the States, the Gordon family owned the coal mines that would become Cole City. The Gordon family also owned and operated a thriving plantation in nearby Walker County, Georgia, with the aid of slave labor. Gordon's attitude toward slave labor undoubtedly took root from his earliest days living the plantation life. During the war, Gordon served as one of Robert E. Lee's most trusted generals and rose to prominence not only in Georgia but also throughout the region. Gordon, a lawyer by profession, had been a US senator and was elected governor of Georgia in 1886. But

Gordon lost his bid to be reelected governor earlier this year and would yield the office to William J. Northern come January.

Gordon had deep ties to Cole City that went well beyond his family's early ownership. And in addition to his links to Cole City for more than twenty years, his scheduled departure from the governor's mansion just a few short weeks away lent urgency to his search for a new Cole City superintendent. But the political urgency was not his only motivation. Gordon needed the right person to serve in the role of Cole City superintendent. Coal production had been steadily lagging for more than a year, and the governor was anxious to get someone in the superintendent's role that could turn things around. The mines yielded the coal, but it was the coke from the ovens that produced the operations revenue. Since the coke ovens depended on coal as its raw material, revenues relied first and foremost on coal production. The workforce at the ovens was mostly white free laborers who were paid by the ton of coke produced. The oven workforce could, therefore, be depended upon to work hard most of the time. It was reasonable to believe that the workers at the ovens were not the source of the problem with production. Such knowledge dictated that management's attention was directed to coal production as the means of improving revenue.

Mine production depended upon how much work was done by the Negro prisoner labor force. The governor understood, with good reason, that the Negroes who worked the mines had little incentive to put forth any great effort. And from his days as a slave owner, he knew that the prisoners, being mostly former slaves, were adept at being "slackers and layabouts."

As an outgrowth of the Coal Creek War, the coal mines in East Tennessee had phased out convict labor in favor of a paid workforce. The result there being that their production now far exceeded that of Cole City. Coal production from the free mines in East Tennessee cost less than one quarter of the coal produced by Cole City. More than anything else, the purpose of using convict labor was to keep production costs down. Since free laborers were now proven to be more cost-effective, the better alternative for Cole City was to discontinue the practice of using leased convicts to mine the coal. But the lease agreement with the state of Georgia had another five years to go. Understanding all this, the governor concluded that to make Cole City competitive again, the new superintendent would have to increase mine production both quickly and significantly. And to do this means getting greater coal production from the prisoners.

Gordon was well known as someone who didn't shirk his responsibilities. But the choice of a new superintendent proved to be a formidable task. Uncharacteristically, the governor labored over the decision on a new superintendent. Compounding his dilemma was the fact that he was not in a position to act unilaterally in appointing a new superintendent. Ever since the organization of Cole City in 1873, there had been the involvement of other powerful forces. Chief among them was Joseph E. Brown. Brown was the president of the state-owned railroad, which in partnership with Cole City was essential to operations. The railroad owned the right of way for the rail spur serving Cole City's coke ovens, thereby controlling the shipping of coke. Brown also had an ownership interest in the Dade Coal Company, the coal mines, and the land on which Cole City resides. Brown, it was often said, had much more to do with the management of Dade Coal Company than Gordon or anyone else. It was Brown, acting behind the scenes, who controlled the appointment of the new superintendent.

Before the War Between the States, Joseph E. Brown's family operated a prosperous plantation in Cherokee County, Georgia, with the aid of slave labor. Brown, an attorney with a practice in Canton, Georgia, grew up enjoying the benefits of slave labor and like Gordon had undoubtedly carried a particular attitude toward slave labor from an early age. He rose to political prominence well before the war and was elected governor at the young age of thirty-six in 1857. Brown didn't support the war and did not play a significant political or military role in it. Then during reconstruction in 1865, he was appointed chief justice of the Georgia Supreme Court. Brown went on to become the president of the state-owned Western and Atlantic Railroad in 1872. In 1873, he together with John Brown Gordon formed the Dade Coal Company, incorporated Cole City, and began to lease convicts from the state of Georgia to work the mines there.

103

Brown was a shrewd and ruthless businessman who understood the economics of convict labor. Like Gordon, Brown felt the need to seat a superintendent who could increase mine production.

Gordon and Brown served in the US Senate together. But the two were more than just political contemporaries and business partners in Dade Coal Company. They were the two most powerful political forces in Georgia. They made up two thirds of the "Bourbon Triumvirate," a political alliance that held great sway over Georgia politics ever since the days of reconstruction. Both Gordon and Brown were known to have held leadership roles in the Ku Klux Klan and were outspoken white supremacists—a fact that surely had some bearing on all aspects of life at Cole City.

While the new superintendent must have the overt approval of Gordon, it was Brown who was pulling strings behind the scene, and in the end, it was Brown's man that Gordon would appoint as superintendent. It was with great certainty that the need for increased coal production from the mines was the main goal in selecting a new superintendent, but it was not the only consideration. Brown would dictate the specific required personal attributes of the next superintendent. These attributes included having an iron will, being a strong disciplinarian, having considerable business acumen, and having the proper attitude toward Negroes and the use of slave labor.

Chapter 24
The New Superintendent

Just before relinquishing his position to the new governor, Gordon appointed Dudley C. Reed, a lawyer in private practice in Dallas, Georgia, and the son-in-law of one of Brown's close friends, to be the new superintendent at Cole City. Reed had the qualifications that Brown sought, and he was the Grand Titan of the Ku Klux Klan in northwest Georgia. Within a week of his appointment, Reed arrived in Cole City with little more than a suitcase for his clothes and a satchel for his prized possessions, a copy of the Cole City charter, his law degree, and a King James Bible. This last possession turned out to be a mere tool for Reed to use in his work as he was most certainly not a godly man.

Reed was a rather squat individual standing a little more than five feet in height with truncated arms and legs that presented a somewhat dwarflike resemblance. Reed was clean-shaven and bald with only a ring of lead-gray hair around his scalp. His hair, which had a lank and unkept appearance, extended to below his collar, suggesting a lack of personal hygiene. His eyes were squinty behind thick spectacles such that the color of his eyes could not be readily determined. His manner was abrupt and his demeanor quite stoic. His clothing seemed to be tailored for someone else, fitting him loosely in some areas and overly tightly in others. His shoes were scuffed and caked with mud. Reed was an altogether unappealing sight.

I would later learn that his disposition matched his appearance quite well. Rumor has it that his marriage was a sham and that he preferred the company of young men, although this cannot be fully confirmed from his observable actions. His wife did not accompany him to Cole City.

Reed seemed, at first, to be ill at ease with his surroundings and unsure of himself in his dealings with the captain of the guard and with Wilcox, the trustee who served as company clerk. Reed was seldom observed about the camp and then only in the company of both men. Reed did not carry a weapon, instead relying on the protection afforded by the captain of the guard, who served much like a personal bodyguard.

Reed spent his first several days at Cole City, keeping to himself. Occasionally he was observed walking about in the company of the guard captain and Wilcox, from whom he solicited much information. Reed displayed an intense interest in all aspects of Cole City life and had a habit of instructing Wilcox to make detailed notes on a pad of paper that was ever-present.

Then, in his third week at Cole City, he began to institute changes that reflected mostly his desire to increase coal production. One after another, the changes were posted in the mess hall for everyone to read. To reinforce the new rules and for those who cannot read, the captain of the guard announced the rule changes during the evening meal.

The first thing Reed changed was putting an end to Sunday church services. Sundays would be just another workday in the mines at Cole City. Also, Reed extended the length of the workday to sixteen hours.

A strong proponent of temperance, Reed, with the support of the new governor, immediately shut down the saloons in Murphy Hollow. Soon afterward, the casinos and whore houses closed as well. The folks who depended upon the operation of these establishments quickly and quietly moved on. Murphy Hollow became a ghost town almost overnight.

The number of trustees at Cole City was significantly reduced in favor of adding more bodies to the task of actually mining. There would remain but five trustees. The remaining trustees would have autonomy to manage the kitchen, hog farm and garden, medical orderly, and oven operations and serve as the superintendent's assistant. I was fortunate enough to keep my job as trustee over the hog farm and gardens, but would soon learn that this responsibility would be somewhat different from now on.

In the mines, the designation of straw boss was discontinued entirely. Mining crews would now consist of six members—two pickers, two shovelers, one mule handler, and one "float." The "float" would work as either a picker or a shoveler, depending on where he was most needed. Each crew would have a designated seam of coal to work and a particular tunnel in which to work. Each crew would have a set production quota, and a guard at the mine entrance would keep track of each crew's daily production.

The jobs held by free laborers were mostly eliminated except at the ovens. Negro prisoners would work only in the mines. White prisoners or free laborers would handle tasks outside the mines.

Miners would now work from 4:00 a.m. to 8:00 p.m. with a ten-minute break every two hours.

The whipping of prisoners for misconduct ceased. This action came not as one of benevolence but as a practical matter. The new superintendent's purpose in discontinuing the practice of whipping prisoner came from his concern that whipping caused a prisoner to be less productive. A prisoner who was beaten couldn't go back to work right away, and often when he did go back to work, he was less than fully productive. The practice of whipping was replaced by "water torture," where water was poured over a cloth covering the nose and mouth of a restrained prisoner, causing the prisoner to feel like they are drowning. Such torture was useful in gaining prisoner compliance, and the recovery was immediate, allowing the prisoner to return to work right away. Occasionally, this type of torture could result in the drowning of the prisoner, but to the new superintendent, this was a small price to pay.

At roll call, the new superintendent reinforced his message to the prisoners. The message was a clear threat to all, but mostly to the Negroes.

> Your only value lies in the work you do with your
> hands. If you're not willing to work, then you're
> of no value. Each crew is responsible for a set ton-

nage of coal every day. Any prisoner not carrying his weight will result in the whole crew missing its quota, and any crew missing its quota will be reprimanded severely. The crew must make sure that everyone does their share, and it's up to the crew to motivate their members as necessary. Reprimands include exposure to water torture as well as the elimination of breaks, and working longer hours. Ongoing failure to make quota will result in the guilty party being met with swift and severe punishment. You will work or you will die here in Cole City. There's no going back to the way things were and there is no life beyond Cole City for those of you who don't produce. Slackers will be buried in a side tunnel of one of the abandoned mines never to be found.

But increased production wasn't the only issue. Along with increased production, there must also be a corresponding reduction in the cost of coal production. The new superintendent would also have to find ways to cut costs. Cutting costs meant cutbacks in all areas of the camp's budget. The cost of housing, food service, and medical must all be reduced.

The hog farm was downsized by selling off more of the piglets. The ration of pork for prisoner consumption was significantly reduced. The herb garden was plowed under. The focus of the vegetable garden shifted away from growing a variety of different vegetables to just potatoes, cabbage, and turnips. Meals would be restricted to include only these vegetables and just a hint of pork for dinner and grits and gravy for breakfast. Negroes and whites would have separate eating areas.

Corn would continue to be grown in the fields, but it was earmarked for feeding the hogs and mules.

These and other changes made by the new superintendent further eroded the already poor quality of prison life at Cole City and was met with universal distain by prisoners, free laborers, and everyone else who depended upon Cole City for their livelihood. Even the guards were disgruntled by longer working hours and other changes. But as intended, the changes had an immediate and ongoing impact on coal production and overall costs. The mines were producing more coal than ever before and the ovens were abuzz with constant activity.

John Brown Gordon was undoubtedly congratulating himself on Reed's appointment.

Chapter 25
Rebellion

From his very first day as the superintendent at Cole City, Dudley Reed was hated by prisoners, free laborers, and guards alike. But being liked was not the new superintendent's concern. It seemed that he went out of his way to earn the disaffection of everyone he met.

The free laborers lost most of their jobs, and the jobs that remained called for more work for less pay. The reduction in the number of guards caused the ones that were left to have more work, and to add insult to injury, their pay was reduced as a camp cost-savings measure. But the most enraged were the Negro prisoners. In the pursuit of increased production, the Negro prisoners found themselves treated like indentured slaves, impotent instruments of the oppressive moneyed class to be worked until they drop and then be cast aside.

It didn't take long for the guards, feeling somewhat oppressed themselves, to adjust to the new order. More and more guards placed themselves on the sick list, leaving the camp short-staffed. The guards responsible for keeping track of the mining crew's daily production quota began to extort favor from the mining crews in exchange for padding their production numbers. Negro prisoners had precious little with which to bribe the guards, but that didn't seem to matter to the guards. It was something of a personal victory for the corrupt guards regardless of how small the bribe. Occasionally, however, a prisoner would get a package from outside, which might contain tobacco, a most prized commodity.

The rise in resentment toward the superintendent by the guards was surpassed only by the growing discontent of the Negro prisoners for anyone in authority. The deteriorating morale of the guards did not go unnoticed by the Negro prisoners. Mental notes were made of the most lackadaisical guards and their propensity for distraction while on duty. At night, the Negro prisoners gathered in small groups and quietly strategized ways to take advantage of the new order. Leaders emerged, and various plots were developed and considered.

It was evident to the Negro prisoners that the superintendent applied a different set of rules to the Negro prisoners and the white prisoners. The white prisoners were, therefore, excluded from the Negro prisoners' plans being developed. So I had no idea what they were planning. Whatever was to happen would be led by the Negro prisoners. The white prisoners, including me, were nevertheless suspicious of all the planning and convinced that trouble was on the horizon. We, white prisoners, were lying low and playing a game of wait and see. We didn't have to wait long.

After that one time, the superintendent never attended morning roll call, and taking their cue from their boss, several of the guards were often a few minutes late for the ritual. And it wasn't until roll call that any guards electing to go on the sick list for that day were identified. Roll call had become an undisciplined exercise carried out by disinterested guards. It was here that the Negro prisoners had wisely decided to make their first strike.

With a level of organization and a swiftness of action that took the guards entirely by surprise, the handful of guards at roll call were quickly and bloodlessly overwhelmed. The guards were wrestled to the ground and disarmed and then moved to the stockade. One group of prisoners went directly to the office, busted down the door, and stripped the armory of all weapons. While there, the prisoners busted into the superintendent's quarters, rousting him from his bed and walked him to the stockade. A small group of prisoners went straightaway to the blacksmith shop and, using the tools they found there, removed their leg irons. One after another, small groups followed the others to the blacksmith shop. The prisoners who have had their leg irons removed took up arms and quickly formed a defensive perimeter around Upper Cole City. With the superintendent and several guards secured in the stockade as hostages, the prisoners were now in complete control of Upper Cole City.

A handful of guards, who were late to roll call or had otherwise been occupied, avoided capture and hid out in the woods nearby. The guards remained hidden until nightfall when they sneaked away down the Hales Gap Road. These guards made it to Murphy Hollow in a short while but found everything closed down. So they continued on foot to Slygo and eventually made their way to Trenton where they awoke the sheriff and raised the alarm.

Meanwhile, back in Upper Cole City, circumstances took an unexpected turn. Not knowing the Negro prisoners' plan, we, white prisoners, were surprised that the freed Negro prisoners did not attempt to escape Cole City. Instead, they were content to maintain fortified defensive positions and simply waited. The Negro prisoners selected one of the sequestered guards to be set free and deliver a message to the local sheriff to give to the governor. This written message, composed by one of the few Negro prisoners who could read and write, stated that the Negro prisoners sought relief from the oppressive regime of Dudley Reed. The message went on to say that if "push comes to shove, we are willing to die before we return to the way things have become under his [Reeds'] rule." And if it comes to it, they'll take the lives of their hostages along with them. They pledged to lay down their arms and submit provided their list of demands were met. They demanded that the plantation culture created at Cole City by Dudley Reed be done away including the following:

- Restoration of Sundays as a day of rest with church services
- Return to twelve-hour workdays
- No more water torture
- No more production quotas
- No more mistreatment by the guards.
- Adoption of a system that allowed prisoner grievances to get fairly heard and action taken against guards who mistreated prisoners

The sheriff telegraphed the prisoners demands to the new governor. Gov. William J. Northern, who was only recently elected, was a staunch Baptist and a vocal promoter of better race relations. He held a much more enlightened view of race issues than his predecessor, and the Negro prisoners hoped that they might find him to have a sympathetic ear to their plight.

Three days passed with no word from the governor, and the Negro prisoners grew increasingly impatient. The more militant ones were voicing a preference for using the hostages as a shield and making a run for it. But cooler heads continued to prevail at least for now. The Negro prisoners, after all, had food and water that would last them for a great long while, and they could afford to wait.

Upon learning of the rebellion, Governor Northern sent a telegram to the commander of the army at Fort McPherson near Atlanta to request that troops be dispatched to Cole City. The fort commander immediately replied to the governor pledging military forces and dispatched four companies of heavily armed soldiers comprising almost five hundred troops under the command of Major John J. Thompson. Troops were organized and sent by train to Chattanooga and then split in two with half the troops each going on the Birmingham Railroad line toward Trenton and the other half going on the Nashville Railroad line to Shellmound. The troops sent to Shellmound disembarked on the third day of the rebellion and acted decisively to cut off the only route of the possible escape of prisoners via the rail spur at Lower Cole City. The two companies were bivouacked at the coke ovens with sentries set on the footpath leading from Upper Cole City to Lower Cole City and at the base of the inclined railway. The operation of the railway and the ovens was curtailed. The other two companies who were sent toward Trenton on the Birmingham Railroad line disembarked the train at Slygo and marched up the Hales Gap Road to Murphy Hollow where they bivouacked. Sentries were set along the Hales Gap Road and at the footpath leading up the mountain from Murphy Hollow. Here the amassed troops remained, awaiting further orders.

Governor Northern, having received the demand letter from the Negro prisoners, remained at the governor's mansion to contemplate the dilemma he faced. Northern was a vocal critic of the convict lease system that had lined the pockets of his political rivals. Northern was a particularly outspoken critic of Joseph E. Brown, who held controlling interest of Cole City as well as being president of the state-owned railroad. The state legislature had only recently begun to hold hearings on the convict leasing system, and based on their initial findings, Northern felt confident that the corrupt and abusive system had ceased to curry favor with the legislature or the voters of Georgia. Northern sought out the advice of John Brown Gordon, whom he had just defeated in the race for governor and was pleased to discover that Gordon had also concluded that the convict lease system was near the end of its useful life. Gordon confessed to having become disillusioned with his involvement in the Bourbon Triumvirate, the convict lease system, and Joseph Brown. After hearing the Negro prisoners' list of demands, Gordon was quick to tell Northern that he believed their requests were reasonable, and he encouraged Northern to find some way to give them all that they sought. Fortified with this knowledge, Northern felt that the Negro prisoners' case against Dudley Reed, Joseph Brown, and Cole City was worthy. On a personal level, he was inclined to acquiesce to the demands of the Negro prisoners at Cole City. But things were never as simple as they may seem, and consenting to the Negro prisoners' demands was immensely problematic.

First and foremost, the governor could not be seen as giving in to threats from anyone, but especially from convicts. Doing so in a staunchly Conservative Southern state would likely mean the end of his political career. The simple act of going to Cole City to negotiate with the Negro prisoners would be political suicide. Any action by Northern to appease the Negro prisoners would pit him against Joseph Brown. Joseph Brown would be a formidable adversary wielding considerable influence in the state and was not someone that Northern wished to antagonize needlessly.

The governor weighed his options for dealing with this crisis carefully before finally hatching a plan. He sent the lieutenant governor, Robert A. Godfrey, to Cole City to sit down with the leader of the rebellion. The lieutenant governor was authorized to hear the

Negro prisoners' grievances and to represent the governor in considering their demands. The army organized the meeting at Hales Gap in three days.

On the appointed day, the lieutenant governor was escorted by an army contingent to the meeting place where he met with Rev. Lucas Armstrong Smith, leader of the Negro prisoner rebellion. Godfrey was taken aback by the presence of Smith, a former slave, Baptist minister, and a self-educated man who was composed and well-spoken. Godfrey was also impressed by Smith's courage to come to this meeting alone in the knowledge that he could get captured. The lieutenant governor offered Smith whiskey, which Smith refused, saying that he was not a man who imbibed. The two men, having little in common upon which to exchange pleasantries, got down to business without delay. Godfrey took the initiative to state emphatically that the state of Georgia would not negotiate with the Negro prisoners because doing so would open the current administration to demands for negotiation from every quarter and undermine the administration's position to affect positive change for all its citizens. Smith countered that the country had fought a war to free the slaves and that the current convict leasing system was nothing less than a way for the plantation class to circumvent all that had gone before. Smith emphasized that he was not here to negotiate but to demand that Negro prisoners have the rights that so many people, both black and white, fought to preserve. Godfrey countered that the Negro prisoners had lost all rights by committing crimes against society. Smith paused and then began slowly to enumerate the litany of minor or invented offenses that had landed one Negro after another in Cole City and that most importantly, no white men had ever gotten sentenced to Cole City for a similar crime. A smile appeared on Godfrey's face for the first time as he realized that Reverend Smith would be an imposing negotiator in the debate to come.

A spirited give and take went on for more than an hour with neither side seeming to yield any ground to the other. The debate drew to a close for the day with the understanding that tomorrow would be another day and further discussion would have to wait until then.

Smith returned to Upper Cole City where he led the assembled Negro prisoners in a Bible reading and prayer service. From Psalm 37, Smith reads, "Be still before the Lord and wait patiently for him; do not fret when people succeed in their ways when they carry out their wicked schemes. Refrain from anger and turn from wrath."

Godfrey received a communique from US president Benjamin Harris, a strong advocate of Negro rights, extolling him to seek a rapid conclusion to the rebellion with due consideration to the Negro prisoners' plight and without bloodshed. The next morning, Godfrey returned to his meeting with Smith with renewed enthusiasm and optimism. Smith, by contrast, remained true to his quiet and thoughtful nature.

Smith laid out the Negro prisoners' demands one at a time. After each demand, Smith paused momentarily to allow Godfrey to comprehend the significance of his words entirely. Godfrey fidgeted but remained silent until Smith had finished and then rose from his seat at the negotiating table and repeated each demand in the same order as he had just heard Smith recite them.

Smith went on to say, "Each of the Negroes incarcerated at Cole City has been convicted in a court of law of committing a crime against society for which a debt is owed. We are not here to discuss whether the charges were justified. We are here instead to consider what the proper punishment should be."

Godfrey decided to play his ace card now in the hope that he can move the conversation forward. Godfrey asked Smith, "If the convict lease system gets abolished in its entirety, would you're people prefer to be returned to a life behind bars where their waking hours get spent in a tiny cell without daylight, where they are allowed out of their cell for only a short time each day? Because that is what the prisoners who are not in the convict lease system do. If that is your people's choice, then I can make that happen without further debate, and all the Negro prisoners at Cole City will get sent to prisons around the state."

Smith was genuinely surprised by Godfrey's gambit. Smith had assumed that the limiting aspect of their conversation was the continuing existence of Cole City. Smith was momentarily speechless.

What Smith did not know was that this was a bluff. The state prison system could not absorb the hundreds of convicts presently working at Cole City.

Smith took a long moment to consider Godfrey's words and then said softly, "It is not our desire to bring down the convict leasing system or to render Cole City a relic of a bygone era. Our demands focus on the basic rights of prisoners and to eliminate the dehumanized practices in the process. Let us agree to remain concentrated on the question as to how prisoners at Cole City get treated."

It was a significant concession from Smith, and it came without prolonged debate. Godfrey's ploy had worked, and such an early success buoyed him. Godfrey offered magnanimously that this was a point upon which the two could build a dialogue of compromise. And indeed, it was. Over the next few meetings between Godfrey and Smith, each one of the Negro prisoners' demands were addressed, and one by one, middle ground was found and agreed upon. Each night Smith held another Bible reading and prayer meeting with the Negro convicts and then told the assembled prisoners about that day's discussions and agreements. In the end, what they decided redefined life for the Negro prisoners at Cole City for the future. And the decisions made by these two honorable men served as a basis for change throughout the state's convict leasing system. This Negro prisoner bill of rights included the following:

1. Prisoners will be allowed to attend a Sunday morning church service should they wish to do so, or they can simply take the time to use however they please. Then starting at noon, the prisoners will go back to work for a half day as a way to help bolster production.
2. The workday will be reduced by two hours each day, subject to the prisoners meeting their production quotas.
3. Water torture will be discontinued. It will be the responsibility of a new Cole City Advisory Board to determine when prisoner disciplinary action is called for and what that disciplinary action would be.

4.   Production quotas will remain but will be negotiated by an advisory board made up of three Negro prisoners elected by the prisoners for one-year terms and three senior guards appointed by the superintendent. The superintendent will serve as the head of the board and have the vote that settled any ties.

5.   Prisoners will have the right to bring a grievance against any guard regarding unfair treatment before the Cole City Advisory Board for action. Likewise, guards will have the right to bring charges against any prisoner for their failure to comply with camp rules, instructions from the guards, or meet fairly set production quotas.

6.   An oversight committee, to be appointed by the state legislature, will be created to review and report to the governor on operations at Cole City. Members of this committee will make regularly scheduled visits to Cole City to assure that there are no violations of prisoner's rights. Also, this committee will serve as a last resort of appeal in mediating any disputes that cannot be resolved by the Cole City Advisory Board.

Based on this agreement, the superintendent was released from custody and reinstated immediately. It was the superintendent's responsibility to see that the points of the agreement reached were fully and vigorously implemented without delay. The superintendent's performance in this regard would be the subject of the Cole City Oversight Committee that would make its initial visit to Cole City within thirty days.

It was also agreed that there will be no retaliation against the Negro prisoners who participated in this rebellion if the rebellious Negro prisoners lay down their weapons and return to their barracks.

Just like that, the rebellion ended. Hostages were released, and prisoners returned to their barracks to await the following day's roll call. The four army companies remained in position for an additional week just to be sure that the deal stuck and then returned to Fort McPherson.

The governor's office was able to keep the entire affair out of the press, allowing the changes in the convict leasing system to occur out of sight of the general public and the state legislature.

Gordon sold his interest in Cole City to Joseph Brown soon after the rebellion ended amid reports that he had grown weary of his affiliation with Cole City and his kinship with Brown.

As a bystander to the whole affair, I was left with a profound respect for the dignity and capability of Rev. Lucas Armstrong Smith, who held the Negro prisoners and prison administration alike to a higher standard and in so doing won for his people the right to be treated more humanely.

Coal production significantly improved over the performance experienced under Colonel Towers, but it didn't rival that of the mines worked by free laborers in Tennessee. Joseph Brown would no longer be able to earn the previously attained level of earnings from Cole City, but he would nevertheless continue to be one of, if not, the wealthiest man in Georgia.

Chapter 26
The Next Chapter

The following year passed without any overly significant crisis at Cole City. Oh, there were the usual instances of wrongdoing, much of which was mediated by the advisory board. And the oversight committee found enough of the expected underlying rights violations that justified their existence. Insubordination was the most common charge made by guards against prisoners, and acts of aggression by guards were the prisoners' most common grievance. Especially egregious prisoner conduct including attempted escapes and prisoner on prisoner violence still occurred but with much less frequency than before. These more egregious matters were outside of the advisory committee's charter and were handled as criminal matters for the judiciary.

The corrupt guards thankfully moved on, for the most part, leaving such duties to those more adept at the task. The adversarial tensions of the past had given way to a pervasive attitude among guards and prisoner that we're all in this together, so we might as well make the best of it.

Don't get me wrong. Cole City is still a penal colony. And being sent to Cole City means hard labor in the coal mines. Longtimers are still falling victim to the black lung, which still takes far too many lives. It's still an unsafe place to be, and all too often, prisoners lose their lives to misfortune. But prisoners are finding, for the first time, a dignity in work.

The advisory committee was working out pretty well, so much so that the three prisoner representatives were asked to serve a second year. Only the reverend choose to do so. As for me, while I was quite proud to have been a part of such a significant positive change at Cole City, I felt strongly that the purpose of the advisory committee could be best served by enlisting the participation of other prisoners. Abraham Lincoln Jones took my place on the committee. I was content to continue in my role as trustee over the hog farm and garden and happy to have more time to devote to this role. The things that I've been learning about butchering a hog would hopefully serve me well when I eventually get out of Cole City and look for gainful employment.

Smith now delivers the sermon at Sunday church services regularly, and the church tent overflows with prisoner whenever he does.

There's still plenty of coal under the mountain, and even though the convict lease system has fallen into disfavor with the state legislature and the public, in general, there's no reason to think that Cole City will not endure for some time to come.

While I still have years to serve on my sentence, I now believe that if the good Lord is willing, I may make it to the end.

List of Characters

Oliver Tobias: A prisoner working in Upper Cole City; the storyteller

George Prosser: A prisoner working in Upper Cole City; the leader of Oliver Tobias' crew

Ernest Shackleford: A prisoner working in Upper Cole City

Henri Moran: A prisoner working in Upper Cole City; Prosser's second in charge

Daniel Hardy: The murder victim for which Oliver was convicted

Bernard Waller: The person who murdered Hardy

James Sobel: A prisoner working in Upper Cole City

Col. Willard Towers: A superintendent over all of Cole City

Doctor Steele: Cole City's camp doctor

James Wildeman: A prisoner working in Upper Cole City

Robert Wilcox: A trustee; company clerk

Pretty Boy Dupree: A prisoner working in Upper Cole City

Cuzzort: A trustee working at the coke ovens

Major John J. Thompson: Commander of US Army companies at Cole City siege, 1891

Reverend Lucas Armstrong Smith: Leader of the Negro prisoner rebellion in 1891

Lieutenant Governor Robert A. Godfrey: Chief negotiator for the state at the rebellion of 1891

Sarge: The trustee over Oliver's crew

Fanning: A prisoner working in Upper Cole City

Ahrens: The trustee responsible for the hog farm

Weissman: Trustee; company clerk

Abraham Lincoln Jones: First prisoner to lodge a grievance against a guard

Cole City

Book 2
A Different Path

Chapter 1
My Last Years
at Cole City

During my last years at the prison mining camp at Cole City, I served as a trustee, managing the camp farm and livestock. During this time, I gained the trust of the prison camp administration and enjoyed freedom of movement within the camp. Times were hard for the prisoners at Cole City, but they were, from a prisoner's perspective, easier than the prior years at Cole City. The sacrifices made by the prisoners who came before paved the way for a life with less strife than Cole City had come to know. Stark differences continued to exist between the way that black prisoners and white prisoners were treated. Still, such differences were reflective of society as a whole in the Deep South at the time. Being one of the few white prisoners, I benefited from a less arduous existence than most prisoners merely because I am white.

By the late 1890s, I came to be relied upon as a steadfast member of the Campbellite Church congregation at Cole City and, over time, took on an increased role in ministering to the flock and even filling in for the Pastor Goodwin on occasions to deliver that Sunday's sermon. The pastor observed that I had been called by God and encouraged me to follow the path of righteousness toward the fulfillment of God's plan for me. I officiated at baptisms, which, like the Baptist Church, were integral to the Campbellite Church. I found myself drawn to the absence of doctrinal encumbrances within the Campbellite religion and began to immerse myself in the ancient teachings of the gospel. Under Pastor Goodwin's tutelage, I became a much more spiritual person.

After the conclusion of church services one Sunday morning, Pastor Goodwin came to me very distressed. He had been asked by a member of the congregation to comfort the congregate's teenage daughter, who had increasingly become irrational and demented over the past weeks, and it was felt that a man of God could bring some comfort to the young woman. The pastor admitted to me that he had seldom interceded in such a situation and that he would like for me to accompany him as he visited with the young woman, not so much to contribute to whatever transpired, but more as a witness. The young woman lived with her family in one of the residences constructed along Cole City Creek in the Nickajack gulch near the coke ovens. Having the freedom to move about Cole City, it was within my discretion to visit the young woman's home if I chose to do so. I had no idea of what was to come or how I may be able to assist the pastor, but I felt compelled to consent to the good pastor's request to accompany him.

It took us about half an hour to negotiate the footpath from Upper Cole City where the church was located to the young woman's home in Lower Cole City. During the walk, the pastor took the opportunity to share with me the Campbellite Church's views on spirituality. Like most matters of the Campbellite Church, there was precious little doctrinal guidance offered in issues of spirituality. The church's founder, Thomas Campbell, sought to minimize or remove entirely the trappings associated with organized churches such as the more established Baptist or Methodist churches and return to what he considered the "ancient" teachings of the Christian church. Accordingly, the Campbellite Church held that immortal spirits, angels and demons, were real and that they existed within the realm of the living. Our role this day is to determine whether the young woman's melancholy is of common origins, such as a mental defect, or substance abuse, or it is from some spiritual source. And if the origin of the melancholy is spiritual, then we would call upon the power of our Christian faith to cast out the unclean spirit. Just exactly how we would go about the casting out would be considered after we were sure that the young woman was indeed possessed. The pastor confided in me that he had only faced the need to determine whether an unclean spirit was present on a few occasions and that there had always been a reasonable explanation for what he had observed. Based on his experience, he expected that we would not find convincing evidence of demonic possession of the young lady we were about to meet.

When we arrived at our destination, we were quietly ushered into a small dark bedroom. The young woman we came to see was lying in the middle of a double bed centered on the wall opposite the door where we came in. She was lying still on her back with her head turned away from us. Her arms and legs were fully extended with her wrists and ankles bound to the bed frame. Her father called her name, but she did not respond. He called out again, and the young woman slowly turned her head toward the inquiring voice. Immediately I could tell that the young woman was in extreme distress. Her face is drawn and distorted by pain. Her eyes are deep-set and dark. Her hair and her night clothes were drenched in perspiration even though the room was uncomfortably cold. She bore a hideous grin that revealed yellow teeth and bloodied gums. In a deep male voice that was unexpectedly familiar and not normal to the young woman, she declared, "The one you seek is no longer here." The voice was that of the long-dead former superintendent of Cole City, Col. Willard Towers. The colonel had been murdered by a prison trustee many years ago, long before the pastor had arrived at Cole City, and I was sure that the pastor did not recognize the voice as I had.

The young woman's father explained that his daughter had been struck suddenly by some unknown malady two weeks prior and that she refused to speak with anyone, except in the voice that we'd just heard. At the same time, she had begun to claw at her breasts with her fingernails drawing blood, which explained her wrist restraints. She had run barefoot into the woods nearby, leaving her feet and ankles scratched and bleeding, which explained her ankle restraints. The young woman's father went on to tell the pastor that his daughter was timid, pious, and devoted to the church but that she had become course, suggestive, and vulgar. She had ripped her clothes off and offered to perform the most repulsive sex acts on her father, mother, and brother. The young woman had repeatedly soiled her bedclothes with complete disregard for the filth in which she lay.

The pastor began by asking and learned that the young woman had taken littlefood or drink since this episode had started and that before taking ill, she had not had anything unusual to eat or drink. The pastor learned that there was no alcohol in the house and that the only medicine was a small amount of rubbing liniment used topically for sore muscles but that the young woman had not had access to this.

While I watched, the pastor asked that everyone leave the room except me and then pulled a chair up near the bed and sat there without speaking for what seemed to me to be a very long time, but in reality, it only lasted ten minutes or so. The young woman did not look at the pastor and did not speak. When the pastor reached out to take hold of the young woman's hand, she withdrew as far as her restraints allowed, still not making eye contact.

The pastor rose from his chair and motioned for me to leave the room with him. Once outside, Pastor Goodwin asked me what I thought, and I confided in him my recognition of the voice I'd heard and that I found this phenomenon frightening and disturbing. The pastor nodded impassively and, after a brief moment, told me that what we'd observed couldn't be easily explained and that it could be a case of possession by an unclean spirit. Possession by an unclean spirit is most often associated with a dead person such as Superintendent Towers or of a ruined place such as Cole City. The pastor suggested that this was a case of possession by an unclean spirit as opposed to a demon. Demons are fallen angels, described in the Bible as having great power. Lucifer himself is a demon. So the young woman's possession was most likely by some lesser unclean spirit. Her possession was not by a "revenant" or ghost because such spirits are not malevolent, and whoever or whatever is possessing this young woman is malevolent.

Pastor Goodwin explained that such possessions were chronicled in several places in the Bible and that in the book of Mark, it is written that Jesus cast an unclean spirit out of a man. The pastor went on to say, "Regardless of the particular nature of the possessing unclean spirit, Jesus gives us the guidance needed to cast it out. In the book of Luke, we are told that casting out an unclean spirit is like a sick person being healed of some illness." He went on to say, "Jesus has vested the ability to cast out unclean spirits in all his believers and that as such we would appeal to him to help us as we attempt to cast out the unclean spirit possessing this unfortunate young woman."

The pastor smiled slightly and said, "The Campbellite Church eschews doctrine in favor of strict adherence to the scripture. So we will be on our own to act in a way that casts out the unclean spirit. But the task is not as daunting as it may seem." With that having been said, the pastor led me back into the young woman's bedroom. The pastor pulled his chair near the bed, took the young woman's hand again, and began to speak softly, quoting Ephesians 6:12 saying, "We seek to wrestle not against flesh and blood, but against the rulers, against the authorities, against the powers of this dark world and against the spiritual forces of evil."

The pastor went on to say, "The Lord has entrusted the souls of the redeemed to act in the casting out of unclean spirits from his flock. Strengthened by the holiness of our ministry, we exhort the unclean spirit possessing this child of God to release her and be gone. In the Name of the Father, and of the Son, and of the Holy Ghost. Amen."

Nothing seemed to happen, and the pastor repeated his simple prayer. The young woman began to stir and, turning to face the pastor, vomited foul-smelling green bile that splattered against the pastor's clothing. Undeterred, the pastor repeated the same prayer. Now the young woman began to shiver as if cold and strain against her bindings. With obvious contempt, the young woman started to speak in the superintendent's voice letting loose the vilest and most vulgar string of expletives imaginable.

Then the young woman turned her piercing gaze toward me, saying, "You have no power over me or the darkness I bring, you who knew about and concealed my murder at the hand of Robert Wilcox, you who murdered Daniel Hardy and betrayed Bernard Waller."

Without saying a word, the pastor urged me to leave the room, which I did right away. I could hear him repeating his prayer and guttural sounds coming from the young woman in the next room. As the daylight began to wane, the pastor's repetition of the prayer continued, and eventually, the young woman's protestations weakened and she became silent. The pastor emerged from the young woman's bedroom drenched in sweat and looking haggard. But there was satisfaction in his facial expression. He turned to me and said, "Our work here is complete." The pastor advised the young woman's father that her restraints should be removed and that she should be given only water for now. Starting tomorrow, she should be given broth until her strength begins to return. The pastor promised to revisit the following day and bid his host good night.

On the climb back up to Upper Cole City, the pastor, in a matter-of-fact tone, said that the unclean spirit was a liar but that even the worst liar will tell the truth if it conveniences him. He said that he knows not of what the spirit spoke but that if I was to continue on the path that God has chosen, I will have to confess my sins, whatever they may be. I will have to confess to any role I may have played in the murders of Superintendent Towers or Daniel Hardy or my betrayal of Bernard Waller and ask for forgiveness.

The pastor went on to say that he "was sure that he'd encountered the unclean spirit of Colonel Towers in Cole City before and that he expected that this evil spirit was attached to this place. If so, then it is likely that we will encounter the evil spirit in the future and that each time we encountered the spirit, we could expect it to be stronger." He added that unconfessed sins would work to the spirit's advantage.

Chapter 2
Early Encounters with the Unexplained

Several times during my ten years at Cole City, I was witness to bizarre and unexplained behavior by those incarcerated there. Much of this behavior was attributable to melancholy from the abuse endured and the atrocities witnessed. Cole City is a living nightmare from which some found escape from the harshness of their reality by fabricating a world of their own from their imagination. Such cases were referred to by the catchphrase on melancholy. Melancholy was broadly used to describe any mental defect from catatonia to maniacal violent outbursts. Many of the prisoners at Cole City came there with a long history of mental illness.

A few of the most maniacal prisoners claimed to be possessed by some evil spirit. Such claims got dismissed and their symptoms ignored. Some prisoners got better on their own, and some sunk more deeply into melancholia. Some were unable to work, and like prisoners with any other debilitating illness, they simply disappeared and were replaced by the more able-bodied ones.

I never gave much thought to the question of unclean spirits until the experience with the pastor and that unfortunate young woman possessed by an unclean spirit connected with the former superintendent. Looking back in time from my new perspective, I now recall several instances when the afflicted prisoner mentioned the superintendent's name or spoke in a voice reminiscent of the superintendent. Some possessions now seem obvious, and the pastor confirmed that such was the case. None of these prisoners survived very long.

But the pastor told me that it wasn't the obvious cases that were the most problematic. In some cases, the possession was not apparent for some time, leaving the unclean spirit to work his evil deeds in secret. The possessed remained unnoticed until the spirit's evil intent blossomed into some malevolent act. Sometimes this meant the loss of innocent life.

Considering what I now know, I have confidence that the colonel's spirit is real and that it is not through with Cole City. I am hopeful, however, that it may be possible to recognize those unfortunate prisoners who are possessed by the superintendent's spirit and with the pastor's help cast the spirit out.

I committed, at that precise moment in my life, to follow the path that God had laid out for me, to redeem myself, and to act as a servant of God in casting out unclean spirits and demons. At the next church service, I rose from my seat and walked down the aisle to the altar at the front of the church and before the congregation confessed my sins and asked God's forgiveness.

From that moment, the pastor took me under his watchful eye and guided me in the ways of righteousness. I spent every idle moment studying the scriptures and seeking understanding. In particular, I sought out scripture in the Bible related to possession and exorcism. In doing so, I learned that some verses bear a stand-alone truth, while others require consideration of their context in order to understand better and apply them. Developing an understanding of the context of a verse can be challenging and time-consuming. I found it tempting to ignore the context of the verses I studied. I'm sure that I tried Pastor Goodwin's patience time and again, but he proved to be a trustworthy source of biblical wisdom for which I was most grateful.

In my studies of the Bible, I found many references to demons and exorcism. Among the verses that I found to be most meaningful were as follows:

- The need for the possessed to resist the devil (James 4:7).
- The devil can be driven out by prayer (Mark 9:29).

- The devil prowls around like a roaring lion, seeking someone to devour (1 Peter 5:8).
- We do not wrestle against flesh and blood, but against the powers over darkness (Ephesians 6:12).
- That an unclean spirit can be cast out at the command of a righteous person (Acts 16:16–18).
- Even the demons believe in the one God (James 2:19).
- If we confess our sins, we will be forgiven (1 John 1:9).
- Do not believe every spirit. Test the spirit to see whether it is a false prophet (1 John 4:1).
- God's power has granted to us all things (2 Peter 1:3).
- What demons could do in Bible times, they can still do today (Luke 8:30).

As my ten-year sentence at Cole City draws to a close, my path is now clear. I believe that it is God's will and my destiny to comfort and guide his believers and seek to convert the nonbelievers. But most of all, I am God's instrument in exorcising unclean spirits and demons among God's children.

Chapter 3
Free at Last

In the late summer of 1900, I completed my sentence at Cole City and got released.

Once again, good fortune shined a light on me. The prison at Cole City releasing a healthy man in the prime of his working life rarely happens but I had, and my good works and faith in God gained the approval of the prison camp's administration. More importantly, by the year 1900, the coal production by the mines had begun to drop, and there was less need for workers in the mines and at the ovens. A limited number of prisoners, who had completed their sentences, got released. Releases and normal attrition due to age or poor health resulted in the prison population dropping to less than four hundred.

As my release became a reality, I was saddened to learn that during my time at Cole City, both my mother and father had passed away. Not having siblings, I was left with no family to go home to. My family had been poor farmers with little to pass along except for a small piece of land. With me in prison, there was no one to pay the taxes on the property, and the county took it for back taxes. So I had no place to call home when released. For ten years, Cole City, as bad as it had been, was my home, and I was finding leaving to be more of a problem than I ever suspected. I wasn't prepared for the freedom that I'd earned.

As my last few days of incarceration wound inevitably toward their end, I turned to the one person whose wisdom and guidance I valued, my pastor. Having served the congregation at Cole City for several years, he had, on occasion, been witness to my circumstance. As I sat with the pastor one Sunday after church, he shared with me selected Bible verses that offered the sought after guidance. He quoted scripture saying, "Therefore, if anyone is in Christ, he is a new creation. The old has passed away; behold, the new has come" (2 Corinthians 5:17).

We discussed the context and meaning of this verse and how I could apply it to my pending life change. I found this conversation buoyed my spirits. Then he quoted another verse by saying, "I can do all things through him who strengthens me" (Philippians 4:13). The meaning of this verse seemed immediately clear to me, and again, my spirits were lifted.

Our conversation then turned to the more pragmatic concerns about where I would live and how I would make a living. It was clear that the pastor had something specific in mind for my future, and I sat transfixed as he began to lay out this plan.

A small contingent of the pastor's congregation traveled to Cole City every Sunday from the rural community of Morganville in the valley about ten miles from Cole City. The pastor told me that these congregants had decided to build a small church in Morganville and had sought the pastor's approval as well as his recommendation for someone to serve as the little church's first pastor. The pastor told me that he knew I'd been called to preach and that he thought I was ready to take the next step by becoming the pastor of the new church now being formed. I could take a room in one of the Upper Cole City boarding houses and travel to the new church to minister to the small flock as needed.

The pastor had arranged with the camp superintendent for me to work as a free laborer tending to the camp's livestock starting right away. As a trustee, I had been given a free hand to tend to the camp's livestock, which I had done for the past few years. Now, I'd have the same responsibilities but as a free man rather than a prisoner. And I'd be paid for my labors. I would continue to study with the pastor to better serve my new flock and, in particular, become one who could exorcise demons and unclean spirits.

I couldn't help but feel that God had preordained the path I was on and that I was fulfilling his will. For the first time in my life, I felt that I had a purpose. Praise the Lord.

Chapter 4
The Mines Close

For the next few years, my life followed the path that God and the pastor had defined for me.

The mining operations at Upper Cole City declined steadily, and the numbers of prisoners diminished. Likewise, the church at Upper Cole City fell increasingly into decline. And as the pastor aged, his health began to slide. The pastor began to rely upon me to battle the forces of evil that persevered in Cole City, especially the unclean spirit associated with the murdered superintendent that never seemed to relax his pursuit of those whom he could possess. I rarely encountered the need to exorcise a spirit with my small congregation at the Morganville Church but was faced with a steady stream of such at Cole City. Only by virtue of the diminishing population of prisoners and free laborers at Cole City did the demands for my particular talents abate.

Then in 1908, the mines closed. Prisoner sentences got commuted except for the worst offenders, such as murderers and rapists, who were transferred to state prisons to finish their sentences.

Most of the Negro prisoners released from Cole City were taken on the narrow gauge rail line from Lower Cole City to Shellmound, where they boarded a train on the mainline to Chattanooga or Nashville. A few Negro prisoners were taken by wagon down the Hales Gap Road to Lookout Valley and then north to the Tennessee State Line where they were released. Most of the Negro prisoners released readily agreed to never return to Cole City. But a handful of prisoners stayed around to create a small settlement community that they named Hooker, after a deceased straw boss who was loved by all the Negro convicts. Hooker was located near the state line well off the most traveled road through Lookout Valley. Here the Negroes would farm the land and cut timber to build something of a village occupied by Negroes only.

Without the mines, there was no purpose in the free laborers staying on at Cole City, especially since there were other options for making a living elsewhere. Almost overnight, Cole City became a ghost town.

As the homes and other buildings were abandoned, they were, one by one, burned to the ground. The burning of abandoned buildings was carried out at the direction of the matriarch of the West family, who owned large tracts of land in and around Cole City. Their purpose was to discourage new settlers from occupying the abandoned homes. The motive for this being that the West family business was making moonshine whiskey, and it was in their best interest to keep people away from Cole City.

The church was too burned to the ground. The pastor had succumbed to old age and poor health long before the church was torched, sparing him the insult.

Most of the mining equipment was salvaged. Rail cars were shipped out to parts unknown, and the rails that were the easiest to get too were taken up. The tracks located deep in the mines were left behind to rust in place. There were a few free laborers who lingered in Cole City after the mines closed to try and make a living from small privately owned coal mining operations. Such endeavors were mostly unsuccessful, and by 1910, the once vibrant town of Cole City was little more than a series of ash piles where buildings had once been. Already, the forest had begun to retake the land.

In nearby Morganville, my church's membership grew slowly but steadily. I found work at a sawmill and lumber company situated in Morganville and rented a room at a boarding house. I wasn't paid well, but nevertheless was able to save enough money to buy a small house and five acres of land near Lookout Creek. I raised pigs and chickens and had a milk cow. By most any measure, my life, which only a few years ago had seemed forfeit, was now comfortable, if not prosperous.

I became acquainted with a virtuous young woman named Lilly in my congregation, and although she was several years my junior, I began to have feelings for her. I consulted the scriptures and found many references to marriage. But the one verse that moved me the most said, "He who finds a wife finds what is good and receives favor from the Lord" (Proverbs 18:22).

We were married in the church in 1912, my forty-sixth year, and her twentieth. And over the following eighteen years, Lilly gave me ten children that lived, five boys and five girls; the last, being a girl that we named Louise after Lilly's mother, was born in 1930.

In 1920, my congregation, having grown to a respectable number, became increasingly disillusioned with the Campbellite version of Christianity. Their neighbors were Baptists and Methodists who often referred to Campbellites as pejorative with little adherence to church doctrine. The church elders brought to me a proposal to accept an invitation for our church to join the Southern Baptist Convention. The church elders argued that Baptist and Campbellites are so near in belief and practice that they should unite. The only significant difference between the two, in the minds of many, is that Campbellites believe that if it isn't mentioned in the Bible, then it shouldn't be in the church. And since music is not mentioned in the Bible, it shouldn't be a part of the church service. Baptist, on the other hand, had long since embraced the presence of organ and piano music in worship services. The elders didn't consider this one small difference to be insurmountable. Throughout the region, other Campbellite churches had merged with their Baptist brethren. I viewed this as just another curve in the path set out for me by God and offered no objection to the elders' desire to become Baptist.

I found that the Baptist Church had a broader appeal to the people in Morganville and beyond and witnessed growth in church membership that exceeded my expectations. With this growth came more social interaction, more church doctrinal issues, and inevitably more problems. I found myself longing for the relative simplicity of my small congregation and the relative lack of doctrine of the Campbellite Church.

The Southern Baptist Convention, which had formed a generation before the Civil War, had favored slavery. The Campbellite Church at Upper Cole City had, by contrast, welcomed Negrors and whites alike, and all were welcome to worship together. But like many other Southern institutions, the Southern Baptist Convention held Negroes to be inferior and barred them from attending church services. The growing Negro population at Hooker was therefore not welcome at the little church in Morganville.

Once the last of the Negroes got removed from Cole City, a large handmade sign was erected alongside Hales Gap Road at the base of the mountain proclaiming, "Niggers Are Not Welcome." I always suspected that the West family had built the sign for their purposes and had little or nothing to do with skin color and everything to do with keeping prying eyes away from Cole City and all of Sand Mountain.

As time went on, I found the changing responsibilities of the emerging church to be more and more tedious and burdensome. I found myself being more surly and quick to anger and inflexible in my dealings with the church's business. My loving wife Lilly added new words to her vocabulary describing me, such as sullen, irritable, and ungracious. I blamed the change in my demeanor on the modern church. I began to consider leaving the church to start a smaller congregation where I could find peace. As it turns out, however, God's plan for me had yet to be completed.

Chapter 5
New Home Community Rises from the Ashes

In 1938, the state of Georgia decided to open up the land in and around the ghost town of Cole City for homesteading and arranged a lottery by which individuals, who qualified, could receive a forty-acre land grant. The only condition for land ownership was a commitment to build a house on the property and occupy the home within two years. I entered the lottery and was granted a tract of land located directly across the road from the old Cooper farm just southeast of Upper Cole City's center. I was then seventy-two years old, and while many men my age were looking toward scaling back their level of activity, I looked forward to the work that I knew this undertaking would require.

Some years earlier, I had bought a well-used 1927 Ford Model T truck from the widow of a recently deceased farmer. The widow told me that her husband had paid almost $300 for the truck when it was new, but that because I was doing God's work, she'd sell it to me for just $65. Considering the grief that that old "Tin Lizzie" would give me for years to come, I suspect that the truck had been used a bit more by the farmer than his widow had let on. But I wasn't a man to give up on something that I'd committed to, and I had committed to that old truck. Out of necessity, I learned much about truck repair. But the old truck served me well as I began the process of homesteading the land I'd been granted. It served as my stump puller, my hay hauler, and my Sunday go-to meeting truck. A few years later, I'd build wooden benches on the bed as a place for school children to sit on the eight-mile ride over dirt roads to the new school that we built.

During World War II, when we couldn't get gasoline, we just let Tin Lizzie sit out in the field, and when the war was over, the old truck, being completely worn out, was left to sit right there as something of a monument to its years of usefulness.

The mining operations and associated land abuse from generations past had left Cole City denuded, but in the years since the mines closed, vegetation had made a comeback. Hardwood trees grew among the Cole City ruins to reach up to six inches in diameter. Substantial though they were, these trees were not large enough to make it practical to harvest them for timber. Fortunately, there were large stands of old-growth forest covering vast areas outside of Cole City. Old-growth oak trees in the Cole City area grow to a maximum diameter of about thirty inches. When Cole City homesteading began in 1938, there were ample old-growth hardwoods on land now owned by the homesteaders.

I was one of the first three homesteaders to take possession of the granted land. The other two homesteaders, Charles Bowman and Ben Putnam, were equally anxious to start new lives in Cole City, and the three of us worked together to timber the lands we'd been granted and mill the lumber needed to build homes and barns. We used a crosscut saw handled by a man on either end of the saw to fell the large hardwoods and, after cutting the logs to length, used a mule to drag them to a cleared area where we'd set up a sawmill powered by Tin Lizzie's gasoline engine. My years of having worked in the lumber business gave me the skills needed to manage the operation, and the other two men provided man power. We turned logs into one by twelve and two by six lengths of lumber that we stacked and covered to let air cure. Over the first year of our endeavor, we built modest wood-frame homes and large wood-frame barns for each of us, quickly meeting the state's only condition of land ownership.

While we were at it, we cut enough lumber to build a church, and with the help of my sons, we built a fine church on a property on the hill overlooking our home on land donated by the state for this purpose.

The number of new homes built in Cole City grew steadily, and soon I had a fair number of congregates at the new church. And within a short time, the new church was admitted to the Southern Baptist Convention, with me as pastor.

Wishing to put the history of Cole City behind us, we named the new community built on the Cole City ruins, New Home.

It wasn't long afterward the church was finished that we had our first funeral and interned our first congregate in the new cemetery. There would be far too many congregants to follow.

Chapter 6
Can This Place be Evil

It had been many years since I'd been called upon to comfort anyone thought to possibly be possessed by an unclean spirit, and when
called upon, I had found that there were other explanations for the
endured maladies. Alcohol abuse and melancholia being the most
prevalent causes. But that was to change.

New Home community grew quickly with one homesteader
after another settling in. Before long, the congregation of my little
church, being the only one there, had grown to a respectable size.
Every Sunday, there would be new people in attendance.

Being true to my years as a Campbellite, my sermons were taken
straight from the scriptures, and without fail, the call to the altar that
ended every service yielded a conversion. Baptisms were many. In the
Baptist tradition, deacons were elected to handle the administrative
needs of the young church.

As the church grew, the number of unexplained malevolent incidents grew with it. At first, these occurrences were not thought to be
out of the ordinary. Still, when the number of events grew to be dis-
proportionate to the small population of the New Home community,
people began to question whether there may be some supernatural
cause. With my reputation for identifying and exorcising unclean
spirits, I was called upon by the deacons to look into the cause of
unusual occurrences.

Chapter 7
A Voice

Sherman Stalcup, a young adult, living with his parents in what used to be Upper Cole City, brutally murdered his father, Troy, with a hammer. The county sheriff ruled the death a homicide and locked Sherman away. From what I could learn about the incident, it was clear that the underlying cause of this tragedy wasn't supernatural, but moonshine whiskey. Troy was well known as a moonshiner and equally well known to partake of his handiwork often and to excess. Sherman had followed in his father's footsteps as a maker and consumer of moonshine whiskey. During a drunken argument between Father and his son, the conflict grew out of control resulting in Sherman taking his father's life. At his trial, Sherman said that in his drunken stupor, he thought that he'd heard an unfamiliar male voice tell him to take up the hammer and strike Troy and that the voice had said to him that Troy was going to kill him and that the only thing to do to save his own life was to strike first. Sherman's defense was, therefore, insanity. But Sherman's testimony was discounted by the court as a blatant attempt to dissuade the jury from sentencing him to death.

Denny Gadd, a sixteen-year-old boy, living at home with his parents in what used to be Upper Cole City, shot and killed his older brother Daryl in what was ruled an unfortnate hunting accident. Denny claimed that he had been distracted by a male voice near him at the moment he aimed his rifle at a squirrel on a stump and that it was this distraction that caused him to shoot his older brother by mistake. There was never any evidence of a third person being in the area when Daryl got killed. I learned that the two brothers had a long history of altercations with each other and that Denny had, on more than one occasion, threatened his older brother's life. This behavior was attributed to a sibling rivalry and not as evidence of any genuine animosity between the brothers. Daryl's death was ruled accidental. Although the presence of a distracting voice gave me reason to pause, I could not determine that there was any unnatural influence on Denny at the time. It must have been an unfortunate accident.

Homesteaders relied heavily on the harvesting of hardwood for the building of their houses and barns in New Home community. Walter Goforth was no exception. Goforth relied upon his teenage sons Jimmy and Johnny to aid in felling trees and dragging logs out of the forest to get milled. The brothers would handle either end of a crosscut saw while their father stood off at a distance to warn the boys when the tree began to tilt so that they could move away from the danger of the falling tree. While the boys worked feverously at their task, their father heard a male voice call his name and looked away from the tree being cut in the direction from where the sound came. It was at that exact moment that the giant oak tree being cut snapped at its base and came crashing down without warning. The tree landed on Jimmy Goforth, crushing him to death. This occurrence marked the third time that some disembodied male voice would be heard at just the moment that someone's life was taken. And I was beginning to think that this was not a coincidence. I began to question whether there might be some supernatural force at work here in what was once Cole City.

In the 1940s, an unsuccessful strip mining operation had existed between the center of what had been Upper Cole City and the New Home church. The land had been scared savagely and left as a monument to the mining companies disregard for the land. The deeply gouged pits filled with spring water and became a favorite swimming hole for the young folks of the New Home community.

On one hot summer Sunday, a small crowd gathered at the swimming hole to enjoy the cool water. From the shore, Marcus Leigh, a good swimmer, dove into the depth of the pool and never came up. The water where Leigh dove was more than twenty feet deep, and there were no rocks upon which Leigh could have landed. So there was no apparent reason for Leigh's drowning. Everyone chalked the drowning up to an unfortunate accident.

Remembering the story about hearing a man's voice at the time of other deaths, I asked the people who were there when Leigh drowned if they had heard such a voice. No one had. Then a few days later, a young girl who was a member of my congregation came to me in private and told me that she wasn't entirely sure but that she thinks that she may have heard a man's voice just before Leigh dove into the water and that the voice had said something like, "Dive deep. Dive as deep as you can. Show everyone how deep you can go. Be a man!" The voice was that of a man but was unfamiliar to her. She had not admitted to hearing the voice before because she didn't want to be the one person to have a different story from the rest of the group. The mysterious voice had now been manifest on the occasion of four deaths.

One spring, there had been heavy rains, and the streams in the valley below on both sides of Sand Mountain where Upper Cole City is situated were swollen beyond their banks. The Hales Gap Road ran alongside a small creek at the foot of the mountain. Hales Gap Road had become the main road leading to and from Cole City, and although unpaved, it was well-traveled. The raging waters cut off access to the New Home community from Lookout Valley. Motorists traveling to New Home community had no choice but to wait until the floodwaters receded.

Charles Isom, the adult son of one of the more prosperous homesteaders in New Home community, had been visiting family in Morganville when he got cut off from his only way home. He drove his old Ford as far up the road as possible and, with his wife and three small children in the car, surveyed the flooded roadway ahead. A few other vehicles were also stopped at this spot, and drivers and passengers were standing alongside the road, not knowing what to do. Then without a word to anyone, Isom put his car in gear and began to drive forward. Bystanders screamed for him to stop but to no avail. Isom plunged his car into the floodwaters rushing over the roadway, and his car got swept away. All were lost. Isom was a pragmatic man not prone to risk-taking, and no one would ever know why he did what he did.

I asked those who had witnessed this tragedy if they had heard a man's voice, but none admitted to having done so. So I'll never know for sure whether some otherworldly entity may have influenced him, but it certainly would have fit a pattern that I had come to recognize.

The presence of a disembodied male voice would be associated with the beating of a pregnant wife by a New Home community man. The wife survived, but her baby was stillborn. A midwife attending to the birth of a baby by a New Home community woman claimed to have heard a male voice speaking some unknown language, possibly Latin during the baby's birth. Another woman claimed to have heard the same thing while she was miscarrying.

Soon every mishap or unfortunate circumstance came to be associated with this disembodied voice, and blame got ascribed to it. I have no proof, but I felt sure that the idea of an unclean spirit possessing the New Home community was more a product of some sort of mass hysteria and less an actual occurrence. But there were too many unexplained events to believe that they were all a product of overactive imaginations. I am therefore convinced that an unclean spirit possesses the New Home community and is preying on the weak-minded to facilitate malevolent deeds.

In my next sermon, I implored the congregation to resist the voice that they may hear. Citing John 8:44, I reminded my flock, "The devil is a deceiver and a liar."

I am convinced that my evil nemesis, Colonel Towers, is still in Cole City and that he has found a new way to torment those who live there. Rather than possess the flesh, this unclean spirit has by more subtle means begun to influence those he targets. He distracts them from their obligations, such as the case with the Goforth boy and Gadd boy's deaths. He lies to them about their invincibility, as was the case with Charles Isom and Marcus Leigh. He creates false threats, as was the case with Sherman Stalcup.

My tools for exorcising demons are powerless against this new tactic. I can't fight the beast because he chooses not to allow me to confront him. He hides in the darkness, subtly influencing those he targets. I never heard the voice, but I am convinced that others did and that the voice led to death and destruction.

Chapter 8
One Last Battle
before I Go

The demon chose, for whatever reason, to not attack my family or me. My children married and blessed me with many grandchildren. In 1948, as I lay on my deathbed at the age of 102, I know that this is the end of my story. I take great comfort and delight that my youngest daughter, Louise, has brought her first child, a boy named Dwight, into the world. She brings the new baby near so that I can have a closer look. As she does so, the newborn begins to wail and thrash about as if he were trying to get away from me. It is at that moment that I sensed something malevolent. Could it be the spirit of Colonel Towers come to wage one last battle with me? Or, worse yet, is he here for the boy?

Cole City

Book 3
The Chosen One

Chapter 1
Evil

Can a place be evil? Can past atrocities cause a place to have a pervasive evil that will be harbored there for generations, enveloping all who call it home? Can horrific events that occurred in the distant past manifest a century later with tragic consequences? Cole City is a ghost town that, without question, is the site of great suffering and evil during its heyday, a place where great evil surely existed. And if one knows just where to look, the scars of that long-ago era are still evident.

Between the years of 1965 and 1971, there were perhaps sixty or so young men between the ages of sixteen and twenty-one living in or around the old ghost town of Cole City. One of every four of the young men would die tragic and violent deaths during this period. But the deaths linked with Cole City are some way or another extended well beyond its geography.

Was it the place? Old-timers, who spent their lives in Cole City, believed it to be so. Some believe that an evil spirit from Cole City's past is ever-present and malicious.

Chapter 2
The Incident

It was late summer in 1961, Dwight's thirteenth year. Little League baseball season had ended, and the new school year had not yet started. Bored and restless, Dwight and three of his classmates decided to go exploring. All of them have heard the ghost tales of Cole City and have explored the ruins of the ghost town where they live. But none of the boys have ever seen the most iconic ruins of the bygone era, the coke ovens. The ruins of the ovens were mostly intact, lying at the bottom of Nickajack gulch, two thousand feet below the mountaintop where the boys live. Making the arduous journey down the old footpath to the ovens required a real commitment of energy and time. But the boys, with nothing else to do, were up to the challenge. They planned to spend the night inside one of the old ovens to give them separation from the ghostly night that envelops the gulch every night. They'll bring sleeping bags, canteens of water, flashlights, and two packages of Oscar Myers hot dogs for their dinner. They'll build a fire inside the oven and roast the hot dogs on sticks.

The climb down the mountain took less time than they expected, and they arrived at the ovens with several hours of daylight left. It was a hot summer day, and the boys had worked up a sweat during their climb down the mountain. They occupied themselves by jumping into the frigid waters of the Blue Hole in Cole City Creek to cool off. They failed to notice the absence of any sounds from the surrounding forest. No birds or insects could be heard.

The boys inspected several ovens and picked one that was mostly intact with few bricks missing from the oven walls. Loose bricks from the walls and roof of the ovens lay scattered about the floor of all the ovens. These bricks had fallen at some time in the past, and other bricks would no doubt fall as well. Finding the oven whose walls were in the best condition will hopefully mean little chance of a brick falling on one of the boys as they slept. The hole in the roof of the oven had to be open to let smoke from the boy's campfire escape the oven. Also, the oven floor had to be flat and free of fallen bricks to offer the boys a place to sleep. Gathering dead limbs for their campfire turned out to be easy enough as the valley around the ovens was littered with fallen trees and branches.

The boys built a fire, and as the sun went down over the mountaintop, they roasted hot dogs on the open fire. Dwight produced a pack of Lucky Strike cigarettes that he'd swiped from his father, and the boys eagerly engaged in the almost ritualistic forbidden deed of smoking. They laughed at one another's jokes and swapped ghost stories until, at last, they settled into their sleeping bags for the night.

Sometime in the wee hours of the morning, the boys were abruptly awakened by Dwight's screams. Dwight was still asleep but having a nightmare. The boys tried to wake Dwight but were unable to do so. Dwight was talking in his sleep, and it was clear that he was carrying on a heated conversation with some unseen person in his dream—all the while, Dwight was thrashing about as if he were trying to push this invisible person away. Then to the other boys' surprise and horror, Dwight's face contorted into a mask of sheer terror, and his voice took on an otherworldly tone. Dwight sat upright and became as still as a statue. Dwight's eyes were wide open, but he didn't seem to see the other boys. And he looked only at the dying embers of the campfire. Dwight's words became garbled and unintelligible. But the tone could not be mistaken, for it was one of malice. Then as suddenly as it had begun, it is all over. Dwight settled back into his sleeping bag and went back to sleep. The other boys were unsure of what to make of all this. There was little choice, however, but to try to ignore what had happened and to go back to sleep.

Sunrise comes late to the floor of the valley and the boys, as was their nature, enjoyed sleeping late. It was midmorning before Dwight awakened and began to stir. The other boys had been up for a while and were, to a man, grumbling about being hungry. They had not thought to bring any food for breakfast, and they were now regretting their oversight. Dwight went outside of the oven and relieved himself without a word to the others. He returned momentarily, rolled up his sleeping bag, and strolled out into the daylight. The other boys relieved themselves on the burned-out campfire and without a word following Dwight's lead headed up the footpath that led back up to the top of the mountain.

It took considerably longer to climb up the mountain than it had taken the boys to descend the day before. Dwight forged ahead at a steady pace, not stopping to rest. No one spoke until they reached the summit. Winded and sweating, the boys collapsed in the shade of an ancient oak tree and emptied their canteens to quench their thirst.

Curiosity finally overcame hesitation, and one of Dwight's friends asked him about the nocturnal episode. Dwight starred off into the distance and remained silent for a long time.

Then quietly, he told his friends, "There was a man inside the oven with them the night before. The man was well-dressed, but his clothes were odd, like something from the 1800s. And the man was smoking a cigar. At first, I thought the cigar wasn't lit because the end of the cigar did not glow, but smoke drifted upward from it, and it stunk to high heaven. The man said little, but his message was somehow clear to me. He said that it was my destiny to avenge the wrongs I endured at the hands of others and that I would be invincible. The man told me that he'd be with me as long as I lived and that because of him watching over me, I would never have to fear getting caught. Nothing or no one would be able to stop me. Then the man was gone like a puff of smoke in the wind, leaving me with a sense of power."

Seeing that his friends did not take his story about the man seriously, Dwight quickly retracted his tale-telling the others that it was just a dream. But Dwight knew that what he'd experienced was no dream. It would be decades before Dwight would ever mention any of this again, and by then, there'd be ample proof of Dwight's invincibility.

In the next few weeks, before school started again, the boys hung out, occupying themselves with the things that thirteen-year-olds find amusing and vital. But Dwight wasn't among them. Whenever one of his friends had attempted to enlist Dwight in whatever they were doing, he declined.

Boys of this age have short attention spans, and it only took being rebuffed by Dwight a few times for the other boys to lose interest in having Dwight participate. Dwight's parents tried to persuade him to take an interest in something but failed. Dwight seemed content to lie on the sofa watching daytime TV. His appetite was off. And he was very irritable. Neither of which characteristics were typical of Dwight's normal behavior.

When classes resumed, Dwight's teachers noticed the changes in his behavior. Dwight no longer took any interest in his schoolwork or in socializing with his classmates. He openly challenged his classmates and his teachers at every turn. Dwight became a regular visitor to the principal's office. Dwight's disruptiveness got him placed on suspension again and again.

On most nights, Dwight could be heard talking in his sleep, but the words were not understandable. Night after night, Dwight would keep the entire household awake with his screams of anguish. The following day, he'd have no recollection of any such behavior. On several occasions, Dwight was found walking about the house aimlessly in his sleep. Dwight quarreled with his parents endlessly. On more than one occasion, Dwight responded to his parent's attempts to discipline him by becoming agitated, striking out against them viciously. Dwight was big for his age, and from the many times he'd been involved in fights, he knew how to handle himself. Dwight bullied everyone smaller or weaker than him, including his younger brother Ollie. Dwight was quick to anger and to use his fists as the first response to adversity. The altercations between Dwight and his father intensified and turned bloody, with both participants inflicting considerable harm to the other and neither gaining an advantage.

Dwight had once been his parent's pride and joy, but ever since that night in the oven, Dwight had become unmanageable. Something had happened to Dwight on that night. There was something terribly wrong with Dwight.

Chapter 3
Cole City

Before the Civil War, the Cherokee of Appalachia were removed and resettled out West. The lands that had been theirs for millennia were parceled out to white settlers. The property in the vicinity of what would become Cole City being rugged, remote, and mostly untenable went largely unsettled and remained in the ownership of the state of Georgia. Then coal was discovered under the mountain in this part of Georgia. Nothing happened with the coal for a long while because of the war, but then, in early 1873, the governor got the sate to grant him the mineral rights for the Sand Mountain plateau. The governor formed the Dade Coal Company, and shortly after that, he incorporated Cole City. To work the mine, the governor took advantage of a convict lease system that the state of Georgia had put in place just after the war.

During the war, the Union Army burned most of the jails and prisons throughout the state, leaving few places to house prisoners. Leasing prisoners to private business was a way to incarcerate prisoners without the need to invest in building new prisons. The state could wash its hands of the prisoners and not coincidentally; the governor could get the laborers that he needed to work the mines at Cole City. At its peak, more than five hundred prisoners were working and living in Cole City.

Of the five hundred prisoners at Cole City, four hundred were black, and most of the black prisoners were former slaves. One in every six prisoners was serving a life sentence, and all the prisoners were serving long sentences. Yet the offenses that brought many of the prisoners to Cole City were relatively minor. Some were guilty of nothing more than a failure to pay some undisclosed fee that they were unaware of before their arrest. These phantom fees were the construct of racial bias meant to subjugate the black population and supply a steady stream of workers for the mine.

Although the stated purpose for prisoner's presence at Cole City was to pay their debt to society, the real reason was much less noble. Prisoners were there to mine coal in support of revenue production for the white owners.

The remoteness of Cole City made it an excellent place to dispose of the unwanted refuse of society. The governor of Georgia, who signed the predatory laws that sent so many innocent black men to Cole City, was also the principal owner of the mine there.

Prison life at the mining camp at Cole City and coke oven operations was brutal and dangerous with murders and deadly accidents commonplace. Malnutrition, unsanitary conditions, and the absence of essential medical treatment doomed the weak and the infirm. Tuberculosis, typhoid fever, pneumonia, and syphilis took many lives. Those too sick or too old to work in the mines would suddenly disappear never to be heard from again. Many were murdered in their sleep to make room for new healthier workers.

Those healthy enough to work toiled for up to sixteen hours a day, seven days a week in unthinkably horrible conditions. Hundreds died from black lung disease. Those who rebelled against authority were beaten. Those who attempted to escape were gunned down by sadistic guards.

Chief among the persecutors was Col. Willard Towers. Formerly a guard supervisor at Camp Sumter in Andersonville, Georgia, during the war, Towers was a ruthless and evil man. Towers, although diminutive, cast a giant shadow over Cole City. Towers was murdered by a trustee who recognized him from their days together at Andersonville. And, although dead and buried, Towers was said to still reside at Cole City, where his spirit claims the weak-minded for his eternal evil doings. Those who came under his influence committed senseless acts of cruelty and murder at his behest with impunity—brother killing brother, son killing father, and friend killing friend.

The mines themselves had numerous openings within a two-mile radius of the main mine entrance and miles of underground passageways, honeycombing the entire area. Coal produced from the mines was transferred via rail from the top of the mountain to the valley two thousand feet below where it was fired in ovens to produce coke. The coke got sent on the railroad to foundries in Chattanooga, Rising Fawn, and elsewhere. At its peak, coal production would reach seven hundred tons per day. But it didn't last. The coal that was easily reached was mostly depleted by the late 1890s, and operations began to diminish significantly. As the mining activities wound down in the late 1890s, the number of convicts needed to operate the mines declined, and one Cole City structure after another got abandoned. The Rattlesnake Mine would close in 1899, and the Ferndale Mine would close two years later. By 1908, all prison camp activity had ceased, and only a handful of small independent mines would remain active. Underground mining would end altogether by the 1920s. Sporadic surface mining would come to Cole City in the 1930s and continue on a limited basis until the 1990s.

Abandonment of Cole City began in the 1890s and accelerated after the turn of the century. Homes, barracks, and other buildings got abandoned in increasing numbers. And as Cole City's citizens left, there were no new settlers. The land reverted to be in the ownership of state government and wasn't open for sale or homesteading. The only other significant landholder in the area was the powerful West family, who owned about four thousand acres of land at the head of Nickajack gulch, dating back to the time of the original land lottery in 1838. The West family, who made their living from making moonshine whiskey, sought to keep the area from being resettled by homesteaders. As Cole City buildings got abandoned, the matriarch of the family, along with two of her sons, would set them ablaze. One by one, the buildings that had defined Cole City disappeared. The ongoing destruction of Cole City was greeted with indifference by local and state officials and law enforcement. The lack of interest by any authority served to encourage the further destruction of Cole City.

Cole City slowly, over the next thirty years, returned to the forest. Trees sprouted and grew in the rubble. Then in 1938, the state opened the Cole City area for homesteading. Poor white Southerners in the region got the opportunity to become Cole City landowners. Between 1938 and the start of World War II, the influx of new settlers to Cole City led a 42 percent growth in population countywide.

Today, if you know where to look and don't mind strenuous mountaineering, you can still find the ruins of the abandoned coke ovens lying along the valley floor of Nickajack gulch. Remnants of the mining operations, including tunnel openings, abandoned railways, and vertical tramways and vertical air shafts, are still visible. Near the coke ovens can be found stone steps that have a groove worn in them from the convict's leg irons rubbing against the stone as the convicts climbed up and down the mountainside between the coke ovens in the valley and their barracks atop the mountain.

A visit to the ruins at Cole City leaves you with a melancholy that can only be explained by a sense of loss in much the same way as a visit to Gettysburg or Andersonville. The somber climate of this place is no doubt a consequence of the many men who endured appalling conditions with such an absence of charity as to make their existence loathsome and hopeless. Those who survived Cole City and got the opportunity to move on were very few and had to be considered the lucky ones. The exact number of prisoners who died in Cole City will never be known for sure. Five hundred is a conservative estimate and a thousand, or more, isn't beyond belief. Over the years, the geographic area now known as Cole City has grown well beyond the limits of the original charter. Cole City now unofficially includes the domain from the Tennessee State Line southward to encompass the Davis and "Happy Hollow" communities and westward to the Alabama State Line at Bryant. The original boundaries of Coal City covered an area of only 3.2 square miles. The area of Cole City shown on modern-day maps is approximately a twelve-square-mile area. The designation of such a larger geographic area came less because Cole City grew than simply because it was the only town designation for miles in any direction.

The real heart of the ghost town of Cole City is the area around the main Dade Coal Company mine. It is this nucleus of all that was genuinely evil about this place. Countless lives got taken, and more than the absence of the trappings associated with a city, it is their souls that make Cole City an authentic ghost town. If there are such things as ghosts, then Cole City, where so many died violently, must be a place that they haunt.

Chapter 4
Dwight Faces Death

The Cole City of today is nothing like Cole City of the past. Almost 150 years had passed since Cole City was founded, and the relatively few people who live here knew little about Cole City's history. My name is Bryan, and I grew up in the ghost town that is Cole City. I am acquainted with everyone in Cole City, more or less, including Dwight. Dwight and I went to the same school, were in the same grade, played on the same sports teams, and went to the same church. My grandfather and Dwight's grandfather were two of the first homesteaders to return to the abandoned ghost town when the state opened up the area for settlement in 1938. Dwight and I had been boyhood friends. I was with Dwight on that fateful night in the coke oven and witnessed the subsequent change in Dwight.

After that night in the coke oven, our lives took very different paths. I became more active in my church, and by contrast, Dwight stopped coming to church at all. Dwight drifted toward the more disorderly and rebellious elements in our world. I went on to graduate from college, where I received a bachelor's degree in theology and spent my life, up until my recent retirement, in the ministry. After graduation from high school, Dwight served in the army during the Vietnam War. I too served in the Vietnam War, but I served as a chaplain and never took up arms. Our paths didn't cross in that faraway land and have otherwise not crossed since. Dwight's path was a secret one and one that didn't lead him back to Cole City until very near the end of his life.

Late one October evening in 2016 while at home in Cole City with my wife, babysitting our two young granddaughters, the telephone rang. Suspecting it to be yet another robo call, I let the call go to voice mail, and as I listened, I recognized Dwight's voice on the other end of the line.

"Bryan," he said, "I know it's been a couple of decades, but I'm hoping that we can talk. I have a question that you are the only person I can ask. Can you give me a call?" And he provided a phone number with a Chattanooga area code before hanging up.

I hadn't spoken to Dwight in over forty years, and while I was delighted to hear from him after all this time, I couldn't help but wonder why he'd be calling me. The following morning, I called the number that Dwight had left and heard Dwight's unmistakable voice. The voice was familiar but tinged with something that at first I thought must be age but later would come to believe was more than just age—it was exhaustion. I learned that Dwight was in hospice a little over a half-hour drive away in Chattanooga. He was dying from stage 4 lung cancer, from which there's no returning. His sickness was ravaging his body, he said, and he didn't have much time. Pain meds kept him sedated much of the time, leaving him short intervals of lucidity as the drug wore off and before the pain returned. It was in one of these lucid moments that I'd been lucky enough to reach Dwight.

Dwight asked me to visit him at hospice so that we could talk, and I felt compelled, both as a minister and as a boyhood friend, to do so. So we agreed that time being of the essence, I'd visit him the next day.

When I arrived at hospice, I found Dwight in a hospital bed in a private room with an IV connected to his arm. An emaciated old man had replaced the robust young man that I remembered. I pulled up a chair and took his hand. He slowly opened his eyes, and a faint smile crossed his lips.

For the next little while, we reminisced about the days of our youth and got caught up on the past forty years. Dwight had married and divorced and had two adult sons and one grandson. His ex-wife and sons lived just outside of Charlotte, North Carolina, where, by Dwight's account, they all lived relatively normal, happy lives. Dwight was somewhat estranged from his immediate family, who, according to him, were unaware of his late-stage cancer. Like many things in his life, Dwight had kept this a secret from them. But soon, his secret would be known to all, regardless of his preference.

Dwight had never been close with his extended family of aunts, uncles, and cousins, many of whom lived in the Chattanooga area. Most of the aunts and uncles had long since passed away, and he'd lost touch with the many cousins who remained. None were aware of Dwight's death sentence or even his presence in the area. And I sensed that this is just the way Dwight wanted it. Dwight had succumbed to the reality that he was no longer invincible and that he would soon die, as did everyone.

When Dwight had finally given in to the reality of being unable to care for himself, he arranged to come back to Chattanooga, nearer to Cole City, for reasons that even he didn't fully understand, to live out his final days in the place meant for such a purpose.

We'd been together for more than an hour, and I could sense Dwight's pain meds beginning to wear off. Then, finally, Dwight came to the question that he'd alluded to in our phone call the day before. Dwight said to me, "In the Bible, it says that God so loved the world that he gave his only Son, that whoever believes in him shall have eternal life." And he asked pointedly, "Bryan, is that true?"

As a minister, I had often heard John 3:16 paraphrased and gotten the same question from those facing imminent death. They all wanted to know whether, regardless of their past sins, they could get into heaven. I asked Dwight whether he'd made his peace with his maker and truly believed in Christ almighty. Dwight's smile was absent as he paused and confided that he thought that there was a God in heaven and that his Son, Jesus, had died for our sins but that he was unsure as to whether his sins could be forgiven.

I did not hesitate with the follow-up question that I always ask. I asked Dwight if he had confessed his sins and asked for forgiveness. Dwight smiled and said, "I was hoping you could help me with that part." And in hushed tones that lacked any specifics, we began to discuss the nature and extent of his past sins. I explained that I was not a priest and that neither of us were Catholic but that there was a catharsis to be gained from confessing one's past sins and asking for forgiveness.

Dwight hesitated for a long moment and then asked if I would make a record of his confession and after his death share that confession with those that he had wronged.

I thought this an odd request until it occurred to me that Dwight was looking to negotiate his way into heaven and he wanted me to help him do so. He was ready to confess his sins and needed someone to listen. Dwight wanted to unburden himself but only to me. He wanted me to keep the truth of his sins a secret until after he dies and then share them with those he has wronged. In so doing, Dwight has the best of all circumstances. His confession buys his way into heaven, while he doesn't have to face those that he has sinned against.

Rather than debate the finer points of theology with a man whose emotional needs are clouded by powerful painkillers, I acquiesced to his wishes and promised to listen to his confessions. From the time we spent together as teenagers, I believe that Dwight has sinned, but I don't yet have any reason to believe that his sins are of any more significance than those of others. I would be wrong about this.

That's how we got here! What follows is my chronicling of Dwight's life story as told to me from his deathbed. The truth of Dwight's confession lies somewhere behind a shroud of pain meds and memories that are decades old. Over the next several evenings, Dwight and I sat together in his tiny room, and I listened as he told me one horror story after another about his life. Never once did he falter to share his secrets, and I struggled to keep up with my note-taking. As Dwight neared the end of his life, the stories he told me ran together, and some of the facts became muddled, but Dwight was undeterred. It seemed that he would not give into death until he'd finished the story. At first, I was not sure whether I heard a truthful confession or the ramblings of Dwight's drug-addled mind. I listened carefully to see if I could find any verifiable facts in what

Dwight told me. I found just enough truth in what I heard to begin to take Dwight at his word. And Dwight's story was spellbinding.

Once our conversation drew to its inevitable end, I could sense a sort of letdown in Dwight. Perhaps he was finding some peace of mind in having said what he wanted to say. Or maybe it was just the meds. Either way, Dwight was reluctant to say more at the moment. I promised Dwight that I'd be back again the following day.

For the next few weeks, I'd visit Dwight almost every day, and with every visit, I could see that Dwight was slipping away. I could easily have sat in judgment of Dwight's evil deeds, but my Savior tells me that regardless of one's sins, a professed genuine belief in Jesus Christ, confession of one's sins, and asking forgiveness are the keys to heaven. I don't know what Dwight truly believed in his soul or whether Dwight made it to heaven or not, but I will, as promised to him on his deathbed, tell his story as best as I can. You should know that some of the gaps in Dwight's story got filled in with my knowledge of past events and the results of research that I took upon myself to conduct.

As Dwight continued, his memories failed him more and more. Two inevitable conclusions came to me—first, Dwight's monologue had become indecipherable, and secondly, Dwight was very near death.

Chapter 5
Boone

The rifle shot caught Boone just behind his right shoulder, passing through muscle and lung tissue before stopping near the dog's racing heart. The small-caliber shot was right where Dwight had aimed, but it wasn't a powerful enough weapon to bring down the big dog. Instead, Boone lumbered through the dense underbrush in the direction of where he lived. Dwight cursed below his breath in disappointment at not having brought down the dog with a single shot, and knowing that a second shot would not fit the story, he hoped his family would believe about the dog's murder.

He'd planned the dog's death meticulously, waiting patiently until his mother, father, and younger brother were away from home. Then, he lured Boone into the woods across the road from where the family lived in a small aging farmhouse in the direction of the neighboring Smiths' house a quarter of a mile away. The dog had to be found dead here to blame the killing on Mr. Smith. Mr. Smith was an easy patsy, no one liked him, and he was often heard threating anyone who dared tread on his downtrodden hobby farm, be it man or beast. Only the week before, Mr. Smith had run into Dwight's dad at Garner's Country Store and had proclaimed loudly for all to hear, "That damn dog has been chasing my chickens again. I'd hate to have to shoot him!"

Boone wasn't Dwight's ultimate target. Dwight had had several run-ins with his neighbor Mr. Smith, but Dwight was only fifteen years old, just a boy really, and still lacking the self-confidence required to confront Smith directly. Dwight would blame Smith for the unthinkable sin of killing Dwight's loyal dog. Dwight would fain outrage at this evil act and use it as a pretext to justify retaliating against Mr. Smith. Mr. Smith would undoubtedly deny any involvement in killing the poor animal. Still, he was an ill-tempered and threatening individual by nature, and Dwight was confident that he could escalate a confrontation with Mr. Smith to justifiable violence. The real goal here was to inflict harm or maybe even kill Mr. Smith. In Dwight's view, Mr. Smith didn't deserve to live.

Boone was a yard dog who spent his entire existence running loose in Dwight's yard, as was the custom for dogs belonging to countryfolk in those parts. Occasionally Boone ventured into the nearby woods to sniff, crap, and chase whatever furry creature he wanted and otherwise do what dogs do. It was true that Boone sometimes wandered into Smith's yard and chased the free-range chickens he found there. Boone never caught any of the chickens, and it could be argued that it was all just sporting fun to Boone.

A ten-year-old mutt, Boone was an unremarkable dog whose only redeeming characteristic was his unwavering loyalty to Dwight's family. Not knowing why he was in such pain, Boone's single thought was to get home, hoping that doing so would result in his pain being somehow relieved. Boone had no understanding that his life would be forfeit for Dwight's grand plan.

Dwight waited at the edge of the woods, listening to the whimpers of the wounded dog as it lay dying. It wouldn't be long before the family returned home, so Dwight was growing more and more anxious. Dwight watched dispassionately as the big dog's life slipped away. Dwight felt nothing. Once he was sure that the dog was dead, Dwight went into the house where he lived with his family and interrupted the silence of the empty house by turning on the TV. It was a new RCA color model, and Dwight tried never to miss an episode of *Where the Action Is* that played daily on WDEF-TV channel 9 broadcasting from Chattanooga, some twenty-five miles away, at 4:00 p.m. daily.

Dwight's mother had taken his younger brother along with her on a trip to the grocery store a half hour away and didn't arrive back home until after five. Upon arriving home, Dwight's younger brother, as he always did, called out for Boone as he approached the front door of the house. But Boone couldn't come. Not giving Boone's absence a second thought, Dwight's younger brother helped his mother carry the groceries into the house and, once this was done, went outside and called again for Boone. Dwight never rose from his comfortable place on the sofa and didn't acknowledge the presence of anyone.

Dwight's father got home from his factory job in the city a bit later. It wasn't his dad's practice to call for Boone upon his arrival home, but hearing his youngest son call out for the dog repeatedly, he felt a pang of concern. Ordinarily, he wouldn't have given the dog's failure to come when called a second thought, but the distress in his young son's voice gave him pause. It wasn't like Boone to wander beyond the sound of a voice calling him home.

The family spent the evening involved in the mundane tasks associated with the end of an ordinary work and school day. The family might have forgotten about Boone's failure to appear except that Boone's dinner went untouched, and as could be concluded from his sizable girth, Boone never missed a meal. As darkness approached, Dwight's dad and younger brother stood on the front porch of their home and called and whistled for Boone. Dwight's dad wanted to search for Boone, but Dwight's mom convinced him that rattlesnakes often being about in the evenings, it was too dark and risky for such an undertaking. Everyone agreed, although tacitly, that they'd wait and see if Boone showed up the next day.

As Dwight's dad left the house for work the next morning, he once again called out for Boone. Dwight's younger brother also called out for Boone for several minutes until the school bus arrived. The youngster was sure that something must be wrong!

That evening, Dwight's dad began to search for Boone. He first patrolled the yard and then ventured into the nearby woods where he soon found the dead dog's stiff, lifeless body. It was evident that Boone had been shot.

Dwight feigned heartbreak at his dad's news but failed to shed a tear. Fortunately for Dwight, no one seemed to notice. As he'd so carefully planned, Dwight expressed outrage, blaming Mr. Smith for killing Boone. Dwight grabbed the same rifle that he'd used the day before, a single-shot .22-caliber J. C. Higgins model that his dad had given him on his twelfth birthday, and rushed out of the house and into the woods between his home and Mr. Smith's house with murder in his heart. Killing someone's dog was a capital offense in these parts, and Dwight would blame Boone's death on Smith and be justified in taking Smith's life then and there. It was a plan that Dwight had worked out in his mind bit by bit after each of his previous encounters with Smith. Now his plan was coming together.

Dwight stormed up on the porch of Mr. Smith's house and pounded on the front door, all the while screaming out in false anguish over Smith's accused killing of his beloved dog. Then something that Dwight hadn't counted on happened. No one answered the door. Dwight's plan suddenly began to unravel; Mr. Smith was not at home. Everyone would learn later that Mr. Smith had, in fact, not been home at all that day or the day before, so he had an iron-clad alibi. Dwight went around to the back of Smith's house and tried the back door, but it was locked. Over the kitchen sink, there were two small windows, and Dwight found one of them unlatched. Dwight raised the window and crawled through the open lower half of the window. His heart was pounding, thinking Smith could return any minute. Dwight was hoping to find some loose cash and hurriedly looked in all the usual places that someone would hide money. Dwight searched kitchen pots, the coffee can, dresser drawers, and under the mattress of the unmade bed. He didn't find any money, but he did find an old Charter Arms .38-caliber pistol under the mattress. Dwight stuffed the gun into his waistband and made his escape through the open window, being careful to close the window behind him. Dwight's plan had failed, but at least he'd gotten a pistol for his effort. The old gun might come in handy later on, he thought.

Dwight was sullen when he returned home. His family assumed that Dwight's gloom was a result of the loss of his dog. But Dwight was sad, not because of Boone's death, but the dog's death had been in vain. Little did Dwight realize that his botched plan would be the launching point for much worse yet to come.

Chapter 6
In The Beginning

Cole City occupies the furthermost northwest corner of the state of Georgia in Dade County.

Dade County Georgia is defined by its proximity to the neighboring states of Tennessee and Alabama, to the north and west, respectively, and by the presence of two vast mountain plateaus that transverse the county.

Lookout Mountain, famous as a Civil War battle site and iconic tourist attractions such as the Incline Railway, Ruby Falls, and Rock City, forms the southeastern boundary of Dade County. Lookout Mountain's diagonal expanse across the corner of the state effectively cuts off Dade County from the remainder of Georgia. Across a narrow valley running from northeast to southwest alongside Lookout Mountain, there is a smaller mountain that runs parallel with its more substantial and more famous neighbor. The smaller mountain known as Sand Mountain is the metaphorical TV sidekick to the serial star that is Lookout Mountain. The valley that lies between the two mountains serves as a rail and highway conduit between the cities of Chattanooga and Birmingham. The small town of Trenton, the county seat of Dade County, is nestled in this narrow valley. A singularly unremarkable town, Trenton was destined to flit and strut across the stage for one brief moment in 1948.

At the northernmost extent of Sand Mountain, just before it extends across the Tennessee State Line, is the ghost town of Cole City, about which much of our story concerns itself.

Before Cole City emerged fully from the forested peaks and gulches of Sand Mountain, the county first had to attend to the matter of what locals refer to as the War Between the States. Sand Mountain and, indeed, the entire county were mostly untouched by strife during the Civil War. Troop movements by both the Union and Confederate armies ran through different parts of the county, but either side fired not a single shot.

At the end of the war, the representatives of each Georgia County met to ratify Georgia's reentry into the Union formally. Dade County sent Bob Tatum to represent the voters of the county at the state assembly. One representative after another took their turn in the spotlight and seizing the opportunity to pontificate on the most pressing of issues in their minds. With a total of 152 counties represented, the procession of one speaker after another would seem interminable. And ultimately, each speaker would reach the same inevitable conclusion by placing his county on the growing list of those in favor of rejoining the Union. Growing tired of the proceedings, Bob Tatum rose to his feet out of turn and without recognition from the Secretary of State overseeing the proceedings addressed the gathered assembly. Tatum loudly declared to the entire assembly, "The rest of ya'll can do whatever the hell you want, but Dade County will never rejoin the Union." Tatum briskly stormed out of the assembly and returned to Dade County to the cheers of its residents. But no one outside of Dade County noticed or cared.

In this way, the story of the "Independent State of Dade" was born that day—a story that, although little noticed outside the county, would endure for the next seventy years.

Things would change in 1948 when the state of Georgia designated a small but geologically stunning canyon on Lookout Mountain in Dade County as a new state park named Cloudland Canyon and constructed a new two-lane paved highway accessing the park from the valley below. The new road extended across the plateau that characterized Lookout Mountain and descended southeastwardly to the opposite valley and the small town of Lafayette. The first and only highway access to Dade County from the state of Georgia was in this way originated. So cut off from the state of

Georgia had Dade County been that before 1948, the only paved roads or rail service leading to and from Dade County came from either Tennessee in the direction of Chattanooga or Alabama in the direction of Birmingham. The small number of county residents, understandably, found the opening of the new state park and the associated completion of the new highway a reason for celebration.

Trenton officials planned a small ceremony in recognition of the new state park. In charge of the festivities was the local postmaster, Allen Townsend. Mr. Townsend, a student of local history, was very familiar with the Independent State of Dade story. Mr. Townsend, a tireless and astute promoter, saw an opportunity, in conjunction with the opening of the new park, to bring public attention to Dade County. Townsend began to promote a more significant celebration, one to recognize Dade County finally reentering the Union. The completion of the park would become a footnote to the much more newsworthy celebration of Dade County, finally rejoining the Union. After convincing the city fathers of his plan, Mr. Townsend took the Independent State of Dade story to the newspaper in Chattanooga, where a small article appeared in the paper there. The small Chattanooga paper was owned by the Ochs family, who had a summer home atop nearby Lookout Mountain. The Ochs family, who also owned the *New York Times*, noticed the story and brought it to the attention of the *New York Times* editorial staff. The story of the Independent State of Dade would become a headline in the *New York Times*. Soon the forgotten Independent State of Dade story had spread across the country, and a grand celebration to welcome Dade County's official ending of the War Between the States was planned. Local folks began to sport State of Dade license plates on the front of their vehicles.

On the day that Dade County was to celebrate rejoining the Union, Burt Hagerty, a still youthful World War II veteran, shaved, put on a clean shirt, and drove his old rattle trap of a car the two miles to Louise Oliver's house. Together they drove the additional eight miles from where they lived in Cole City to the celebration in Trenton. Burt and Louise, who had been seeing more and more of each other lately, were going to meet with Burt's sister, her new husband, and a few friends for the big event later that day.

They encountered a big crowd there, including state and federal dignitaries. Georgia's governor, US senators, congressmen, and reporters from as far away as New York City were all in attendance. It was an event for the ages, and just about everybody who lived in or around Dade County was there. Dade County had never seen such an auspicious occasion, and likely never would again.

Burt and Louise, having had more than a few drinks, were washed away in the celebration and absorbed in each other's company, so much so that when Burt's sister suggested that perhaps Burt and Louise should "go on and get married," it was considered to be a great idea by all.

Conveniently enough, Trenton was widely known in the region as a place to get a quick marriage. A state-required premarriage blood test and marriage license could be had at almost any hour on any day without waiting. And the local justice of the peace was easily persuaded to officiate for a few dollars. The marriage industry in Trenton was such that on most days, dressed-up brides and grooms, from hundreds of miles around, would often be seen making the short walk from Avacian's lab to the courthouse carrying their lab test results or having an equally quick post ceremonial hamburger across the street at the Busy Bee Café. What was good enough for all those impatient brides and grooms turned out to be good enough for Burt and Louise. And in a matter of just a few minutes, it was official. Burt and Louise were married.

Years later, when asked about the events of the day, Burt's sister would characterize Burt and Louise's decision to get a spur-of-the-moment, quickie marriage with what was a popular cliché of the era saying, "They thought it was a good idea at the time." She would also reveal that she and her husband were asked to sign Burt and Louise's marriage certificate as witnesses, because, as she said, they "were the only ones sober enough to do so." The day's festivities would long be remembered by those who were there as the county's legacy of independence was solidified. Burt and Louise had embarked upon the creation of an enduring legacy of their own that day.

Burt and Louise started to get to know each other in the way that newlyweds do. And though their honest affection for each other granted them the customary amount of tolerance and acceptance of each other, they found many aspects of their marriage to be tremendously challenging. But they were bound together, and there could be no doubt that they loved each other. There's no other explanation for why two so poorly matched people would spend the rest of their lives married to each other.

Louise was overly sensitive and prone to fits of anger that could ignite without warning and burn with an intensity and duration that defied reason. Burt honestly believed that he knew what was best, regardless of the subject. And while he didn't overtly manifest his belief, his pension for being passive-aggressive was textbook dysfunction. While this is a gross oversimplification of two complex individuals, it is central to the volatility of their relationship. Ozzie and Harriet, they weren't. But even though they fought often and spent many quarrelsome nights apart, they were bound by their shared desire to have a family. All grievances with each other were put aside, eventually, in favor of their dedication to starting a family. And less than a year after they were married, they shared the bliss and wonder of bringing a new life into the world. All other considerations were set aside in deference to the needs of their new infant son named Dwight. Dwight's arrival, coming less than a year after Burt and Louise were married, left little time for Burt and Louise to get to know each other before they became parents. There were no courses in parenthood that they could take, and the examples set by their parents left them ill-prepared for what would be the next twenty or so years of their lives. But ill-prepared or not, they both knew that having a family was by far the most important aspects of their life together.

Dwight would arrive in August of 1949 in the usual way. An unremarkable child, Dwight would be witness to and often the subject of the epic struggle between Burt and Louise. Dwight would have a ringside seat to screaming matches that would sometimes last for days. The conflict would be a regular part of his young life.

But life wasn't all bad for young Dwight. He was the apple of his father's eye and was doted upon. And more importantly, Dwight would be incapable of doing anything wrong in his father's eyes. No matter what, his father always overlooked Dwight's wrongdoings. Louise, who was much more prone to disciplining the young man, was forbidden to do so by Burt. Dwight would grow up in the knowledge that he could do whatever he pleased without fear of retribution from his parents. As a result, he was, even as an infant, a quarrelsome individual, prone to bouts of histrionics in support of getting whatever he wanted. By any measure, Dwight, as an infant and later as a growing boy, was a handful. In school, Dwight was disruptive and malicious, but his teachers learned early on that any attempt at discipline would get met with Louise's fury. Dwight would come to understand that Louise was always ready to go to war on his behalf, regardless of the situation. As a consequence of this contentious dynamic, Dwight became a pariah among the school's teachers and staff.

Restart Here
Chapter 7
Brushy Mountain

In the 1890s, the widespread revolt by free miners, whose jobs had been taken by unpaid leased convicts all across the coalfields of Tennessee and North Georgia, led to the bloody conflict known as the Coal Creek War. Free miners attacked and burned state prisons, stockades, and convict mining camps. The lives of many free miners were lost in the revolt. There were also many deaths among convicts, guards, and militiamen. Battles continued to occur into 1892 before the revolt was finally brought to heel by the military.

Brushy Mountain, a maximum security prison designed to hold three hundred prisoners, officially opened near Petros, Tennessee, in 1896 in the aftermath of the bloody Coal Creek War. The prison would hold almost a thousand former free miners and dangerous convicts. Brushy Mountain was only slightly less brutal than the Cole City mining operations. Escape attempts, riots, conflict between the most serious offenders, and abuse by the guards all contributed to Brushy Mountain being a dark and deadly place.

Dwight's grandfather worked as a guard at the Brushy Mountain State Prison in the 1950s and 1960s. And when Dwight was fourteen years old, Burt and Louise drove their 1955 Pontiac the five hours it took to complete the 120-mile drive through the mountains from their home in Cole City to the prison located in the remote north-central Tennessee mountains.

Dwight's grandfather, who everyone knew as Frank, took the family on a tour of the prison. The tour included not only the visitor-approved areas such as the gift shop but also many behind-the-scene areas not usually seen by visitors including the prison cells, dining hall, the fences topped with concertina wire, the bloodhound kennel, and even the electric chair. Louise had a newfangled Kodak camera and would take many pictures.

Granddaddy Frank, as he was known to family members, took great delight in showing Dwight and Dwight's younger brother Ollie around. The two boys were less enthusiastic about the whole affair. Then, during their tour, the two boys were brought into the execution chamber. Sitting alone in the center of the room was the electric chair. The use of an electric chair as a means of execution began just a few years before Brushy Mountain was completed, and the chair in front of them dated from the prison's original construction. The chair itself was configured in a familiar way with a seat elevated on four legs and a rigid back. The chair was somewhat oversized compared to an ordinary kitchen chair with the main components made from oak four by fours. The mass and rigidity of the chair rendered it most uncomfortable, but as Granddaddy Frank pointed out, comfort was not its purpose. There were heavy leather straps to restrain each leg and each arm. There were also leather straps affixed to the back of the chair as chest and head restraints. There was a metal hood large enough to fit over someone's head suspended on a metal cable dangling over the head position. Bulky electrical wires extended from the hood to a metal cabinet attached to the wall behind the chair. There was a metal cuff lying loosely at the base of one of the chair's front legs. Running from this cuff to the same metal cabinet behind the chair was another bulky electrical wire.

Granddaddy Frank sensed a sudden surge in the boy's interest and knowing that Louise was out of earshot seized upon the moment to tell them about the chair and how executions got carried out.

Granddaddy Frank explained that the execution involved first placing a saltwater-soaked sponge about the size of a cantaloupe on top of the prisoner's recently shaved head and then placing the metal hood on the prisoners head. The cuff was clamped tightly to the prisoner's recently shaved ankle. The prisoner's head would be covered with a black hood as the last preparation, and the guards would leave the chamber. At the appointed time, the order was given, and the executioner would throw a switch in the adjacent control room, sending two thousand volts of electricity traveling through the prisoner's body between the hood and the leg cuff. The overhead lights throughout the prison would dim noticeably, which served to confirm to the prison population that the execution had taken place. The current was allowed to flow for thirty seconds and then shut off. The purpose of this electrical jolt was to stop the prisoner's heart, and a doctor would enter the chamber to check for a pulse. If the doctor detected a pulse, then the process of electrocution was repeated. Sometimes it would take two or three tries to stop the prisoner's heart.

Seeing that he had the boys' complete attention, Granddaddy Frank took things to the next level by describing in detail how the act of electrocution affected the prisoner's body.

Granddaddy Frank told the boys that the body convulses with the back arching and the hands gripping the chair unnaturally. Smoke tendrils emerge from the hood. Witnesses hear a sizzling sound like meat cooking in a frying pan and smell the scent of burning flesh.

The boys were wide-eyed and slack-jawed, but their attention did not waver as Granddaddy Frank went on. The prisoner would lose control of his bowels and bladder, and his flesh would become flushed. The hood hid the prisoner's face, contorted in pain.

As Granddaddy Franks monologue drew to a close, he offered the boys the unique opportunity to sit in the electric chair. Eleven-year-old Ollie wanted no part of the experience. Although there had never been an execution at Brushy Mountain, the idea of sitting in the electric chair filled Ollie with foreboding. The thought held a certain gruesome appeal to young Dwight, however. Dwight's felt no apprehension at all, only curiosity and excitement at the idea of sitting in a chair designed to take someone's life in such a gruesome manner. Bug-eyed with sheer delight, it's easy to imagine this having been a pivotal moment in Dwight's life. Granddaddy Frank hoisted Dwight into the chair like it was an ordinary kitchen chair. Dwight's face shined with pleasure as he sat in the chair without speaking.

Louise's voice could be heard as she approached the execution chamber, and Granddaddy Frank quickly helped Dwight out of the chair before she could see what they were doing. As she rounded the corner, bringing her into a direct line of sight with Dwight, she saw nothing amiss. She was surprised and concerned, however, that Dwight's younger brother was in tears for reasons she did not understand. Both Granddaddy Frank and Dwight claimed ignorance. With a wink and a nod, an unspoken pledge of secrecy was sealed between Dwight and his grandfather.

Learned men believe that true sociopaths experience one or more seminal moments sometime early in their lives. The night that Dwight had spent in the coke oven was likely such a moment. That moment left Dwight with an unshakable belief in his invincibility, that someone or something was looking out for him. But here, sitting in the electric chair at Brushy Mountain was assuredly another such moment, one that left him with a fascination with death and for the taking of lives. Dwight could feel the power surging through his body, knowing that he could take lives without the fear of being caught.

Chapter 8
A V8 Ford

Batman had the Batmobile. Dwight had a V8 Ford.

During the 1960s, while most young men between fifteen and twenty years old were protesting the Vietnam War, smoking dope, and trying to get laid, those few who lived in the backwoods in and around Cole City would remain mired in the 1950s fixation with fast cars and drinking beer.

At the end of the Korean conflict, returning soldiers who had learned about car engines in the service and had experienced a reality far from the ordinary brought back with them a different attitude about cars. They wanted fast cars, stylish cars, and cars to be—for the first time in the American auto market—an extension of their fun-loving lifestyles. Hot Rods would begin to appear on city streets. With the Eisenhower Interstate highway system adding easy access to the open road, the automobile market in America would be forever changed. Both Ford and Chevy introduced higher horsepower V8 engines in the mid-1950s. Ten years later, under the innovative guidance of men like Lee Iacocca at Ford and John DeLorean at GM, the first muscle cars, Mustang and GTO, would be introduced to the buying public. Such high-horsepower cars would set sales records.

But the stylish new muscle cars of the mid-1960s were beyond the buying power of most of the young men of Cole City. The vehicles of choice for Dwight and his like-minded buddies would be the Fords and Chevys made in the mid-1950s. These cars weren't as fast as the new muscle cars on their own, but the engines were like Lego blocks; they could be easily and relatively inexpensively modified and upgraded to compete with the modern muscle cars. And compete they did. From Woodward Avenue in Detroit to the lonely stretch of blacktop on the way to Cole City, souped-up cars from the mid-1950s were prized for their style and speed.

On Dwight's sixteenth birthday, his father took him to Trenton, where the state police administered driver license tests. Dwight had been driving for some time without a license and had no difficulty in passing the test and obtaining his first driver's license. When out of sight of his parents, Dwight had practiced his high-speed driving skills along Cole City's few paved roads. Dwight passing his driver's test was a moment that Burt had long looked forward to almost as much as Dwight. It was a rite of passage, something akin to a bar mitzvah. But unlike the Judaist ritual, where a thirteen-year-old boy becomes accountable for his actions, Dwight would have no accountability. Burt bought Dwight a bright-red 1956 Ford with a V8 engine. The Ford was one of the most coveted cars by sixteen-year-olds at that time and place. What you drove defined who you were, and Dwight enjoyed life at the top of the subculture food chain. Burt swelled with pride at Dwight's enjoyment of this beautiful and fast automobile.

There was a direct relationship between how fast you drove and how popular you'd be among your buddies. Largely because of the car he drove, Dwight would enjoy being the top dog, the alpha male, among his buddies. Dwight's enjoyment seemed to stem from how fast he'd drive and how many passengers he had. Soon Dwight had a close circle of several like-minded buddies, any number of whom could be found in Dwight's company most of the time.

Dwight soon developed a well-deserved reputation as a wild man behind the wheel—a fact that didn't go unnoticed by the local insurance agent who promptly sent Burt an auto insurance cancellation notice.

There would be no more riding the school bus for Dwight as he now had a car to drive to school every day. Often, after school, Dwight would pile four or five of his buddies into his Ford and drive to the local pool hall, the Tip Top restaurant, where they'd spend the remainder of the afternoon, smoking, shooting pool, and "cutting up." The Tip Top was a guy's place, offering a jukebox, a couple of pool tables, and a dining room where a cheeseburger could be gotten. The Tip Top, like all establishments in the county, did not have a license to sell beer. In spite of this fact, the Tip Top was the most popular of such places in the county. Dwight spent much of his free time at the Tip Top and made several new friends there. He would also make some new enemies there.

Dwight's expanded circle of friends included some who'd dropped out of school and some that were much older. One of these new friends introduced Dwight to a local bootlegger and the pleasures of beer drinking. As background, Dade County was what was known as a dry county, meaning that there was no sale of beer, wine, or liquor in the county. The official status as a dry county gave rise to a countywide cottage industry for bootleggers, who met the market demand for "illegal" alcohol. Bootlegging was done with a wink and a nod from the local sheriff and under the blind eye of the teetotaling evangelically inclined. Developing a relationship with a local bootlegger was, like getting a driver's license, a rite of passage for many young men in Cole City, at that time.

Saturday nights at the Tip Top had a less than wholesome appeal. Beer runs to the bootleggers yielded a steady flow of booze, and the parking lot was a de facto lounge.

The combination of alcohol and fast cars had been the storyline of many a tragedy, and Dwight's tale, in this regard, would be much the same. The V8 Ford would become an extension of Dwight's persona, a weapon for Dwight to use, and a curse upon him.

Burt would have many opportunities to contemplate the wisdom of putting such a lethal weapon in Dwight's hands and the dangers of his drinking and driving. There was, however, no attempt to throttle Dwight's destructive behavior.

Chapter 9
False Start

Looking back on the time just after Dwight got his V8 Ford, several episodes underscore the emerging darkness in Dwight. One such event might have easily been mistaken as little more than mischievousness at the time but would prove to be prophetic.

While in high school, Dwight and his buddies were always looking for ways to create fun for themselves and cause chaos. Pooling their mental abilities, they came up with the idea that would turn their fun into a life-threatening episode.

The Idea

They would "borrow" a starter pistol used by the track coach along with some blanks and see what kind of fun they could have.

Near the end of classes, one day, they snuck into the coach's office and took a starter pistol from his desk drawer. There were no high school track events planned in the foreseeable future, so their thought was that no one would notice their theft and they could return the gun before it was missed. This last part of their plan would prove to be the only part that worked out the way they hoped.

They took the gun behind the gym and fooled around with it for a while, pointing it at one another and firing blanks, but soon they grew bored and began to look for different ways to have fun.

The Plan

Dwight suggested that they could point the gun at unsuspecting folks and pull the trigger just to see what would happen. Someone else suggested that they couldn't point the gun at anyone who knew them and could get them in trouble. Here's where these Darwin Award winners plan took on the dimensions of a tragedy in the works. They decided to drive down East 38th Street in nearby Chattanooga and "shoot" at strangers along the way. There was no danger of anyone along East 38th Street recognizing Dwight or any of his buddies because East 38th Street runs through the heart of the projects. Both the shiny white faces and the flashy red car were unfamiliar to folks living in the projects. Dwight and his buddies planned to hang out the window of Dwight's car and shoot the starter pistol at random black people walking along East 38th Street. What great fun, eh? And what could go wrong?

The Execution

The starter pistol was hidden away under the car seat, and the boys were off. It was a forty-minute drive to East 38th Street, and they spent another fifteen minutes to stop for beer at a bootlegger's along the way. They had almost an hour to reconsider their plan, but no one did.

Drinking beer and driving slowly along the street, in broad open daylight, they first pointed the starter pistol at a group of four teenage boys who understandably scrambled behind whatever cover they could find or hit the dirt. Dwight and his buddies were delighted at the effect of putting their plan into motion. Next, they targeted a middle-aged man carrying a brown paper bag. Startled, he dropped the bag and ran for cover when he heard the shots. Again peals of laughter rolled from the speeding Ford. The boys hadn't imagined how much fun this little game would be.

There's no doubt that the choice of targets had racial overtones. The boys had grown up in a whites-only area, and they held attitudes of superiority toward black people that they'd learned from their parents and other white adults. The use of the N-word was common to their vocabulary and was shouted from the windows of the Ford as they harassed the folks they found on East 38th Street. The motivation in targeting black people was also based on their belief that no black people would recognize a carload of white teenagers from Cole City. And, sure enough, the eyewitnesses couldn't give the police who investigated enough of a description of the car or its passengers to identify Dwight and his like-minded buddies. So they had that going for them.

What the boys had never considered was that someone that they targeted might fight back.

The boys' last target was a group of three men in their late teens. When these young black men saw a gun pointed at them, instead of running for cover, two of them pulled out guns of their own and began firing back at Dwight's car. The difference being that these young black men were firing real bullets. While bullets pinged the Ford, no one, fortunately, got shot. Dwight sped away and drove back to Cole City straightaway. The laughter among Dwight and his buddies had ceased, and the ride back was in silence.

The starter pistol was returned to the coach's desk the next day. For as long as Dwight owned that car, people would ask him how he got the bullet holes in the trunk lid. Neither Dwight nor any of his buddies ever revealed the truth.

This episode served as something of a trial run for Dwight. The next time Dwight shot a pistol, it would be firing real bullets.

Chapter 10
Jail

In addition to being the source of legal authority, the Dade County sheriff held sway over the county's wrongdoing. He collaborated with the moonshiners who made their illicit product in the remote hollers of Sand Mountain. Bootleggers paid tribute to the sheriff in late-night exchanges along back roads. It was a role played by county sheriffs throughout the North Georgia mountains for generations and accepted by the county's citizens as usual. There was an expectation, however, that the sheriff would thwart violent crime, including assaults and robberies. In the absence of such felonies, which were rare, the sheriff had little in the way of official duties. And making the sheriff's job even more relaxed, there is also a chief of police for the town of Trenton. The chief, named Hot Rod Hutcheson, was an uneducated man who could not write a traffic ticket. Instead, he'd offer the offender the option of signing a blank ticket or being taken to the local justice of the peace straightaway. If the justice of the peace wasn't available, then the offender would be locked in a cell at the old city jail.

Other than the occasional out-of-town motorist who had made the mistake of speeding within the city limits, there were few occasions to lock up a wrongdoer.

The old city jail is a two-story brick building that faces onto the courthouse square in the middle of the tiny town. Offices occupy the ground floor, and the second-floor houses barred cells. The building was built in the 1890s but lacked the charm of many such antiquities. And it didn't have many of the modern conveniences such as air-conditioning. On hot summer nights, internees would open the barred casement windows overlooking the courthouse square to draw a little breeze.

Hot Rod, who years later would be struck and killed by a motorist during a routine traffic stop, spent his "on-duty" time behind the wheel of his aging patrol car parked out in front of the jail. Trenton was a quiet little town, and Hot Rod spent most evenings struggling just to stay awake.

One hot summer night, Dwight and his buddies made the mistake of being drunk and disorderly inside the Busy Bee restaurant, and Hot Rod got summoned to restore order. Hot Rod tossed the lot of them in a jail cell, probably just to sober up. The group was just drunk enough to be having a good time and didn't seem to mind. They weren't about to let getting locked up put a crimp in their party. But being stuck in a jail cell without access to booze was undoubtedly a disagreeable complication that required a fix. Dwight called out the open window to one of his buddies below who was comparatively sober, and a plan was quickly hatched.

The Plan

One of Dwight's like-minded buddies would drive his car slowly around and around the courthouse square in full view of Hot Rod, who was at his usual parking place in front of the jail. Being careful not to break any law, the driver would continue to circle the courthouse until Hot Rod's curiosity got the best of him, and he'd start his patrol car engine and turn on his bubblegum machine roof light. At this point, Dwight's friend would continue to drive southbound on the main street away from the courthouse until he was out of sight of the jail and would stop, awaiting Hot Rod's approach. Hot Rod would follow the same routine of asking for the driver's license— even though he couldn't read it—looking at the license plate, and sniffing inside the car for the smell of alcohol. This routine would occupy Hot Rod's full attention for a few minutes, but ultimately, he'd have no reason to detain the driver.

While Hot Rod was occupied, just out of sight of the jail, Dwight's other buddies would rush onto the lawn in the front of the jail and toss cans of beer up to Dwight's waiting grasp.

After a few minutes, a different friend in a different car would begin the deception of Hot Rod all over again.

When the boys were released, Hot Rod could only scratch his head and wonder how all the empty beer cans got in the cell.

Such pranks were mostly harmless and fell under the heading of boys will be boys. But it got Dwight acquainted with the inside of a jail cell and led him to the conclusion that he wouldn't want to spend much time behind bars, a finding that would get revived later on when Dwight's life takes a much more sinister, darker turn.

Chapter 11
They Drowned

In the spring of 1965, Dwight, not yet having a driver's license, was still riding the school bus to and from school every day along with his younger brother Ollie. The school had six defined bus routes, but only three busses, so each bus had to make two trips to and from school every day. The time between the earliest bus arrivals and morning classes beginning afforded the students from the first buses about forty minutes of free time. Most of the early arrivals would hang out in the schoolyard with their classmates. Dwight and Ollie were among the early arrivals. On these occasions, Dwight avoided Ollie as best as he could because he found his younger brother to be a pain in the ass. On this particular morning, Ollie had a bug up his butt about something and simply wouldn't leave Dwight alone. He followed Dwight around the schoolyard nattering and whining about whatever injustice he felt at the time, until, quite understandably to most, Dwight grew frustrated and lashed out at his younger brother, knocking him to the ground and leaving him bloodied and crying there. Such an occurrence wasn't anything unusual since Dwight was often seen whaling on his younger brother. What made this day different was that an older boy named Jack saw what Dwight did and decided that he would intervene. Being older and bigger than Dwight, Jack was able to do to Dwight what Dwight had done to Ollie. Jack left Dwight sprawled upon the ground humbled and embarrassed. As Jack walked away, Dwight swore under his breath that someday Jack would pay. And Dwight had a long memory.

Dwight would get his driver's license that summer and never have to ride the school bus with Ollie again.

Across the Alabama State Line from Cole City, there's a little-used road on the "back side" of Sand Mountain that leads down into the Valley made by the Tennessee River. Along the east side of the river is Hog Jaw Road, which takes you to a bridge over the creek at Long Island Cove. Just beyond the bridge, the creek merges with the river. It is here that our story picks up.

It was a pitch-black night with no moon, and cloud cover blocked out the stars on this spring night. It was quite a warm night for late spring with no wind. Jack and his friend Ken muscled a small aluminum johnboat out of the back of Ken's dad's old pickup and dragged it to the edge of the creek. The creek's current was less swift here but nevertheless a treacherous spot to launch a boat. But this was the best launch site for a few miles in either direction up or downstream. Since he'd been old enough to drive, Ken had come here several times. His experience gave him the confidence to launch the small fishing boat here in spite of the known perils. For Jack, this was a fist trip to the spot with Ken, and he proceeded with an abundance of caution. Neither Ken nor Jack knew how to swim, and Jack's mother had insisted that the two of them bring along life jackets, which they obediently did.

Ken slipped the small boat into the water, and Jack handed him the five-horsepower Evinrude outboard, which Ken expertly attached to the boat transom. Next, Jack gave Ken the five-gallon metal fuel tank, which Ken connected to the motor and squeezed the rubber bulb pump several times, dropped the foot of the motor and propeller into the water, and gave the starter rope a yank. The motor started in a cloud of blue smoke. While the motor sat idling, Jack handed Ken the equipment and provisions they'd need to go out into the creek fishing—a couple of rod and reel outfits, a tackle box, a minnow bucket with the bait they'd need, a cooler with ice and beer, a single anchor tied to the boat with a fifty-foot length of rope, a couple of flashlights, and the two life jackets. A second cooler with ice and sandwiches was left in the cab of the truck for them later. They planned to stick to the submerged brush piles along the creek bank and stay out of the swifter current. Their hopes were high. It was the best time of the year for crappie fishing, and the weather was perfect. Jack and Ken pushed the small boat into the creek with the bow pointed upstream, and as Ken dropped the motor into gear and revved the motor, they moved upstream quickly. Jack played the light from one of the flashlights along the shoreline like an old-time hand on a river barge.

Two other fishermen had built a fire on the bank overlooking the creek where it flowed into the river even though the heat from the fire wasn't needed on this warm night. The light from the fire cast a faint glow toward the creek bank where Ken and Jack had launched their boat. They had watched with little interest as Jack and Ken went about their own business.

No one is entirely sure of exactly what happened later that night. But from the account given by the two fishermen on the bank, we know that two or more hours passed with no sign of Ken and Jack's lights, but this was no reason for concern. Only one car had crossed the bridge over the creek heading upstream on the dead-end road that ran alongside the creek bank. Later the fishermen on the bank thought that they heard the sound of an occasional firecracker coming from upstream—a sound that was out of place in the serene stillness, but not something that the fishermen on the bank would give a second thought. Then in the distance from upstream, they heard the whine of the tiny outboard. The Doppler effect changed the pitch of the sound as the boat drew nearer. But still, no light appeared. And instead of the motor slowing as it approached shore, it continued to rev at full throttle. Suddenly just before reaching land, the motor was shut off abruptly. From the dim light of the campfire, the fishermen on the bank could see the small boat, at first with the bow high in the air as the motor revved and then, as the motor stopped the wake trailing the boat swamping the transom. Both Ken and Jack were pitched into the water only a few feet from shore. The boat sank immediately, and the two life jackets could be seen floating away. But there was no sign of Ken or Jack. The fishermen on the bank shed their jackets and boots and jumped into the water to save the boys. But their efforts would be to no avail. Eventually, the two fishermen returned to shore. While the two fishermen tried frantically to save Jack and Ken, the car that they'd seen pass by earlier slowly went by in the opposite direction. The fishermen on the bank weren't sure of the type of car or color but thought that it might have been a mid-1950s Ford.

Ken and Jack's bodies were found the next day just downstream of their sunken boat, only a few feet from shore and in only five feet of water.

When the boat got pulled from the water, no one noticed the two small holes in the side just above the waterline. These two tiny holes would be the only clue to what had happened. The holes were of the size that would be made by a small-caliber bullet. And being shot at explained why Jack and Ken were rushing to shore without the benefit of their flashlights.

Earlier that day, Dwight had overheard Jack's younger brother, with whom Dwight was friends with, talking about how his brother Jack was going fishing later that night with Ken. Jack's brother was unsuspecting as Dwight asked for details about where and at what time. Dwight saw an opportunity to get the revenge he sought against Jack and hatched a plan to do so. The idea was to find Jack and Ken in their fishing boat, which shouldn't be difficult as there would be no other boats on the creek at that time. Dwight planned to shoot Jack, who would be a sitting duck, just the way he'd shot Boone.

Dwight, as it turns out, wasn't as good a marksman as he would have wanted to be, and although he'd tried several times, he'd only been able to hit the boat and not the occupants. It didn't take Jack and Ken long to figure out that they were being shot at from the bank, douse their lights, and make for shore. Neither they nor Dwight had counted on the small boat getting swamped, but that's what happened. As a result, Jack and Ken drowned. The event didn't unfold as Dwight had planned, but the outcome nevertheless gave Dwight a rush of mixed emotions. Dwight felt euphoria at having succeeded in what, up until now, had only been in his imagination. Dwight harbored hatred in his heart for how Jack had treated him and the sweetness of knowing that he had his revenge. Jack had gotten what he deserved. Dwight felt invincible, having absolute power over life and death. At the same time, there was a tinge of melancholia at the thought that it was over. And a sense of emptiness was beginning to take hold and a gnawing ennui that crept into his thoughts confounded his satisfaction at having succeeded and replacing it with feelings of disappointment and emptiness that led to Dwight's first realization that this wasn't enough—there had to be more.

The local authorities ruled the deaths accidental and never investigated further. Dwight made a clean getaway.

Chapter 12
Eddie

Eddie Cook was a couple of years younger than Dwight. Both attended the same school, and while they were acquainted, Eddie wasn't in Dwight's circle of close friends. Eddie was a popular kid who hung out at the same pool hall as Dwight. Like Dwight, Eddie liked to drink beer and shot pool, and like Dwight, what he loved most was to drive fast. Eddie's dad had bought him a brand-new bright-red 1969 Chevelle Super Sport with a 396-cubic-inch engine that was easily faster than anything driven by anyone at the pool hall, including Dwight. Eddie loved to show off, and Dwight didn't like what he considered to be Eddie stealing his limelight.

Being jealous of Eddie's popularity, Dwight wanted to put him in his place, and the way he chose to do so was by challenging Eddie's driving skills. Eddie took the bait and accepted Dwight's challenge, and soon Eddie was following Dwight's old Ford along a lonely stretch of road not far from the pool hall at a high rate of speed. This road had a two-mile stretch with no houses or side roads. This stretch of road was mostly straight and level, making it a favorite place for those inclined to drive at high speed. Dwight knew this stretch of road very well because it was the route he took every day on the way home from school, and he'd driven it at high speed many times before. Eddie, however, lived in a different direction from the school and had no reason to travel this stretch of road. But Eddie was confident in the speed of his car and his driving skill, so he was undeterred by the thought of racing Dwight on an unfamiliar road.

Dwight's old Ford had reached more than 80 mph by the time he drifted down Raines hill onto the lonely stretch of the two-lane road.

Eddie was right on Dwight's rear bumper. Reaching the flat stretch of road, Dwight accelerated, reaching 90 mph and then 100 mph. Eddie was still on Dwight's tail. Roughly halfway along the two-mile stretch of road, there was a slight curve to the right, and midway through this curve, there was a dip in the road. Dwight who was very familiar with this subtle nuance in the road knew just how to enter the curve to void having the dip in the road and send his vehicle reeling. Dwight entered the curve at near 110 mph and easily drifted through the dip without losing control of the Ford. Eddie, being unfamiliar with the road, took the curve a bit wider than Dwight, when the Chevelle crossed over the dip in the road, it was launched skyward. The trajectory took Eddie's car off the left shoulder of the road, and Eddie tried to correct, but it was too late. The Chevelle overcorrected and shot back across the road into the ditch on the near side, flipped over, and skidded on its roof for almost a hundred yards before hitting a tree and coming to a stop. Dwight saw Eddie's headlights disappear from his rearview mirror and smiled. Dwight didn't go back to check on Eddie.

It was almost a half hour later that another motorist happens along and spots Eddie's crashed car. It would be another half hour before an ambulance arrived at the crash site where attendants found Eddie entangled in the destroyed car and near death. A crowd gathered, and it wasn't said aloud, but no one at the scene gave Eddie a chance of surviving his injuries.

Eddie suffered severe head trauma in the wreck and lingered near death for ten days in Erlanger Hospital's ICU before finally succumbing to his injuries.

Dwight showed no interest in Eddie's recovery and did not visit Eddie in the hospital. As Eddie's coffin got lowered into the ground, Dwight was shooting pool at the Tip Top and losing badly. Dwight's mind was not on the game, and he didn't seem to mind loosing for a change. Dwight had much more to be happy about than winning at pool. Dwight smiled as he thought that Eddie deserved what he got!

It would be the first time that Dwight tested his invincibility and the first time he'd used his Ford as a weapon with lethal results. Dwight was emboldened.

Chapter 13
Carlos

Cole City, indeed all of Dade County, has been economically depressed ever since the prison camp closed more than fifty years prior.

It's a truism that regardless of the economic status of any group, a socioeconomic hierarchy will naturally emerge within the group. In a caste system, class structure gets determined by birth. In contrast, Cole City's class structure consists of the relative haves who occupy the top tier and the relative have-nots who occupy the bottom tier. By any other standard, Dwight's family would reside near the bottom of most any socioeconomic stratification. However, compared to their neighbors in Cole City, Dwight's family would be counted among the haves. Dwight's parents owned a home and two cars and had decent jobs. Most of their neighbors and friends were not as well off. Dwight was a big fish in a little pond.

The Williams family, who lived nearby, were among the have-nots. The home they lived in was a small run-down rental. The adults in the family didn't have steady jobs, and the family survived mostly on food stamps. The family car was a worn-out old Oldsmobile. The household included several children of varying age with Carlos, at sixteen, being the oldest. Dwight and Carlos were not friends and, for the most part, did not share their social orbits.

Carlos had his own small group of friends who shared his socioeconomic status. They didn't attend school regularly, didn't play sports, and were not active in the local church. They were, in fact, a dreadful lot, destined to be among the underbelly of society serving as fodder for the war in Vietnam. Until their selective service numbers got called, they'd be content to do as little as necessary to support their vices of drinking beer, smoking dope, and shooting pool.

Dwight was pursuing the affections of a young lady who lived on Lookout Mountain, and he had been making the drive from his home to hers frequently. The young lady was attractive, by local standards, and was pursued by another somewhat older man who also lived on Lookout Mountain. Dwight found himself confronted by the other man at the young lady's home, and the result was one of the very few times that Dwight didn't come out on top. Beaten and dejected, Dwight decided that rather than going directly home, he'd stop at the nearest beer joint. Underage drinking was the only attraction at this otherwise unpleasant establishment. Dwight would have a couple of beers to mellow out. Dwight's decision would cause his orbit to intersect with Carlos Williams for the first and only time.

Dwight left the bar for the long drive home in the dark and only a mile or so from the bar got passed in a blur by Carlos' Oldsmobile heading home as well, no doubt. Dwight could see that Carlos had three passengers as they hooted and yelled at Dwight as they passed. Dwight saw this as a challenge and immediately sped up to catch the offenders. Dwight's Ford was much faster than the Oldsmobile, and he caught up and overtook the offenders soon enough, passing them and cutting them off. The two cars raced one after the other along the narrow two-lane stretch of the paved road at speeds nearing 100 mph with Dwight in the lead. Dwight could have easily left the Oldsmobile in the dust, but what would be the fun in that?

Up ahead, there was a narrow one-lane bridge over a creek, and as they approached the bridge, Dwight had an idea. He slowed the Ford just a bit, and as expected, Carlos pulled into the oncoming lane to pass. As he did so, Dwight sped up just enough to keep Carlos from getting around the Ford. Racing downhill toward the bridge side by side, it became a game of chicken. The Ford edged ahead just slightly to prevent Carlos from getting in front of Dwight. Only at the very last moment did Carlos realize that the approaching bridge only had one lane and that he would not be able to beat Dwight to the bridge. Carlos instantly understood his mistake and braked the Oldsmobile hard, throwing it into a skid. As Dwight darted across the bridge, the big Oldsmobile swerved and fishtailed, leaving the road just before the bridge and plunging headlong into the creek below. Dwight, with a broad smile, watched Carlos' wreck in his rearview mirror. Dwight slowed down but didn't go back to check on Carlos.

It would be a week before anyone noticed the rear deck of the Oldsmobile protruding slightly from the surface of the creek. When the car got pulled from the water, the bloated bodies of the four missing teenagers got discovered. From all appearances, it looked like Carlos had just lost control of the Oldsmobile resulting in a fatal one-car accident.

Having suffered a beating and lost the young lady of interest to a rival put Dwight in a very foul mood. The incident with Carlos had, however, turned an otherwise shitty day into a cause of celebration. Fate had delivered four more victims for Dwight's growing list. Dwight's latest victims, just like those who had preceded them, deserved what they got.

Dwight never went back to visit the young lady who lived on Lookout Mountain. It would be some time before Dwight would have interest in another young lady.

Chapter 14
Inola

The presence of the Cherokee in western North Carolina, North Georgia, and eastern Tennessee and the influence of their rich culture on white settlers in that region have always gotten understated. The Cherokee were a peaceful agricultural society that had assimilated the culture and customs of white settlers in the 1800s. A matrilineal society whose members took their name from their mothers, extended families were linked within the Cherokee's seven clans.

Five generations after the Trail of Tears, an elder woman in the tribe of the Eastern Band of the Cherokee in North Carolina was called upon, as was the custom, to bestow a name upon a newborn girl in the Wolf (a-ni-way-a) Clan, the largest among the seven Cherokee clans. In the native language, the old woman proclaimed that the child would be named Inola (Black Fox). The name bestowed by the tribal elder would get carried throughout the child's life, which would be both long and eventful.

The Wolf Clan had survived the Cherokee removal in 1838 by hiding out in the vast and rugged mountains of North Carolina, centered in what is now Graham County, by living off the land. Over subsequent generations, members of the Wolf Clan came to own and farm lands along the Yellow Creek, where they prospered.

Inola would have two sons whose Cherokee names have been lost to history. The sons grew up in the Wolf Clan in the Snowbird Mountains near the small town of Robbinsville in the late 1920s.

In 1938, Inola would unceremoniously and unexpectedly pack up the entire family and move a hundred miles west to sparsely populated Cole City. The family's move was rumored to have been precipitated by the involvement of a family member in the killing of a man in Graham County. Inola would change the name of her family to Stalcup in an effort, some said, to remain hidden from law enforcement. Inola would maintain that the family's move to Cole City was singularly motivated by the opportunity to take advantage of Georgia opening the land to homesteading.

One of Inola's sons built what the Navaho would have called a hogan and settled on a small piece of land within sight of the home where Dwight would grow up in a few years. The other son would build a small "stick-built" house and settle on a slightly larger piece of land on a hilltop overlooking the road along the abandoned Cole City Tramway. Here Inola's two sons would come to be known as "Biggun" and Roy Stalcup.

The newly christened Stalcup family had the distinctive facial features of the American Indian, but in their new home, they steadfastly clung to their claim to be white. They would forego any association with their Cherokee heritage and forever remain estranged from the Wolf Clan. There were no Cherokee within fifty miles of Cole City, and both Roy and Biggun would marry white women. Biggun and Roy's offspring would get accepted in the community as white. Biggun and his wife Mae were somewhat successful subsistence farmers raising primarily corn. There would be two sons born to the couple. Roy and his wife Georgina were less prosperous, living in a ramshackle old tar-papered shack without electricity or running water. Roy was less diligent in his labors and found farming to be too difficult. Instead, Roy took to making whiskey.

Roy and his wife would also have two sons and then much later in life two daughters. The sons were, from an early age, enlisted in the family enterprise. Roy, unfortunately, became his own best customer and fell victim to the addictive power of his product. As his oldest son Samuel grew to adulthood, he followed in his father's footsteps both as a maker and as a consumer of illicit whiskey.

Late one autumn night, Roy, in a quarrelsome mood, got into a drunken altercation with Samuel; and Samuel would, in his rage, strike Roy on the head repeatedly with a hammer. The black aura of death would seem to have followed Roy from the homicide in North Carolina years ago to exact vengeance now. Samuel would be apprehended, tried, and sent to prison where he would remain until his death in 1966. But the tragedy would not end with Roy's death but would haunt the Stalcup family, seeking to quench its thirst for more lives.

Just over a year later, the members of the Bowman family, on their way to church on Sunday morning, would make a gruesome discovery.

The Bowmans' home is on the high ground just to the southeast of the main Dade Coal Company mine entrance at Cole City. This mine entrance was slopped rather than horizontal as is usually the case, and the flat land surrounding the mine entrance for a half mile in each direction would become generally known as the Slope Mine. The area was covered in loosely scattered shale tailings from the mining operations with a castlelike rock tower surrounding an open pit serving as an air shaft for the mine below the surface. The slope mines were otherwise nonremarkable in every sense of the word.

As the Bowman family drove along the road that ran northwesterly from their home through the Slope Mine and up the ridge on the other side toward the church they attended, one of the children noticed something unusual. A few yards off the road, there was what appeared to be a bundle of clothing. The site was curious enough that they stopped the car alongside the road, and their teenage son got dispatched to take a look.

What the lad found beside the road was the crumpled body of Douglas Stalcup, youngest son of Roy Stalcup and brother to Samuel Stalcup. The body laid in a pool of coagulated blood. The body looked undamaged except for a hole in the head at the right temple. It was immediately evident that Douglas Stalcup was dead and had been so for some time.

The county sheriff got summoned to the scene. The sheriff's arrival was accompanied by his usual level of disinterest in investigating the young man's death. Douglas Stalcup had only been back from his enlistment in the army for a few months and wasn't known to be involved in the whiskey-making enterprise favored by his father and brother. Douglas, a quiet and unassuming young man, didn't have any friends to speak of, didn't have a girlfriend, and didn't attend the local church. He didn't even own a dog. No one could think of any enemies that Douglas might have.

By the time the sheriff arrived, the site around the body had been trampled by numerous onlookers, so there was no way to know whether any of the footprints were made before Douglas Stalcup's death. The coroner was called to the scene, as was required by Georgia law in such circumstances, and upon first glance, he pronounced the death to be a suicide. The coroner's proclamation came even though there was no gun found at the scene. The absence of a weapon was explained as an instance in which someone happening upon the body and taking the gun. Case closed? Well, not quite.

The coroner was not an overly exuberant civil servant, preferring to do no more than that which was required of him. So it was a little out of character when he decided to save the bullet retrieved from Stalcup's body. When asked why he had done so, he said that "it seemed like the thing to do at the time."

No one would know that Douglas had a sexual preference for young men, although, in retrospect, his life could be easily explained by such a bias. It would never be known that he and Dwight were acquainted or whether their relationship was a romantic one. Dwight was well known for having a sexual interest in the opposite sex, but he may also have had a sexual interest in men as well.

Dwight was disinclined to admit to any same-sex tendencies. For someone like Dwight, there could be nothing worse than to be outed, and thusly, a motive for Dwight to take Douglas' life may have existed.

It was a .38-caliber bullet that killed Douglas, the same caliber as that of the pistol that Dwight had taken from the Smiths' house.

Dwight never came right out and admitted that he'd killed Douglas, and his reason for recounting this dark episode in Cole City history or his particular role in it was never made clear. There is reason to suspect, however, that Douglas Stalcup got lured to the remote spot where he was killed by Dwight so that the true nature of their relationship would forever get sealed in secrecy. It is possible that Douglas Stalcup was Dwight's seventh victim.

Chapter 15
Jon Pruitt

Everyone referred to it as a cave, but in reality, it was just a shallow cavity in the rocky cliff face of no more than thirty feet in depth from front to back. But it just sounded better to call it a cave. And with all the talk about it, you needed a handy handle by which the spot could be easily referenced in conversation. So it was known simply as "the cave."

The rock cliff face ran along the crest of Sand Mountain at its northernmost extent. It overlooked the Tennessee River far below, and because of the view and the easy access from the end of Dennis Road, it was a popular place for local teenagers to hang out. It was away from prying eyes and sufficient enough of a destination for their purpose, which was to drink beer and tell lies. Young boys were the only visitors to the cave as the young ladies, even the most notorious of which, knew to stay away. The absence of female visitors to the cave led to speculation that the cave may be a rendezvous for young men seeking a sexual liaison.

It was in the late morning hours that the call came in. The sheriff grudgingly picked up the phone in his office at the jail and gruffly said, "Hello." The next few seconds was indelibly marked on the sheriff's life for as long as he lived. A muffled voice on the other end of the line said, "I think he's dead."

The sheriff gathered himself and, now on high alert, asked, "Who's dead?"

The voice on the other end of the line said, "Jon Pruitt."

The conversation after that was a back and forth between the sheriff and the caller as the sheriff tried to find out what this was all about, and the caller tried to remain anonymous. The sheriff learned that there was a body in the cave at the end of Dennis Road belonging to Jon Pruitt, a local teenager who lived with his family in Cole City.

The sheriff of Dade County had very few occasions to operate the light atop the roof of his cruiser or to have the siren blast the customary warning. He didn't like to make a scene, but today he'd have to do so, as getting to the scene, some ten miles away, as quickly as possible seemed like the thing to do. The sheriff's route to the scene passed directly by Dwight's house. Dwight was home but showed no interest in all the commotion.

Lying on his back with his legs folded underneath him was the body of Jon Pruitt. His left arm was underneath his body, and the hand at the end of his outstretched right arm held an old .38-caliber pistol. The body lay in a puddle of blood from a single head wound. There was no doubting the caller Jon Pruitt was surely dead. The floor of the cave was littered with empty beer cans, and there was a still warm burned-out campfire. Footprints were everywhere in the dry sandy soil of the cave floor.

The sheriff didn't enter the cave itself but stood outside its mouth to make these initial observations. He was trying to memorize all that he saw because he'd surely need to recount his arrival at the scene to the state police, whom he'd have to call. He walked up the trail to the road and on to the nearest house. The sheriff knocked on the front door and asked the elderly woman who came to the door if he could use her telephone. He never considered using his radio since there was no one in his office, and besides, this far out in the county, he'd be out of the radio's range.

While the sheriff waited for the state police and the local coroner to arrive, he struck up a conversation with the elderly couple who lived here, all the while keeping a watch on Dennis Road.

The sheriff asked the couple if they'd seen or heard anything unusual the night before as it seemed like the kind of question that someone should ask. The sheriff had to ask the husband the same question three times as his hearing wasn't very good, and he wasn't wearing his hearing aid. Finally, the wife answered for him, telling the sheriff that she was sure he hadn't heard anything for obvious reasons. She further confided that it wasn't unusual for cars to drive by and park down the road so that the occupants could walk down the trail to the cave and that it happened enough to be unremarkable to her. She hadn't noticed anyone coming or going. Neither had she heard anything sounding like a gunshot. The sheriff thought to himself that since the cave is well below the crest line of the mountain, any sounds would likely carry away from the cliffside. Such a conclusion was evidence of a level of astuteness uncommon to the sheriff, and he took a moment to soak in the moment. He was shaken from his self-indulgence by the old woman's offer of a glass of sweet tea. The sheriff accepted the old woman's offer and settled comfortably into a rocking chair on her porch to await the arrival of those he'd summoned.

No curious onlookers appeared.

It took the state police almost an hour to get to the scene and the coroner an additional forty-five minutes. The sheriff continued to sit on the elderly couple's front porch and, when approached by the state police, offered what little he knew in a quiet, measured manner. It didn't take long for the state police to wrap up their investigation of the scene and release the body to the coroner who took it away. The person in charge of the state police's investigation remarked that it looked like a suicide, and that's precisely what the final report completed some thirty or so days later said. The state police did not look any more closely at the circumstances. The sheriff didn't either. After all, it wasn't his job.

Had the state police or the sheriff investigated more thoroughly, they might have been able to identify the caller, but that didn't happen. They also didn't find who had made all the disparate footprints on the cave floor. They did find that the gun had five unspent cartridges in the revolver and one spent cartridge. The weapon was .38 caliber in size, just big enough to assure death even if not well aimed. They didn't bother to look at tire tracks or look for fingerprints. It would, in fact, be many years before such things were routinely done in a case like this.

Most importantly, the state police failed to note that the gun was in Jon Pruitt's right hand and the wound in the corresponding side of his head, but Jon Pruitt was known to be left-handed. No suspects were ever identified, and no motive for murder ever explored. Had this been done, they might have discovered that Dwight had been at the cave the night before and that he and Jon Pruitt had a long history of familiarity. They would never know that Jon Pruitt was rumored to be gay.

Dwight admitted to me that he had met Jon at the cave on that night, that the two had quarreled, and that he had, in a fit of rage, shot and killed Jon Pruitt. Dwight had not planned on killing Jon Pruitt. Had he done so, then he would likely have decided not to use the same gun that was used to kill Douglas Stalcup sometime earlier. But Dwight had come to rely upon his good fortune; he was, after all, invincible. Death had, once again, been riding shotgun with Dwight allowing him to go unsuspected and unquestioned.

Jon Pruitt was Dwight's eight victim.

By the early 1990s, the police force in Dade County had grown substantially. The old days of having a sleepy sheriff and a single illiterate city police chief were, like *Mayberry RFD*, a bygone era. The county had hired additional and more experienced deputies provided ongoing officer training and appointed a detective for the first time. This new detective, Dave Gray, having grown up on Sand Mountain, knew of the Stalcup and Pruitt suicides. When he began to organize the historical case file information for the sheriff's office, he came across the bullets from both incidents that had been preserved by the coroner. On a lark, he submitted the two rounds to the National Integrated Ballistic Information Network (NIBIN) for analysis. In the early 1990s, the NIBIN began working with local law enforcement for the first time to evaluate ballistics data and provide investigators with actionable leads in cases involving firearms. The agency is operated by the Bureau of Alcohol, Tobacco, and Firearms. Coincidentally the ATF is where Gray had worked before coming back to Dade County to work for the sheriff's office. Gray was very familiar with the services offered by NIBIN and conversant in their procedures.

Weeks became months without Gray hearing anything back from NIBIN, and he forgot all about it. Then unexpectedly, the

NIBIN report came back, and it was surprising. The two men killed had been shot with the same gun—the same weapon that was in evidence ever since being recovered from the Jon Pruitt scene. This report wasn't enough to get either suicide reclassified as a homicide, but there was no telling just where this new piece of evidence could lead. Gray rechecked for any history on the gun but found no record of it ever having been registered or reported stolen.

Detective Gray found himself face-to-face with several explanations for the same gun having been used in two suicides. Had the weapon that Douglas Stalcup used to commit suicide been taken from the body by a passerby and found its way somehow to Jon Pruitt, who then used the gun to commit suicide as well? Perhaps Jon Pruitt was the one who took the gun from the Stalcup suicide scene in the first place? Or had there been someone else who had used the weapon to kill Douglas Stalcup and then later to kill Jon Pruitt as well?

Detective Gray knew that according to Occam's razor, if there exists more than one possible explanation for an occurrence, then the simplest one is usually the right answer. In this case, the simplest answer was that the same person had murdered both Douglas Stalcup and Jon Pruitt.

Without any proof, however, this explanation lacked the veracity needed to pursue an investigation. Still, the mystery troubled Detective Gray, and he found himself asking who would have had a motive to kill both men. In most cases, murder is motivated by money, sex, or love. But none of these would explain either death, much less both. This conclusion left Detective Gray with the thought that perhaps the killing of both men had been unrelated except by the killer. This thought led Gray to consider whether the killings had been for sport. Or maybe the killings had been motivated by opportunity and nothing more. Gray would become convinced that there was indeed a cold-blooded killer in their midst. But with the absence of evidence or a motive, these murder mysteries were destined to remain unsolved.

Dwight would never be considered a suspect. Jon Pruitt was victim number eight.

Chapter 16
Dumb and Dumber

Dwight remained close with his like-minded buddies after high school graduation, hanging out at the pool hall, smoking, drinking beer, and cutting up. It was all about having a good time, except when it wasn't. Mostly they were just killing time awaiting the letter from the Selective Service drafting them into the army. It was like a cloud silently hovering over their young lives. They all felt it, but no one talked about it.

One Saturday night, Dwight and three of his buddies were driving back to the pool hall after a beer run when Dwight's car broke down. Dwight coasted the car into a gas station and opened the hood to see if he could spot the problem.

Ever since Dwight was old enough to have an interest in cars, Burt had tried in vain to get him to learn about his car and how to fix it when it broke down. But Dwight's only interest was in driving. Unfortunately, he knew little about how to diagnosis the problem, much less fix it. None of his buddies knew any more than Dwight did. Their lack of knowledge was exacerbated by the amount of beer they'd consumed earlier, leaving the group with little hope for solving their present predicament. They weren't, however, worried. They were too tanked to worry.

And as luck would have it, an auto mechanic on his way home from his job stopped for gas and saw the hood up on Dwight's car. Even luckier, the mechanic, being a Good Samaritan, offered to see if he could help. While the Good Samaritan had his head under the hood, Dwight helped himself to the mechanic's tools and secreted them away in the trunk of Dwight's car. Dwight's buddies struggled to conceal their amusement at Dwight's brazen act.

Let me pause here for a moment to let the stupidity of this senseless act sink in. With his car broken down and being worked on, at no cost, by a Good Samaritan mechanic, these brain surgeons thought it would be smart to steal the mechanic's tools. I doubt that any one of them had the good sense to understand the stupidity of the act or even know the meaning of the term "exit strategy."

Hot Rod Hutchinson came, impounded the broken-down car, handcuffed the lot of them, and hauled them all off to jail. By now, Hot Rod had lost his patience with Dwight and his pals. So in jail, they'd remain for several days awaiting the circuit court appearance for theft.

But Dwight was nothing if not lucky, and while he sat cooling his heels in jail, the Good Samaritan who'd tried to help Dwight with his broken-down car decided not to press charges. So Dwight and his pals were grudgingly set free. Although short in duration, this second stay in jail was just long enough to remind Dwight of the need to avoid jail in the future.

The Good Samaritan possessed some good luck of his own. If he'd elected to pursue charges against Dwight and his friends, he would inevitably end up on Dwight's list of those "who deserved what they got." Almost everyone who had earned this distinction didn't live long.

Chapter 17
Don Smith

On most Saturday nights, Dwight could be found at the Tip Top pool hall hanging out with his like-minded buddies, smoking, drinking beer, and shooting pool. And this particular Saturday night was no different. Dwight, drinking heavily, was becoming more and more belligerent. Over a game of eight ball with an acquaintance named Bennett, Dwight became embroiled in a confrontation that led to the two of them going outside. Blows were not exchanged, but there was much puffery and posturing, and under threat of bodily harm, Bennett withdrew and went home.

Had it not been for his state of inebriation and the fact that he thought his manhood had been challenged in front of his buddies, Dwight might have let it go. But with the urging of his buddies, especially one older buddy named Don Smith, Dwight determined that he needed to exact a measure of satisfaction from Bennett.

Don wasn't usually a combative individual, but on this occasion, he'd also had too much to drink and had allowed himself to get fired up by Dwight.

Feeding on each other's growing combativeness, Dwight and Don got into Dwight's car and drove to Bennett's house. Dwight parked in Bennett's driveway with the passenger side of the vehicle closest to Bennett's house. Don exited the car while Dwight lingered behind the wheel. Dwight's brief hesitation in exiting the vehicle may have saved his life. Don stepped away from Dwight's vehicle and started for the front porch carrying a tire iron in his right hand. The porch light was off, and Bennett stepped out into the shadows provided by the darkened porch and opened fire with a deer rifle. Dwight dove for cover in the floorboard of his car as bullets pierced the metal of his car again and again. A shot from the high-powered rifle struck Don in the neck, and he went down and didn't move. Meanwhile, Bennett's wife was phoning the sheriff.

Dwight begged Bennett not to shoot him and to allow him to attend to his injured friend Don. Under a watchful eye and the aim of his rifle, Bennett let Dwight retrieve his friend from where he'd fallen, load him into the back seat of his car, and hastily drive away. Dwight drove directly to Erlanger Hospital's emergency room, not knowing whether Don was alive or dead. The trip to the ER would take half an hour, during which Don lay bleeding uncontrollably as his life slipped away.

By the time the sheriff arrived at Bennett's house, Dwight was gone. Bennett told the sheriff what had happened, and the sheriff dutifully made a report detailing Dwight and Don's trespassing and assault on Bennett. It appeared to the sheriff that Bennett was within his rights to defend himself and his home and chose not to take Bennett into custody. Bennett accompanied the sheriff back to the jail, where he signed an arrest warrant for Dwight and Don.

The damage to Don's body was devastating. Where Don's throat had once been, there was now nothing but bloody bandages. His larynx, voice box, and neck muscles had been blown away. Had the bullet been a fraction of an inch farther to the right, he would have been decapitated. The ER doc observed that the loss of blood was extreme and began a transfusion. But Don's brain had been deprived of blood flow for too long. Even if he survived the wound itself, he would be brain dead. So it's probably better that he didn't survive the night.

Dwight would not make it past the ER entrance and wasn't there when they pronounced Don dead.

The following day, Bennett, learning of Don's death, withdrew the complaint against both Dwight and Don. Bennett would admit, for years to come, that he felt guilty over the entire episode. He told others that he thought that had he not been quarrelsome with Dwight, to begin with, the whole confrontation might never have happened. Those who knew Dwight best found Bennett's self-imposed guilt to be without basis; they knew that the encounter with Dwight was unavoidable by any measure.

Don was arguably an unintended victim, a bystander if not an entirely innocent one. Intended or not, Don became Dwight's ninth casualty.

Chapter 18
Fire!

There was little work to be had for teenagers growing up in the 1960s in Cole City. There were no factories, retail stores or restaurants nearby. But there were potatoes. Sand Mountain had over the years developed a reputation for growing potatoes, and while truck farmers hauled a great variety of produce to market in Chattanooga, no other crop equaled the annual potato production. A handful of larger farms had comparatively large-scale operations employing dozens of people in late summer to pick up potatoes in the fields, transport them to a grading shed for sorting by size and quality, and pack them into burlap sacks for transportation in bulk to market.

The process of harvesting potatoes is an arduous backbreaking one, requiring workers to bend over and pickup potatoes off the ground and place them in large burlap bags that they carry over their shoulders. It is hot, dirty, backbreaking, low-paying work not suited for those lacking in determination. Few white workers were drawn to this hard work.

The farmers learned long ago that since they couldn't depend on the local labor force to harvest their crops, they would have to look elsewhere for the help they needed at harvest time. Undocumented Mexican migrant workers turned out to be the answer the farmers were looking for.

The Mexican workers were the closest thing San Mountain had to minorities. Sand Mountain had no black population. A large handmade sign proclaiming, "Nigger, don't let the sun set on you on Sand Mountain," was posted conspicuously along the side of the road leading from Trenton up the mountain, placing Sand Mountain communities among those known as sundown towns—a community where blacks had to leave before dark under the threat of violence. Although this sign was removed decades ago, Sand Mountain remains a place where there are no black people living, even now. There can be no doubt that its self-proclaimed status as a sundown town was instrumental in maintaining the white homogeneity of Sand Mountain's residents through the years. So the acceptance of Mexican migrant workers to the area was greeted with a somewhat mixed reaction by the whites who lived there.

The Mexican migrant workers, all of whom had skin color a few shades darker than the locals, knew to keep to themselves. The migrant workers worked hard for little money and didn't cause trouble. They moved on when the harvest was done. No one questioned the worker's rights to be there, and the white folks didn't complain about the jobs going to Mexicans. All things considered, things ran smoothly and to everyone's satisfaction.

The migrant workers were modern-day gypsies traveling from place to place in mass following the next crop to be harvested. They lived in travel trailers that they towed from place to place or would be housed in ramshackle shanties belonging to the farm owners. These accommodations would house several families at a time. The Mexicans would not be invited to attend any of the local churches and were not welcome in the country stores on the mountain. But a handful of merchants in Trenton, including the town's only supermarket, grudgingly took their money in exchange for necessities.

Occasionally one or more of the local white teenagers, hard up for cash, would work in the fields alongside the Mexicans, at least for a time. Dwight, being forever short on cash, would work for the farmer during harvest time, but he got the somewhat easier job of grading the potatoes that were brought in from the fields. This work was much less strenuous and had the added benefit of being in the shade of the grading shed. This job was a step up from work as a field hand and reserved for local white kids. The work was still hot, dirty, and low-paying but slightly less so than working in the fields.

Javier Garcia, his wife, and two sons, who looked to be about ten and twelve years old, were one of several migrant families working at the same farm where Dwight was employed briefly. Because the Garcia family worked in the fields, Dwight had almost no contact with them and had no reason to notice them—that is, until, dissatisfied with Dwight's laziness and habit for missing work, the walking boss moved Javier from the field to the grading shed, taking Dwight's job and sending Dwight out into the fields to pick up potatoes. This news was a source of great amusement to Dwight's friends working at the farm, and Dwight took quite a ribbing. Dwight, failing to understand the need for this change, failed to see the humor in the situation. In a huff, Dwight stormed out of the grading shed not to return. Dwight would spend the remainder of his summer in other pursuits.

After the potato harvest of 1968, Javier Garcia, his wife, and their two young sons stayed behind when the other migrant workers moved on. They set up housekeeping in a small rental home with the agreement of the farmer they had worked for and were preparing to have the children enrolled in school, when late one night, there was a fire. The family narrowly escaped with their lives but lost all their possessions.

Dwight and his buddies, with genuine malice in their hearts, boosted about having run the "Mexican niggers" off the mountain that night.

It's not clear who threw the Molotov cocktail that started the fire in the wood frame dwelling, but all in attendance shared in the conviction that it was right to do so. Working here during the harvest was one thing, but to make this their home was more than the white folks on Sand Mountain could go along with.

The family left the area the following day and never returned.

The Mexican migrant workers returned the next year at harvest time, but the Garcia family was not among them and would never to be seen again.

Chapter 19
Jacksonville State

Before the Selective Service instituted the draft lottery, anyone who was attending college could get a deferment. None of Dwight's closest friends were college material, but college enrollment offered a refuge from being drafted into the army and likely ending up fighting in Vietnam, at least for a little while. A couple of Dwight's buddies enrolled as freshmen at Jacksonville State University, a small school in northern Alabama mostly known as a teachers college located about a hundred miles southwest of Trenton. They weren't so much interested in furthering their education as they were in staying out of the army for a little while longer and having a good time along the way. Along with a couple of other students that Dwight did not know, they rented a house off campus and settled into a routine of skipping classes and partying. They were able to succeed in achieving their main goals of regularly scoring weed and occasionally getting laid.

Dwight's high school grades weren't good enough for him to be admitted to college, but the lifestyle of sex and drugs being enjoyed by his buddies at Jacksonville State had a genuine appeal, and Dwight spent as much time as he could hanging out with his friends there. On one of Dwight's visits, he was disappointed that his old Ford wasn't able to make the trip, and he had to borrow his dad's car. Instead of driving his hot car, he was stuck with a dowdy family car, Burt's four-door 1969 Plymouth Fury. It was a beast of a car. Even by the standards of the day, the Fury was a behemoth of a car—a fact that Dwight found inconsistent with his self-image but that, ironically, would save his life.

On the first night of Dwight's visit, he and one of his buddie's drove to a secluded overlook in the company of two young coeds. There they would listen to music on the Fury's radio, drink beer, and smoke dope. Soon enough, there came a time to move things back to the relative comfort and privacy of the house Dwight's buddies had rented, and the four of them made a move to do just that.

Perhaps the promise of sex caused Dwight to rush. Perhaps things hadn't gone the way Dwight would like with the coed, and feeling dejected and angry, he abandoned all caution. He'd had so many close brushes with death and escaped that he felt invincible. Whatever his thinking, Dwight's old habits of driving fast were in full bloom as he sped southward at an excessive rate of speed on an unfamiliar country lane. Dwight saw out of the corner of his eye the lights of a car approaching on an intersecting road. Dwight recklessly continued without slowing on a collision course with the other car. Dwight ran a stop sign at the intersection with the state highway and struck a Chevelle traveling west on the highway toward the university, broadside. Did Dwight see and ignore the stop sign? Did he see the Chevelle coming and decide to use the Fury as a weapon? Was it a case of malice or a thoughtless mistake? Either way, the results were tragic.

The Chevelle carried six university students returning to campus from a movie.

The oversized Fury literally ran over the smaller Chevelle and, continuing across the main road, spun around and struck an ancient oak tree about two hundred feet farther on. The top half of the Chevelle disappeared. Five of the six students in the Chevelle died instantly. The sixth student would survive, but her injuries were severe and left her totally disabled for the rest of her life. Dwight's passengers were luckily not seriously injured and would go on to live their lives. Dwight suffered broken ribs and a punctured lung that required hospitalization but from which he would recover quickly and completely. It is likely that the size of the Fury in combination with the speed and the fact that the Fury flew over the top of the Chevelle on impact saved the lives of Dwight and his passengers. As a result of the crash, Dwight felt more invincible than ever.

The local police, possibly thinking that Dwight wouldn't survive his injuries, didn't test his alcohol level right away. But before Dwight could recover from his injuries enough to leave the hospital, the sheriff came for a visit to his hospital room. Dwight was being charged with five counts of vehicular homicide. The college kids that lost their lives in this horrible accident were from families that were well respected in the community and who held sway, to some degree, over the sheriff's office. The sheriff here was an elected official who would be up for reelection soon. It looked like Dwight's luck may have finally run out and that he would be in Alabama for a trial. Dwight was read his rights and told to not leave the jurisdiction.

As Dwight slowly recuperated, he hatched a plan to flee from the state of Alabama thinking that all he had to do was get across the state line into Georgia to avoid prosecution. The sheriff had not seen a need to place an officer at the hospital to discourage Dwight from fleeing. It's likely, in fact, that the sheriff would welcome an attempt by Dwight to flee as this would only serve to deepen Dwight's predicament. Dwight, with a little help from his friends, was able to slip away from the hospital in the dead of night and return home to Cole City where he would continue to recuperate.

Then one otherwise unremarkable afternoon a few weeks later, the Dade County sheriff came knocking on Dwight's door with a warrant for his arrest. An order of extradition had been executed, and Dwight was taken into custody and returned to Alabama to face the charges against him.

At his arraignment the next day, the judge made Dwight an offer. It was the height of the Vietnam War, and America's youth was being decimated by the war. The judge offered to suspend all charges against Dwight provided he went straight away to the army enlistment center and volunteered.—a tough choice, risk going to prison if convicted of his crimes or join the army and go to Vietnam.

That very day, Dwight enlisted in the army and, after bringing the enlistment papers back to the judge, had all the charges against him suspended. If Dwight fulfilled his two-year commitment to the army, the charges would be dropped. If for any reason Dwight failed to fulfill his commitment to the army, he would be brought back to

Alabama and tried on all charges against him. Dwight was given two weeks by the army to say his goodbyes and get his affairs in order and was then placed aboard a bus to Fort Benning where he would spend the next several weeks in basic training.

The body count, a term popularized by the military and media in the war to come, was now fourteen people dead plus one crippled and a murdered dog, but Dwight continued to slip the gallows as if he were imbued with some dark power.

Chapter 20
All I Know I Got from TV

Dwight found himself growing less and less apprehensive about the prospect of becoming a soldier. Could this turn out to be the kind of opportunity he'd secretly always longed for, to be able to take the life of those who deserved it without remorse, without fear, without being held accountable?

Some of Dwight's buddies, who had flunked out of school, had already been drafted. Others seeing limited socioeconomic prospects at home chose to volunteer for the military with several having joined the navy as well as the army and one heroic young man becoming a marine. Luckily all, except the marine, completed their tours in Vietnam and returned home albeit somewhat worse for the wear. The marine was not so lucky.

Dwight wasn't as close to these friends as he'd once been but was close enough to know their stories and was aware that fortune had been a fickle companion for each of them.

Dwight's friend Benny, who had been involved in the brush up with the law over the stolen tools two years prior, was among the first of Dwight's pals to join the army under similar circumstances to those faced by Dwight. Benny had amassed a sizeable police record, with offenses ranging from vandalism, to breaking and entering, to car theft, and eventually to assault over a bar fight. The judge in Benny's case had paved the way for Benny to join the army and have his record expunged. And Benny turned out to be a good soldier.

His time in the army was spent without incident, that is, until a Viet Cong sniper's bullet changed his life forever. Benny's wound was life-threatening, requiring extensive time in military hospitals and a long rehabilitation. But survive he did, and a few months later, Benny was well enough to be sent home for thirty days of R&R. But Benny's mind was permanently damaged beyond repair. We didn't know what PTSD was back then, and Benny's mental state would go undiagnosed for several years.

When Benny was discharged from the army hospital, he had almost a year left on his enlistment, and near the end of his leave, Benny was ordered to return to Vietnam. Considering his mental state and all that he'd been through, most understood when Benny simply said no. Benny had few options. Failure to report for duty as ordered was, and is, a court-martial offense. Such action would cause Benny to be arrested and sent to federal prison as a deserter. But going back to Vietnam after having almost lost his life was something that Benny's mind would not accept. So he ran. Rather than give himself up to the military police with the prospect of spending the rest of his life locked up at Leavenworth, Benny disappeared. Over the next few years, Benny would work at cash-paying jobs that didn't require a social security number as a way to make ends meet. But money was scarce, and he eventually returned to the life of petty crime he'd lived before his stint in the army.

Then, one fall, just over a year after his desertion, Benny was apprehended by local police in Americus, Georgia. By the time the judicial system and the army got through with Benny, he would spend more than twenty years of his life in prison. But survive he did!

Dwight's friend Carl came home from Vietnam addicted to heroin. Within a couple of weeks of his return, Carl's drug habit was like Audrey in *Little Shop of Horrors*, screaming, "Feed me!" Carl was perhaps Dwight's most intelligent buddy, and he hatched an ingenious and effective plan to get the money he needed for drugs. Carl, who was handsome and charming, asked the somewhat dowdy daughter of the president of Trenton's only bank to go with him to see a movie in nearby Chattanooga. During the movie, Carl excused himself and telephoned the girl's father to say that if he ever wanted to see his daughter alive again, he'd have to come up with $50,000 in cash before midnight. The horrified bank executive entered the bank under the cloak of darkness, retrieved the money, and dropped it exactly when and where he'd been instructed to by Carl. Carl picked up the money, dropped off the young lady who had no idea that she's been a kidnap victim, and disappeared. The FBI was called in and agents interviewed all of Carl's friends including Dwight. Off and on for several weeks, FBI agents would be observed in the area, but they didn't catch Carl.

Unfortunately, Carl's drug habit would do him in. Five months after his crime, Carl died of a fatal drug overdose in San Francisco.

Dwight and his buddies had their brushes with death, but Carl would be the only one to die of a drug overdose.

With these thoughts in the back of his mind, Dwight approached his induction into the military with mixed emotions. On the one hand, he didn't want to end up like Benny or Carl or even worse. But on the other hand, the army was going to give him a gun, teach him how to use it, and have him kill people—a thought that, more than any other, would be the fuel Dwight needed for his coming journey to become a soldier.

Chapter 21
The War

The war had its own lexicon that was a common touchstone for all who were a part of it, a language shared by all those who were there. Remembering the experience, Dwight fell comfortably into the use of words and terms that were common to the time and place but mostly unused in everyday life away from the war.

Such words and terms are as follows:

- AAR: After-action report
- AIT: Advanced Infantry Training
- ARVN: Army of the Republic of Vietnam
- Barbecue: Armored cavalry units requesting Napalm on a location
- Bivouac: A temporary camp without tents or cover
- Boom boom: Sex
- Bong Son Bomber: Giant-sized joint or marijuana cigarette
- Bush: Jungle
- Charlie: Abbreviation of Viet Cong
- Charm school: Initial training and orientation upon arrival in-country
- Cherry: Designation for new replacement from the states
- Coka Girl: A Vietnamese woman who sells everything except "boom boom"
- DEROS (Date Eligible Return from Over Seas): Acronym used in Vietnam to determine the date a soldier can go home

- Flower Seeker: Describing men looking for prostitutes
- Heads: Troops who used illicit drugs
- Ho Chi Minh Road Sticks: Vietnamese sandals made from old truck tires
- Hooch: A hut or simple dwelling
- Idiot Stick: A rifle
- Indian Country: Area controlled by Charlie
- Lager: A night defensive perimeter
- Juicers: Alcoholics
- KIA: Killed in action
- LT: Lieutenant
- Little People: Radio code for South Vietnamese Army soldier
- Number One: The best
- Number Ten Thousand: The worst
- RA (Regular Army): Someone who enlisted versus a draftee
- Real Life: Life before the war or before the draft
- Zippo Raids: Burning of Vietnamese villages

Because of the large numbers of draftees and recruits entering the army for the Vietnam War, basic training was carried out at several different military bases in the United States. As an enlistee, Dwight was RA and was sent to Army Infantry Training carried out at Fort Benning in Columbus, Georgia, where he would complete eight weeks of basic training, followed by an additional eight weeks of AIT.

A typical day for Dwight at Fort Benning would begin with a 6:00 a.m. reveille and an early morning run of six miles before breakfast. After breakfast, Dwight would go from one training exercise to another including hand-to-hand combat, obstacle course, and rifle range. Dwight's training involved the handling of equipment he'd be expected to use in-country that, in addition to weapons (M16 rifle or M-60 machine gun, .38-caliber handgun, bayonet, and extra ammo) included wet-weather gear, helmet, and an array of other things to use and wear. Fully equipped, all this gear amounted to about eighty-five pounds, and Dwight's training involved carrying a rucksack with this equipment during training exercises. It only made sense to train this way as this is what could be expected in-country. Additionally, grunts wore flak jackets during training, but upon arrival in-country, the flak jackets were usually the first thing to be discarded because of the heat and heavy load. At the end of the day, each grunt would carry what was necessary, and beyond that, it was up to them to decide what they would carry and how much it would weigh.

After graduation from AIT, Dwight was granted two weeks of leave in which he returned home to Cole City, a newly minted soldier. He looked different, leaner, more fit, and with close-cropped hair. He also acted different, more focused, and his already scant sense of humor was now completely absent. But you could tell that the prospect of being sent off to the war in Vietnam, while very scary, also held fascination for Dwight. Dwight had added several new words to his vocabulary including Cherry, meaning a soldier first arriving in Vietnam; Gook, a contemptuous word referring to all Vietnamese people; Charlie, referring to the Viet Cong, which he used proudly and vociferously; and Grunts, referring to infantrymen. Those who knew Dwight recognized in him a degree of machismo that had not been there before.

In addition to other training, soldiers being deployed to Vietnam were also sent to charm school just before leaving the United States or just after their arrival in Vietnam. Charm school was intended to orient the soldiers to what it would be like once they're in-country. Such orientation was indispensable, but unfortunately Charm school fell well short of providing these newly minted soldiers with all they'd need to know. New arrivals were referred to as cherries by more experienced soldiers. All the cherries' training up to this point was necessary but woefully insufficient for their survival. The real training wouldn't begin in earnest until they were assigned to a unit where this informal training was overseen by more experienced soldiers. This training covered every aspect of life in a war zone from where and when to take a crap to where you could steal the essentials that you needed to how to get laid.

Cherries were there to replace those who'd left by having completed their tour, been wounded, or killed. The cherries were immediately integrated into their new unit where they were expected to pick up where their predecessor had left off. The cherries learned mostly through observation and immolation and often by making mistakes that were quickly pointed out by others in the unit. Every cherry learned what they needed to know to survive, or they didn't survive very long. The weakest cherries were singled out and rode hard by others in the unit. The very worst among these, if deemed to not have what it took to learn what was needed and who were a hazard to their units, were the first to die, usually by their own incompetence but sometimes at the hands of the enemy after having been placed in harm's way by their own men and occasionally by friendly fire. One soldier could take the life of another, usually leaving almost no evidence of the crime. Fingerprints could be destroyed by a fragmentation grenade, and since such grenades did not have serial numbers, tracing the shell was impossible.

Such murderous acts became more and more common as the war wore on and soldiers increasingly questioned the war. The term "fragging" became synonymous with any murderous act against another soldier.

In addition to the general terms of endearment that one infantryman would use for a fellow infantryman in-country, such as grunt, every GI had a nickname by which they were known to others in their unit. Dwight's nickname, which he came by quite understandably, was "Stretch" in recognition of his unusually tall six-foot four-inch frame. Stretch was tall for an American, but compared to the Vietnamese people, he was a giant. It wasn't unusual for curious Vietnamese to stop what they were doing and stare at Stretch. Stretch found no advantage to being tall except for the fact that he was never picked to run point for his unit.

I guess that having such a tall target out front was just asking for trouble. Stretch joked that if he did something incredibly bad or, as the Vietnamese say, Xau lam (Vietnamese slang for "numbah ten thousand"), he'd be put on point for the next patrol. This meant that if he did something bad enough to be fragged by his own unit, then putting his tall frame on point would serve the purpose well enough. It was this fear, more than fear of the enemy or anything else, that kept Stretch honest, at least with his own unit.

Chapter 22
Body Count

The wartime culture in which Dwight found himself was a palpable mixture of righteous indignation and unbridled evil. It molded Dwight's predilections toward the taking of lives and honed his skill for doing so. Righteous indignation sprang eternal from the indoctrination each soldier received from the moment of his commitment to military service and ceaseless bombardment of propaganda they received from that point on. While others back at home may be questioning whether or not the war was right, soldiers were groomed and manipulated continually so that they believed in what they were doing. They were taught that they were the good guys. They were fighting for right. The unbridled evil they accepted came from demonizing their enemy by the US war machine. They were taught and came to believe that the AVN was the embodiment of evil. They weren't human. They didn't deserve to live. Not all soldiers embraced these beliefs but enough did to taint all who served.

Pentagon documents, which are now housed by the US National Archives, detail more than three hundred alleged incidents of mass atrocities during the American presence in Vietnam.

It was under US General Julian Ewell's command that soldiers committed the atrocities at My Lai. One Pentagon investigator, whose reports are filed in the US Archives, observed that there was a My Lai every month referring to one of the bloodiest periods of the war in 1968.

During a large-scale operation in the densely populated Mekong Delta under General Ewell known as the Winter Soldier Operation in 1968, an enemy body count of almost eleven thousand KIA was claimed in AARs. These same reports however listed fewer than 750 weapons as being captured. Such numbers leaves no doubt that the military inflated the number of enemy KIA by listing the bodies of unarmed Vietnamese civilians that were killed by the US Army.

The taking of Vietnamese civilian lives was a direct and unavoidable result of General Ewell's policy that the enemy body count had to kept up by killing any Vietnamese whether enemy combatant or civilian, earning him the moniker "Butcher of the Delta." Under General Ewell's command, US soldiers would take the lives of many thousands of Vietnamese, sparing only those who were known to be in the service of the US Military. Anyone found to be in Indian Country was assumed to be ARVN and was fair game. This included unarmed women and children.

In a war in which lip service was paid to winning hearts and minds, the US military had an almost singular focus on one defining measure of success in Vietnam—body count, the number of enemy reportedly killed in action. The American media would announce body count numbers during each evening's TV news cast, and the American people were told that evidence of our winning of the war could be found in the high numbers of enemy KIA compared to the low number of US Army KIA. The military along with the media had created a way to keep score and defrauded the American public by inflating the numbers, a fraud based on the mass murder of unarmed innocent civilians.

There is a saying in the business world that "you get what you measure," and the measurement of choice for the Army was body count.

Many US Army Infantrymen went along with all this, but for most, when it came to killing an unarmed civilian, they drew the line. There are stories about repercussions for soldier who didn't get with the program including being ostracized, demoted, disciplined, and in extreme cases fragged. On the other hand, there were many who embraced the program. Dwight was in the latter group.

Dwight served his entire tour in Vietnam in the infantry under General Ewell, a man who not only embraced these beliefs but also would lead an army to accept them and act upon them. Dwight became the general's poster boy for inflating body count. And even now, Dwight justifies what he did by saying that he was just following orders. But as he shared more of the specifics of his time in Vietnam, his argument weakened.

Chapter 23
Dwight the Soldier

Every soldier who served in Vietnam had their story. Over the decades, since the end of the war, more and more veterans have reluctantly shared their story, and slowly a more detailed picture of what the war was actually like has emerged. But even now, Vietnam War veterans are often reluctant to share stories of the atrocities that they witnessed—not so with Dwight who recounted his actions for me in explicit detail. It was as if, even now at the hour of his death, he remained proud of what he did in Vietnam.

The war is, as has been said before by soldiers in every war, long-haul truckers, airplane pilots, and many others, endless boredom punctuated by brief moments of sheer terror. Even the grunts, who saw the most action, weren't often unlucky enough to see any major combat or even a small-scale jungle ambush during their time in-country. They spent the vast majority of their time on patrol, waiting in ambush, or back at base camp.

Those brief moments of exhilaration became the defining moments of the war for Dwight and were the central theme in his recounting of his time in Vietnam. Dwight shared one story after another of the action that he saw with each story having the same point, someone dying at Dwight's hands. Enemy combatant or unlucky passerby, it didn't matter who.

In one of Dwight's more lucid periods between his pain meds beginning to wear off and the pain becoming so bad that he'd need more meds, Dwight shared the following story.

Stopping at the base of a mountain about twenty clicks from base camp, Stretch's unit settled in for the night in a depression in the ground, possibly made by B-52 Ordinance a day or two earlier. The sun had just set, and a light rain had just started to fall on the lager, dampening the exposed dirt in the crater and the surrounding jungle foliage. The crater wasn't yet the mudhole that it would become. Nevertheless Stretch wisely picked a spot on slightly higher ground, trenched drainage around his chosen spot, and hunkered down for the long wet night. One of the things that cherries found surprising about Vietnam is how cold it was at night when the monsoon rain was relentless.

Stretch's unit had been away from base camp on patrol for three days and nights without incident, and they were just now beginning to stir lethargically in response to the rising sun. The light rain of the night before had thankfully dissipated, and a bright sun was beginning to shine down on the wet jungle, causing a covering of fog along the ground with tendrils rising upward to greet the sun. As mornings in Vietnam go, this was a good one. As he rose from the damp earth where he had slept intermittently, Stretch scratched incessantly at the many new mosquito bites and then began the OCD ritual that he followed whenever he was out on patrol. He shook out his poncho to get rid of any creatures that it may harbor, folded it neatly, and tucked it away. He then checked his uniform, equipment, and boots for any unwanted hitchhikers. After all you can't be too careful when you're in a country that has thirty-seven different venomous snakes. Vietnam is home, in fact, to some of the world's most deadly snakes including the king cobra, which can grow up to five meters in length, and the banded krait, one of the deadliest of snakes. This was of course something of an exaggeration, but not much of one.

Satisfied that he was alone, he sat on a fallen tree log and generously powdered his bare feet and slipped on his filthy and still damp socks. He pulled on his damp boots and stuffed his fatigues into his boots while lacing them up. He hoped that this last precaution will keep ticks, leeches, and spiders from taking up residence, at least for a little while.

Knowing that he'd only been in-country for a total of thirty-five days, Stretch was still considered a cherry. He muttered to himself, "Another f——ing boondoggle, only 296 days to go." Stretch knew that almost all of these days would be spent like this one, out in the boonies, scared, and wet. But scared and wet meant that he had survived another day and that, more than the sunshine, made this a good day.

Oh well, he thought, *it's time to eat*. When on patrol, C rations were the only source of food. Infantry units were resupplied with C rations, water, ammunition, clothes, and other items by helicopter every three to five days; and the unit expected to be resupplied today. This was something to look forward to especially since Stretch was down to the least desirable C rations.

The scrambled egg weren't bad cold, but anything else had to be heated to be edible. And there was no time to heat up C rations this morning as the LT was jumpier than usual and wanted the unit on the move as soon as possible. All Dwight had left was ham and lima beans, which were just god-awful. Using his trusty John Wayne, slang for a military-issued can opener, Stretch quickly wolfed down the ham and beans with a wash of water from one of his canteens.

Stretch had learned in his first days on patrol, which now seemed like a lifetime ago, that he would need fifteen quarts of water a day in order to stay hydrated. Stretch had five one-quart canteens that he carried everywhere. With the sun out, he'd drain all five early in the day and hope to find some resupply along the way. During the monsoon season or in areas with rivers and streams, refilling his canteen wasn't a problem as water was plentiful. But drinking untreated water was asking for trouble of the kind you can't afford. Time and circumstance permitting, grunts would often strain the particles out of the water with a piece of cloth and then boil the water to purify it. More often than not, the circumstances or the lack of time didn't allow for this, so grunts would rely on the use of iodine tablets. The only problem with this technique for dealing with waterborne contagion was the horrible taste. So not all grunts would be diligent about using the iodine tablets and for this many would pay a high price.

Before breaking camp, the empty C ration cans, cigarette butts, and other trash were buried. That task having been accomplished, it was time to move out.

The grunts left their bivouac in a single file behind a veteran point man carrying a shotgun. There were two grunts on the flanks with M16s, of which Stretch was one. It's still early in the morning, and yet the grunts were already wet with sweat. Under the weight of all their gear, they appeared to bow as if to an audience. Their heads were on a swivel, scanning the jungle around them, each more alert than the other. This went on for what seemed like a couple of hours with only brief breaks to catch their breath and rehydrate. By now, the sun was high above and beating down on them as they slogged through the jungle. Sweat ran down Stretch's back and chest into every scratch and mosquito bite, burning and itching.

Then, the jungle seemed to part just a little, and the point man found himself on a hard-packed dirt path. The path was still slick from last night's rain, and the lack of footprints suggested that it had not been used recently. The path wound eastward through the jungle and the unit followed. Stretch fell in behind the point man about ten yards back with the rest of the unit a little farther back. The vegetation on either side of the path was thick and uninviting. So the unit continued along the path for another half hour or so without deviating off course. Stepping out of the jungle, the point man found himself standing in the edge of a clearing about the length of a football field and half as wide. Vegetation, mostly elephant grass, was thick and almost as tall as the point man's head. At the far end of the clearing was a bamboo thicket with six thatched hoochs situated between the clearing and the thicket. The dirt path that the unit had been following extended into the clearing toward the hoochs beyond. The point man stopped dead still and began to scan the clearing. Stretch was motioned up so that his height could be used to advantage, and he began scanning the clearing as well. There was perfect stillness. Not a bird chirping and not a buzzing insect to be heard. Stretch could tell that the veteran point man was uneasy, even though there was no movement around the hoochs up ahead and nothing untoward was noticed by either man.

The unit had spread out on either side of the path and taken cover in the vegetation at the edge of the clearing. Here they waited silently as the point man slowly edged forward toward the hoochs, now less than thirty yards ahead. Stretch followed a few steps behind the point man and to the point man's right.

The silence was broken by the unmistakable report of an AK-47 from somewhere just behind and to the left of the hoochs. Almost every soldier in Vietnam would have seen fellow soldiers that had been killed but far fewer would have actually witnessed the moment in time when their life ended. This would be the first such experience for Stretch, but certainly not his last. The point man lay face down just ten feet from Stretch. Stretch couldn't see it, but half of the point man's face had been blown away. He was dead before he hit the ground, and his lifeless body gave testament to that fact.

The unit, almost in unison, laid a barrage of gunfire into the jungle to the left of the hooch where the sniper shot had come from for what seemed to Stretch like a very long time. In reality, the barrage lasted only about a minute. Stretch regaining his composure leaped up and charged toward the hooch with his M16 at the ready. Stretch could hear the unit behind him yelling and running toward the hooch, but Stretch got there first. At that moment, Stretch had no fear and never considered whether he might be putting himself in the AK-47 line of fire. Even here and now, Dwight felt invincible. All he felt was rage and the overwhelming need to do something. As Stretch neared the first hooch, someone sprang from what must be a bunker and sprinted toward the bamboo thicket. Stretch didn't have enough time to consider whether the fleeing Vietnamese was a combatant or a civilian and, opening fire, cut him down after only a few steps. Stretch burst into the first hooch and saw the shape of three people crotched along the back wall. Without thinking, Stretch opened fire again and saw the bodies jerk as they were struck by the bullets from his M16. By now Stretch's unit was upon the other hoochs, and the yelling was punctuated by gunfire. It was all over in less than five minutes, and cautiously the unit reconnoitered the area. They found no dead enemy combatants and no weapons. In the hooch where Dwight stood, they found a couple of hundred pounds of rice and three dead Vietnamese, two of which were women and the third a young girl. Stretch had shot and killed them all.

Stretch had survived his first skirmish, witnessed a fellow soldier killed by ambush for the first time, and also for the first time had killed noncombatants. All these landmark events would be repeated again and again before Stretch's tour would be over.

A helicopter came and took the body-bag-wrapped point man's body away. The point man wasn't quite a short-timer, but was to rotate out in a little less than three months. He'd almost made it. The bodies of the three Vietnamese were quickly buried in shallow graves at the LT's orders. These three deaths would be added to the unit's body count in the AAR as if they were actual combatants. They were most likely peasants who had no political allegiance. Their village was being used by the VC as a resupply point, and the rice stored there was being watched over by a single VC hiding nearby. But that's not the way this incident would be recounted in the official record.

Years later, Dwight would recount the feeling he had then. He said, "It wasn't like killing somebody… They were Gooks. I looked forward to just hiding in an ambush and popping Gooks who came along. Mostly they were just out after dark, but a few wore black pajamas. You never knew who was a friend and who was an enemy, so my orders were if they're Vietnamese, kill 'em! It didn't mean anything! Just more to add to the body count!

"I lost count of how many gooks I killed. Men, yeah, some of whom were surely VC but there were others. You just couldn't be sure. And the women were just as dangerous, so you couldn't let them slip by. Some had kids, sure, and it was their bad luck to be in the wrong place at the wrong time. Besides, those kids were just gonna grow up to be VC anyway. One less VC to worry about down the road."

This wasn't the only such story that Dwight would share. But the details of the stories would run together, and he'd tell essentially the same stories again and again so that it was difficult to know exactly what had happened. What was clear however was that Dwight had taken many lives and that he felt no remorse for having done so. He seemed to feel that he'd found his true calling and that he was serving a worthwhile purpose.

I asked him if he felt differently about the lives he's taken in Vietnam and the lives he'd taken here before going to war. He shared his belief that his taking of lives before he went to Vietnam had just been to prepare him for what he's do once he got there. He said that "it had been necessary."

There's little to be gained from any attempt to further unravel Dwight's time in Vietnam. The true body count would never be known.

Soldiers returning to the United States from Vietnam were not warmly welcomed. There were no parades, no parties, and no overt expressions of appreciation from the general public. Returning soldiers were considered by many to be baby killers, and in Dwight's case, there was truth in this belief. Dwight would find the return to public life very difficult—not because he felt guilty about what he'd done in Vietnam, but because he felt like he no longer had any purpose. Dwight had a driving need to take lives and could find no way to fulfill that need.

Chapter 24
Uncle Bill

When Dwight was eight years old, his maternal uncle David died from lung cancer. It was a horrible death. David, a lifelong smoker, had lingered near death for weeks before succumbing. It was the 1950s and back then poor people, like David, died at home. His bed had been made in the front room of the old house he lived in with his wife Geraldine. On weekends, David's nine siblings and Dwight's mother would, one by one, visit with David in the front room and try in vain to ignore the fact that he was dying before their eyes.

Some of Dwight's earliest memories were of these weekly visits with David, and the impression made by this experience would be indelible. The grief and sadness that filled David's room would affect all who visited. And as the end neared, visitors would be victimized themselves by the grotesqueness of David's illness. Dwight would not be able to avoid the compulsory paying of his respects on these visits and just by being there would not be spared the most disturbing details of David's demise. Dwight was too young to understand the sadness of these visits but deep down would carry this memory forever, not out of sadness as much as just a morbid curiosity.

The culture of the 1950s embraced smoking on a social level, and the health risk of tobacco use was still not generally known or accepted by the public. We wouldn't learn until years later that big tobacco knew the health dangers of smoking all along.

Over the next decade, we'd all come to understand the link between smoking and lung cancer.

Decades after his uncle David passing, Dwight's maternal uncle Bill would be diagnosed with stage 4 lung cancer. A sixty-two-year-old lifelong smoker, he had long since accepted that this would be how he'd die, but like most everyone else, Bill wasn't ready for this to happen to him this early in his life. Like David before him, Bill would find his world shrunk to first a small room and then a bed. And like David before him, Bill would have his family around him. Dwight wasn't close with any of his extended family and wasn't one to visit with Bill as he'd been made to do with his uncle David years earlier.

From what he's heard from other family members, Dwight knew that his uncle Bill was close to death. So Dwight finally mustered his courage and visited Bill in hospice for the first and only time. He found Bill bedridden and emaciated with an oxygen tube feeding the living gas into his nostrils. Bill was short of breath and would have to pause several times in order to complete a sentence. Bill was however cogent and aware of his surroundings and situation.

Dwight watched with fascination as Bill would remove his oxygen tube and twist the valve closing off the oxygen supply just long enough to light a cigarette in order to have a smoke, a practice he'd repeat again and again right up until his passing.

Dwight himself was a smoker by now, living in a house where both his mother and father were heavy smokers. But until now Dwight hadn't really made the connection between smoking and death. It was an epiphany and a powerful insight that would mold the rest of Dwight's life.

Bill drowned in his own fluids only brief minutes after his last cigarettes. His passing left behind a heartbroken widow and the seed of an idea in his sociopath nephew Dwight.

Chapter 25
Tobacco Road

Dwight had taken lives by his actions and inactions, by his hand, and by manipulating circumstances. Burt and Louise were aware of at least a fraction of what Dwight had done, but mostly they weren't. But it isn't something that was ever spoken of, even among his family or closest friends. Dwight would carry the weight of what he'd done alone. Doing so would give most people pause to reexamine their lives and to possibly choose a path that held greater regard for the lives and safety of themselves and others. There is no evidence to suggest that this was the case for Dwight.

After Dwight's return from Vietnam, he tried to go back to the way things were before, to his same old behavior—drinking, smoking dope, driving fast, getting into fights, and getting into trouble with the law. But he found that things weren't the same as before. The war had brought out the worst in Dwight, and there was no coming back from that. Dwight's social circle had shrunk significantly; some of his past friends were still in the army, and those who had suffered serious injury from their association with Dwight no longer palled around with Dwight. This was a lonely time and troublesome for Dwight. And it was during this time that Dwight met and began to date a young woman who, much like the substance of many a country song, would look past the horrible events of Dwight's life and his disregard for others and seek to make Dwight a better man.

Dwight focused all his attention on his new girlfriend who would come to represent the full extent of his social life. Dwight's first long-term girlfriend would become his wife. They'd buy a trailer and settle into a typical white trash existence in the north end of the county. Dwight would bounce from job to job, making Moon Pies, building cabinets, and such. But all his jobs ended the same way, with Dwight being dismissed for one reason or another. However life would move on regardless. Dwight would become a dad and move his expanded family away from Dade County and into a midcentury ranch house in a suburb of Chattanooga. A second child would soon follow. But Dwight wasn't able to hold a job for long at a time, and providing for his family had become a worry. And the normalcy of Dwight's new life offered him no outlet for the drive that had so consumed him in his life before marriage. Dwight searched an ever-expanding world for meaningful employment, a job that would let him exorcize his demons. Dwight tried finding comfort by being close to death. He worked for a while setting tombstones in local cemeteries for a monument company, but it just wasn't enough to satisfy his needs. An old friend from his youth baseball days had gone into his family's mortuary business and offered Dwight the chance to learn to be an undertaker. Dwight would consider this opportunity seriously, but before committing to this path, fate would yield to him a better opportunity. Dwight, whose faith in his own invincibility had begun to waver, would have renewed reason to believe that his life was charmed.

Dwight couldn't get the death of his uncle Bill out of his thoughts. The seed of an idea placed in Dwight's mind at the time of his uncle's death had germinated and sprouted into a full-blown idea.

Cigarettes had killed his uncle Bill and before that his uncle David. In fact, the news was now full of reports about the link between cigarettes and lung cancer. Helping people along toward their inescapable demise from their use of tobacco might bring Dwight the kind of fulfillment he yearned for. Death would be long in coming and Dwight would mostly not know his victims, but there would be no doubt that working in the cigarette business would make Dwight something of a grim reaper. This idea would grow and grow until Dwight felt compelled to do something about it. Dwight found a job working as a maintenance man on the night shift at a cigarette factory near Charlotte. Dwight approached the new job with an eye toward being the best employee he could possibly be, work hard, get along with coworkers and superiors, and not cause any trouble. It would be a challenge for Dwight but ultimately one he faced and conquered.

Dwight moved his wife and kids to the Charlotte area. Having a steady income served to improve Dwight's homelife. Dwight joined a local Baptist church and eventually became a deacon. He'd coach little league baseball and YMCA basketball. He drove a minivan and took his family on vacation at the beach every summer. From all outward appearances, Dwight was a model dad, husband, and all-around good guy. There was never any hint of the macabre satisfaction that Dwight derived from his work-a-day world.

Dwight was one of approximately thirteen thousand people employed in the manufacturing of tobacco products at the time—products that, according to the Centers for Disease Control, would take the lives of an estimated 480,000 people annually.

Such knowledge didn't give Dwight the same rush as he had gotten from being responsible for the taking of life by more direct means, but the risk of getting caught was nil, and whenever he heard a news report about deaths from lung cancer, he felt just the slightest elation. It was enough.

Dwight would volunteer to work overtime and weekends. Everyone who knew Dwight assumed that he did so for the usual reasons, an overweight, overbearing wife, underperforming children, and/or the need for extra money. Unknown to everyone, Dwight's real motivation to work as many hours as possible was his need to fulfill the dictates of his black aura for more and more killings achieved vicariously through the sickness and death others suffered from tobacco use.

One of the perks of his job was free cigarettes, and Dwight was quick to take whatever his employer would give him. Once or twice each year, he'd pack up his wife and kids and drive back to Cole City for a short visit with Burt and Louise. On these occasions, Dwight would fill all the available space in his car with cartons of cigarettes that he'd give to Burt and Louise, who were lifelong smokers, not inclined to believe the negative press about cigarettes being unhealthy. Burt and Louise would gladly accept Dwight's gift and would put it to the intended use of slowly killing themselves. Burt would die of lung cancer at the age of seventy-eight and Louise from congestive heart failure at age seventy-nine. Both had been told repeatedly by their doctors that smoking would kill them and it did just that. Dwight and his family visited Burt and Louise less and less in the years of their failing health and didn't visit them at all in the last few weeks of their lives. He'd continue to send them cigarettes courtesy of FedEx right up until the very end.

Dwight played the part of the grieving son at both his parents' funerals, but deep down, he harbored feelings of satisfaction at the role he'd played in their deaths. Dwight would work hard to keep his true self hidden from everyone and did so right up until faced with his own imminent demise.

Dwight had long since quit smoking, but in an ironic twist, it was lung cancer that was slowly robbing him of his life.

For more than forty years, Dwight's need to take lives was fed by his choice of vocation. That adds up to almost ten million deaths during the years that Dwight worked for big tobacco. Dwight, along with everyone else, knew full well that cigarettes killed. He knew this and still chose to do what he did. Without remorse, he'd justify what he did by saying that he was just doing his job, doing what he had to do to provide for his family, that he was no different from the thousands of other "good" people working for big tobacco. Arguments not unlike the ones we've all heard from those who committed war time atrocities, Auschwitz, Andersonville, and Vietnam.

Chapter 26
Season Finale

If this were a TV series, this would be the final episode. But real life can seldom be captured in the sixty minutes of a TV episode. Real life is always more complicated. I hope that my parting words can bring some clarity to Dwight's story.

When death approached, Dwight sought redemption, not out of remorse for what he'd done, but for the benefit of his eternal soul—an act of selfishness rather than the selflessness demanded by Christian teachings. Alone in his hospice room, Dwight quietly slipped beyond the grasp of our world and went on to the next where he'd be judged by a power higher than our own.

I declined the opportunity to speak at Dwight's funeral, deferring instead to someone who had not been privy to Dwight's deathbed confessions. Dwight's two sons were at the graveside service, but the service was otherwise unattended except for the officiant and me. I spoke briefly with Dwight's sons after the internment and tried to provide comfort to them by telling them that Dwight had, in the end, sought salvation. Rather than provide comfort, my words seemed to cause the boys to be puzzled. As far as they knew, their father was a good man and a faithful servant of God, who would not need redemption at the time of his death. From this, it was clear to me that neither of Dwight's sons knew anything about his secret life. Even still, I therefore thought it inappropriate to share any of the details of Dwight's final days with them. To do so at this time and place didn't seem right.

A few days later, while having lunch at the Busy Bee on the square in Trenton, I spotted Detective Gray having a cup of coffee in one of the restaurant's booths. I took my sandwich and slid into the booth across from the detective. We exchanged the usual pleasantries, which were followed by awkward silence. In the silence, I mustered my courage and hesitantly began to speak. The detective sat quietly over the next half hour as I gave him the *Reader's Digest* condensed version of Dwight's role in the murders of Douglas Stalcup and Jon Pruitt. I didn't mention any of Dwight's other wrongdoings as I saw no need to complicate matters by sharing the full text of Dwight's life story just yet. It would be the first time that I'd recount Dwight's story, and there was an immense sense of relief at doing so.

When I finished, the detective had only a few questions. Did I believe what Dwight had told me? Why had I not brought this information to him sooner? And what did I expected him to do with the knowledge that I was giving him? The detective chuckled softly, half to me and half to himself, and said, "That clears up one very old and puzzling mystery, at least." That's when the detective told me how he'd matched the bullets from the Stalcup and Pruitt's deaths years before. In these two cases, the deaths had been ruled as suicides, but both the physical evidence and Dwight's confession now strongly suggested otherwise. But as the detective pointed out, Dwight's passing had precluded any chance of prosecuting him for any crime. Had Dwight still been alive, then reopening of these two investigations would be more than justified, but dead men can't be prosecuted. Proving that Dwight had murdered Stalcup and Pruitt might give surviving family members some closure but would have little benefit otherwise. The detective told me that he'd bring what I'd told him to the attorney general but that he doubted that the AG would want to bring it before the grand jury. It had taken Detective Gray less than five minutes to justify doing nothing with Dwight's confession. I realized then that I had assumed that the authorities would have an interest in knowing about Dwight's wrongdoing. Such was not the case. The detective summed it up by saying that he'd prefer to "let sleeping dogs lie."

For months after my encounter with Detective Gray, I struggled to come to terms with the need to share Dwight's story. I had promised him that I would do so. As far as I know, Dwight never tried to reach out to anyone who he had wronged in his life to ask their forgiveness. So if Dwight's story is ever to get told, I would have to do the telling.

My Christian beliefs have always provided me with the guidance I sought in matters of uncertainty, and it is to my faith that I turned for guidance now. Most fundamentally, I am a man of God and a true believer. As such, I have suspended disbelief in favor of the supernatural. While I have never witnessed it, I believe that angels are manifest. And if angels are manifest, then so are demons.

I am reminded of a verse in the New Testament. Matthew 13:25 says, "While everyone was sleeping, his enemy came and sowed weeds among the wheat."

Looking back, I now see that the night we spent in the coke oven as boys was a turning point for Dwight. In Dwight's fugue state that night, he kept calling out the name of Colonel Towers. In researching the name, I found that a Colonel Towers who was a sadistic Cole City Prison Camp superintendent was murdered there in the 1890s. Through the years since his death, there have been many stories of his spirit coming to the weak-minded. These stories told of evil deeds conducted and of the good fortune of those who carried out these acts. I believe that it is possible that the spirit of Colonel Towers lingers at Cole City and, recognizing that Dwight was a sociopath, set up residence in Dwight's soul that night in the coke oven and forever guided and protected him along his lifelong path of destruction.

If a place can be evil, then Cole City is such a place. If a person can be evil, then Dwight was just such a person.

I believe that the unclean spirit of the long-dead prison superintendent Towers continues to look for souls to influence in the ruins of Cole City.

As I promised to Dwight on his deathbed, I am sharing his story.

About the Author

Garry Hundley grew up amid the remote ruins of what is now the ghost town known as Cole City. As a boy, he endlessly explored the scattered ruins of what was once a vast prison coal mining camp and hiked the mountain trails made by countless lost souls who once toiled there. Although he holds two degrees in engineering from the Georgia Institute of Technology, his passion has always been history. As an avid history student, he has traveled throughout North America and thirty-five other countries to learn about the people, culture, and events that have shaped our world.

Before his focus turned toward writing historical fiction, Garry achieved worldwide acclaim as a successful technical innovator and corporate executive. Garry lives on a remote mountain lake in North Carolina with his golden retriever, Nell.

CPSIA information can be obtained
at www.ICGtesting.com
Printed in the USA
LVHW041709120621
690064LV00004B/388

9 781098 063634